Democracy and the Future

Democracy and the Future

Future-Regarding Governance in Democratic Systems

Edited by

MICHAEL K. MACKENZIE, MAIJA
SETÄLÄ AND SIMO KYLLÖNEN

EDINBURGH
University Press

Edinburgh University Press is one of the leading university presses in the UK. We publish academic books and journals in our selected subject areas across the humanities and social sciences, combining cutting-edge scholarship with high editorial and production values to produce academic works of lasting importance. For more information visit our website: edinburghuniversitypress.com

Edinburgh University Press Ltd
13 Infirmary Street,
Edinburgh, EH1 1LT

First published in hardback by Edinburgh University Press 2023

Typeset in 10/13 Giovanni by
Cheshire Typesetting Ltd, Cuddington, Cheshire

A CIP record for this book is available from the British Library

ISBN 978-1-3995-1274-9 (hardback)
ISBN 978-1-3995-1275-6 (paperback)
ISBN 978-1-3995-1276-3 (webready PDF)
ISBN 978-1-3995-1277-0 (epub)

CONTENTS

FIGURES AND TABLES

Figures

Tables

CONTRIBUTORS

Didier Caluwaerts is Associate Professor of Political Science at the Vrije Universiteit, Brussels. His research and teaching deal with Belgian and comparative politics, democratic innovations and democratic governance in deeply divided societies.

Sven Ove Hansson is a Professor of Philosophy at the Royal Institute of Technology, Stockholm. His research interests include decision theory, the philosophy of risk, moral and political philosophy, the philosophy of science and technology, and logic.

Kaisa Herne is a Professor of Political Science at Tampere University. Her research focuses on political behaviour, political psychology, decision-making, experimental methods and deliberative democracy.

Vesa Koskimaa is a Research Fellow in Political Science at Tampere University. He specialises in the study of political elite networks, parliaments and party politics.

Katariina Kulha is a project researcher and a doctoral candidate in political science at the University of Turku. Her work focuses on the issues of climate justice and deliberative democracy.

Simo Kyllönen is university lecturer in research ethics and open science at the University of Helsinki. His main research topics are related to intergenerational justice, democratic theory and ethics of climate change.

Eerik Lagerspetz is a Professor of Practical Philosophy at the University of Turku. He has published widely on political and legal philosophy, the history of political thought and theories of collective decisions, especially with respect to the philosophical implications of social choice theory.

Claudia Landwehr is Professor of Political Science at the Johannes Gutenberg University, Mainz. Her work focuses on institutional design, democratic innovations and citizens' conceptions of democracy.

Michael K. MacKenzie is an Associate Professor of Political Science at the University of Pittsburgh. His research interests include democratic theory, intergenerational relations, deliberation, environmental policy, political representation, institutional design and public engagement.

Alfred Moore is a senior lecturer at the Department of Politics at the University of York. He works on issues such as the politics of expertise, the role of conspiracy theories in politics, democratic theory and deliberation. Currently, his work focuses on the role of competition in democratic theory.

Lauri Rapeli is the research director in the Social Science Research Institute at Åbo Akademi University. His main research interests are in public opinion, political knowledge and political behaviour.

Maija Setälä is a Professor in Political Science at the University of Turku. She specialises in democratic theory, with a focus on deliberative democracy, different forms of direct democracy and democratic innovations.

Graham Smith is Professor of Politics, University of Westminster. He is a specialist in democratic theory and practice, with particular expertise in new forms of public participation in political decision-making.

Hilma Sormunen worked as a project researcher at the University of Turku. Currently, she works as an assistant to an MP in the Finnish parliament, Eduskunta.

Daan Vermassen is a doctoral student at the Department of Political Science, Vrije Universiteit, Brussels. His research focuses on democratic short-termism.

Mark E. Warren is Professor Emeritus in the Department of Political Science at the University of British Columbia, where he previously held the Harold and Dorrie Merilees Chair in the Study of Democracy. He is especially interested in new forms of citizen participation, new forms of democratic representation, the relationship between civil society and democratic governance, and the corruption of democratic relationships.

ACKNOWLEDGEMENTS

This book is based on papers presented in the workshop 'Democratic Institutions for Long-Term Governance' organised in November 2020. The workshop and the book brought together researchers, advisory board members and other partners of the research project 'Participation in Long-Term Decision-making' (PALO; decision number 312671). PALO was a 4.5-year project (2017–2022) funded by the Strategic Research Council at the Academy of Finland to study political participation and long-term decision-making in democratic systems.

We would like to thank all the participants in the workshop for their contributions and discussions at the workshop. We would also like to thank Mikko Leino, Lyydia Aarninsalo and Mari Taskinen for their help in organising the workshop, and Toni Wessman for his great assistance in editing this book.

The Challenges and Possibilities of Future-Regarding Governance

Simo Kyllönen, Michael K. MacKenzie and Maija Setälä

Introduction

Can democratic institutions help us to act in future-regarding ways? Many people – even committed democrats – have their doubts. Representative democracies, especially those with well-functioning bureaucracies, tend to provide their people with relatively high levels of economic prosperity and social welfare (Norris 2012). Overall, democratic systems fare better in this respect than autocratic ones, even those with high levels of state capacity. But it is not clear that democratic systems are equally good at ensuring the welfare of their people over the long term or acting with the potential interests of future others in mind.

Governments have failed to address climate change, plastics pollution, the loss of biodiversity, generational reproductions of racism and inequality, and many other long-term problems. Most countries also have huge – and growing – public debts that cannot be sustained over the long term. Furthermore, it is now apparent that no country was adequately prepared to deal with the Covid-19 pandemic, despite advance warnings from many public health experts. Even wealthy, stable democracies, such as Switzerland, often have trouble making investments in the future. Recent attempts to reform the Swiss public pension system by raising the retirement age have been rejected several times in referenda, even though it is clear that the system, as it exists, is unsustainable over the long term (Bello and Galasso 2021).

These examples seem to suggest that democracies – like other regimes – are myopic and seek to maximise short-term welfare at the expense of the future. As Alan Jacobs (2008) points out, politics is not just about the distribution of costs and benefits *between* people, it is also about the distribution of costs and benefits over time. But political regimes, of all types, have reasons to neglect the future in favour of the present. As the authors of the Brundtland Report state in their opening chapter: 'We act as we do because we can get away with it: future generations do not vote; they have no political or financial power; they cannot challenge our decisions' (World Commission on Environment and Development 1987: 8).

Most political systems have difficulty making long-term investments and acting in future-regarding ways, but many observers worry that there are features of democratic systems that make them particularly – or especially – myopic. Unlike authoritarian regimes, democratic systems are supposed to be responsive to the interests and preferences of the people they serve. If voters are myopic and democratic systems are properly responsive to their preferences, collective decision-making in democratic systems will be myopic as well – as is illustrated by the failed reforms in the Swiss public pension system. Electoral competition will incentivise short-sighted behaviour if politicians think (or know) that their voters care more about their own short-term interests and less about their future interests or the potential interests of future others. But short electoral cycles create myopic incentives for another reason as well. In democratic systems, governments – and the people who serve in them – frequently change. This makes it possible to revise and reverse policies, which also makes democracies more adaptable than other regimes, and better able to correct mistakes (e.g., Runciman 2013). But the political dynamics of short electoral cycles can make it difficult for political actors in representative systems to make credible long-term commitments because future governments will have the power to reverse or undo any long-term plans or investments that they might make. These are fundamental problems because they imply that democracies will be short-sighted *not when they are working badly but when they are working well*. Which is to say, when they are responsive to the demands of voters, and when elected politicians are accountable, and may be replaced by new ones (MacKenzie 2021b: ch. 1).

These features of democracy have led many scholars to conclude that democracies cannot solve long-term problems such as climate change (Shearman and Smith 2007; Randers 2012; Bell 2016; Mittiga 2021). These scholars argue that we will need authoritarian regimes (or practices) to impose unpopular but necessary costs on unwilling publics for the benefit of the future. We reject this option at the outset for at least two reasons. First, calls for authoritarian solutions to our long-term problems typically underestimate the capacities of democracies to act in future-regarding ways, while also overestimating the capacities of authoritarian regimes to do so. Authoritarian leaders may be future-regarding, but then again, they might not be – and there is little that anyone outside the inner circle of power in an authoritarian regime can do to influence the decisions of powerful insiders. Authoritarian governments also typically lack diversity. But it is not possible to identify – and then create – mutually agreeable futures (i.e., futures that might be good for everyone, or as many people as possible) without giving diverse groups of people some means of making their voices heard and influencing future-making decisions. The futures that authoritarian leaders create might be good for themselves and a range of others – and they might be better than any number of alternative futures. But the futures created by authoritarians will, by definition, be narrow: they will reflect the relatively narrow visions of the few people empowered to make the future in those regimes.

The second reason that we reject the authoritarian option is because we are interested in how we might make inclusive, mutually accommodating, or agreeable futures together. For this we will need democracy, but we will also need to make the democracies we have more future-regarding. We need democracies in which people consider future-regarding reasons in their collective decisions and are motivated to act on those reasons. Can this be done? If so, how? These are the questions that we address in this book.

The Aim and Scope of the Book

This book is about *future-regarding* democratic governance. This choice of terms is deliberate and highlights the nature of our approach. We reject the idea that our political systems should be more 'future-oriented' (e.g., González-Ricoy and Gosseries 2016). When we are oriented towards something, like the north or the future, we are necessarily oriented away from something else, like the south or the present. Addressing political myopia is about correcting presentism, which involves focusing on the present to the exclusion of the future. But this does not mean that we should focus on the future to the exclusion of the present (or the past). When we are future-regarding we are not turning our backs on the present or the past. The proper objective, in our view, is to strike a balance: We need to do what is right or necessary for the present without disregarding the future in the process, hence the term 'future-regarding'.

The concept of the 'future' itself is ambiguous and needs some clarification. First, the future is not one thing. It is a collection of knowable and unknowable potentialities. When we are talking about the future we are talking about possible alternative futures, of which there are many (e.g., Gidley 2017). Secondly, the term 'future generations' is ambiguous. It can be used to mean young people who will be social, economic and political actors in the future. Or it can be used to mean future people who do not yet exist. When the authors in this book talk about 'future generations' they are normally using the term in the latter sense. There are, however, further distinctions to be made between generations of people who will exist in the near future, versus those who will not come to exist until some point in the far future. It is also important to acknowledge that future generations will not be monolithic. The people who comprise future generations will have conflicts of interest amongst themselves, and they will have divergent life experiences and beliefs. This means that what we (might) do for 'the future' – or for 'future generations' – is likely to have differential impacts on differently situated future people.

Thirdly, the idea of the 'long term' is ambiguous. What we consider the 'long term' to be will depend on the issue at hand. Long-term planning during war, for example, might entail thinking strategically about the next weeks or months of combat – even though wars themselves always have long-term social, economic, political and environmental impacts. Long-term plans in education might look twenty or thirty years into the future. Long-term plans to mitigate climate change must look hundreds of years into the future, and nuclear waste must be stored safely for tens of thousands of years. When acting as morally responsible decision makers, we must consider the likely timeframes of the effects of our decisions, as well as whether the negative consequences of our decisions are irreversible (Caney 2018). It is becoming increasingly clear that *all* our collective decisions have long-term consequences of one sort or another, which means that the familiar distinction between short-term and long-term issues may be untenable (MacKenzie 2021a).

In order to deal with issues that will have long-term consequences, such as climate change, governments must make long-term commitments and investments that have some reasonable prospect of being maintained long enough to do some good. As explained above, making credible commitments in democratic systems can be challenging because democratic governments must be re-elected at regular intervals or replaced by new governments. On this view, democracies have – and always *must* have – a commitment problem. To address this problem, independent institutions (such as central banks or constitutional courts) may help safeguard long-term commitments within particular policy domains. This approach can help societies to maintain collective commitments over time, but this strategy risks de-politicising certain policy domains and thereby preventing decisions within those domains from being influenced by changing preferences or beliefs. If *all* our decisions have long-term consequences, we cannot rely on independent institutions to support credible commitments in every policy domain without also undermining the democratic character of our political systems. What is needed – as we argue in the concluding chapter – is a balance between independence and politicisation. We need independent institutions that can protect our long-term commitments from being too easily overthrown by changing governments. We also need politicised institutions (such as political parties and legislatures) to subject those long-term commitments to regular processes of review and critique, with the possibility of making changes when changes may be needed or justified.

In more general terms, we view future-regarding governance as an ongoing process of balancing – and re-balancing – goods and objectives which are (or may be) in tension with each other. We need to balance the legitimate concerns of the present with the potential interests of the future (as we understand them). We need to maintain our long-term commitments while also being willing (and able) to adjust those commitments as circumstances require. We need to invest in the future at some cost to the present, and we need to address the needs of the present without neglecting the future. We need to trust that government officials will not plunder our long-term investments to service their own short-term desires, and we need to trust experts to help guide us though complex long-term decisions. But we must also ensure that decision makers of all types are subject to scrutiny, critique and accountability. Future-regarding governance is difficult to do well, but we argue in this book that democracy may be particularly well suited to navigating the tensions that exist at the heart of this challenge.

This approach departs from much of the existing literature on future-regarding governance and intergenerational justice. Many justice theorists do not focus on governance at all – or, if they do, they see it as a second step to be taken after credible and widely acceptable theories of justice have been established (for a discussion see Goodhart 2018). Our approach acknowledges the role that justice claims might play in justifying future-regarding decisions and institutions (e.g., Warren, Chapter 1, this volume), but the primary focus in this book is on institutional design and the creation of incentives and structures for future-regarding action.

Among those who are interested in institutional design, many scholars, as explained above, think that we will need to abandon – or significantly constrain – democratic processes if we are going to act in future-regarding ways to solve problems like climate change. Other scholars who are dedicated to the principles of democracy but acknowledge its myopic tendencies have argued that we will need to add supplementary institutions – such as Offices for Future Generations (OFGs) (Smith, Chapter 8, this volume) or randomly selected second chambers (MacKenzie 2016b, 2021b) – to our democratic systems to make them more future-regarding. An alternative option is to think more carefully about how our existing democratic institutions and practices might be leveraged or enhanced to make them more future-regarding.

This book brings these two latter approaches – one focused on supplementary institutions and the other on existing institutions – into conversation with each other. Our existing democratic institutions and practices can either inhibit or encourage future-regarding policy decisions, depending on the institutional forms and practices in which those decisions are made (e.g., Caluwaerts and Vermassen, Chapter 9, this volume). But the structures of our existing systems will also affect how – and to what extent – supplementary future-regarding institutions might be established and empowered.

The chapters in this book focus primarily on democratic institutions and practices *within* nation-states. Future-regarding governance is, of course, an international and global challenge, but – outside the European Union – we do not have examples of empowered international democratic institutions. Nevertheless, the challenges and possibilities of future-regarding governance that are addressed in this book will be relevant to analyses of local, regional, national, supranational or global democratic systems.

With this in mind, the book uses Finland as an example of how future-regarding governance might be done. Finland has one of the most advanced governmental foresight systems in the world. It has a unique parliamentary institution called the Committee for the Future which engages in ongoing dialogues with the government on futures issues. Government ministries conduct regular foresight analyses, and these efforts are supplemented by experts working in non-governmental organisations and research institutes. The whole system is linked together into a comprehensive foresight network (Koskimaa, Chapter 10, this volume). Finland has had inclusive multiparty governments for decades and a political culture characterised by high levels of trust in both government officials and experts. These features of the Finnish system have helped to sustain the country's foresight capacities and long-term policy commitments.

The Finnish system is not, however, an archetypal model that can or should be replicated elsewhere. There are many features of the Finnish system – such as high levels of trust in experts and elites – that are not present elsewhere. This is important because the Finnish system heavily relies on technical experts and elites, and it does not do enough to engage diverse publics in making decisions about their shared futures. In this respect, Finland can be regarded as an illustrative example of future-regarding governance in a particular democratic system with specific social and cultural features. The Finnish case provides some lessons that may be relevant elsewhere, but it also raises critical questions about the limits of expert-driven future-regarding governance, and the need for informed public input.

The Structure of the Book

The book is organised into four parts. Part One deals with some of the conceptual challenges and possibilities of making long-term decisions in democratic systems. Part Two looks at how we might encourage – or incentivise – political actors, experts and people more generally, to think and act in future-regarding ways. Part Three addresses questions of institutional design, and Part Four explores and critiques future-regarding policymaking in Finland, especially its national foresight system.

Part One: The Challenges of Long-Term Decision-Making

Mark E. Warren (Chapter 1) identifies three challenges of long-term decision-making in democratic systems. The first challenge concerns who should be included and empowered in a democratic state or society. Such decisions are normally based on membership or citizenship. But if the consequences of our decisions reach beyond currently existing people to affect those who will live in the future, the question arises as to whether – and how – future people should be included in our democratic communities. This consideration raises the second challenge of long-term decision-making in democratic systems: how can we know or anticipate what the interests of future people might be? Warren responds to these challenges by developing a detailed defence of the All Affected Principle (AAP), which says that all those whose interests are affected by collective decisions should have some meaningful role in making or influencing those decisions – and this, in principle, includes both present and future people. In response to the second challenge, Warren argues that the AAP should be understood as a principle of social justice that is linked to the goods that justify democracy, namely, those of self-determination and self-development. On this account, we do not need to know what future people will want or need in precise terms (which would be impossible). Instead, the AAP compels us to aim at maintaining the conditions of self-determination and self-development such that future people will be empowered to make their own decisions when the time comes for them to do so. In other words, acting in future-regarding ways entails ensuring that we do not unduly or unjustifiably infringe on the freedoms and abilities of future people to engage in self-determination and self-development. This should be our primary objective and motivation in future-regarding governance.

Warren's third challenge has to do with motivating or incentivising people to act in future-regarding ways. He argues that institutions for long-term decision-making will have at least five general characteristics: they must have the scope to deal with the issues; they must have the capacity to address them; they must be trustworthy enough for people to want to invest in the future; people must also have ownership over the institutions so that they see long-term decisions as their own; and, lastly, the institutions must be deliberative so that people understand the issues and their own long-term commitments to them. Warren's analysis shows that the challenges of good long-term governance are not so very different from the challenges and conditions for good (democratic) governance more generally.

Eerik Lagerspetz (Chapter 2), however, challenges the idea that good democratic governance is also good long-term governance. He argues that there is, sometimes, a trade-off between two democratic goods: responsiveness and self-determination (or self-governance). He begins with an analysis of the infamous aggregation problems that social choice theorists have identified, which show how rational individuals can end up making irrational or incoherent collective decisions (or indecisions). Lagerspetz argues that maximal democratic responsiveness (i.e., the requirement that democratic systems respond to the demands and expectations of the people they serve), can preclude the possibility of self-governance rather than uphold it when individuals (acting rationally) express incoherent or indeterminate collective preferences. In response, Lagerspetz argues that democratic systems may have to limit responsiveness – at least in some respects – to uphold self-governance and make future-regarding collective actions possible.

Alfred Moore (Chapter 3) identifies a different but related tension between reversibility and commitment. All democratic decisions are, and must be, subject to regular reassessments. Democratic politicians must face regular elections, and any decisions made by a democratic community can, in principle, be revised or reversed at a later date. But if we are going to achieve our shared long-term objectives, we must be able to make credible commitments and long-term investments. Moore acknowledges this tension but argues that the principles of reversibility that define democratic processes play a critically important role in helping democratic societies achieve (an always shifting) balance between steadfastness (or commitment) and flexibility (or reversibility). He argues that reversibility (as a principle and a practice) has epistemic potentials that enable democratic systems to adapt and respond to dispersed information and thereby make better future-regarding decisions. His analysis focuses on the epistemic advantages that may be obtained in competitive party systems, especially those in which diverse partisan groups vigorously compete in elections but then deliberate and act together in coalitional governments. This analysis challenges the conventional wisdom that partisanship – or politicisation, more generally – inhibits rather than supports future-regarding collective action.

Sven Ove Hansson (Chapter 4) challenges the idea that there are short-term issues, such as pandemics, and long-term issues, such as climate change. Instead, he argues that both types of issues are temporally and politically complex, but in different ways. Both issues have long-term causes and consequences resulting from human actions (and inactions) and addressing these problems will require decision makers to rely on the knowledge and input of scientific experts. However, Hansson identifies several important distinctions between these two issues that make dealing with them challenging in different ways. He argues that national leaders have stronger incentives to deal with pandemics than climate change because the effects of pandemics are more immediately felt and harder to deny, individuals can help protect themselves against the threats of pandemics, and measures taken within a country to deal with them will have their largest impacts within that country, even though addressing pandemics will always, also, require global coordination. In short, although pandemics and climate change both have long-term causes and consequences, they are associated with different political challenges and incentives. Hansson's analysis reminds us that in order to engage in effective future-regarding governance, we will need to unpack the central – unique and common – features of each temporally complex issue.

Part Two: Thinking and Acting in Future-Regarding Ways

The second part of book addresses some of the challenges and possibilities associated with motivating or incentivising future-regarding thinking and action in democratic systems. Kaisa Herne (Chapter 5) argues that we should consider combining perspective-taking exercises and inclusive deliberative forums. The idea is simple but intriguing. Perspective-taking exercises encourage people to think about what it might be like to experience the world as someone else. There is evidence that these exercises can be used to encourage people to more seriously consider the potential interests of future others. But perspective-taking exercises, themselves, do not bring diverse perspectives and interests into contact with each other. Scholars have argued that inclusive deliberative forums, which *do* bring diverse perspectives and interests into contact (and conflict) with each other, can encourage people to more seriously consider the future, but they do not always do so. Herne argues that the solution to both problems is to bring these two approaches together. Future-regarding perspective-taking exercises can be used in deliberative forums to ensure that participants do not neglect the potential interests of the future when they are deliberating issues, such as climate change, that will have divergent impacts on different groups both now and in the future. The next step is to think about how this approach might be scaled-up and integrated into our democratic systems – or legislative processes – more generally.

In contrast to the argument that Alfred Moore (Chapter 3) makes, Claudia Landwehr (Chapter 6) argues that the interests of silent voices, such as future generations, are unlikely to be adequately considered where politics is driven by strong electoral pressures. She frames her analysis around a discussion of statistical victims – that is, victims who are statistically expected to suffer from our policy choices but who are not yet identifiable as individual victims. Although specific future people will not always become statistical victims, statistical victims are always people who may be harmed in the future. Such victims are typically unorganised – or unorganisable – and thus have no clear representation in our democratic systems. Landwehr argues that the representation of statistical victims will have to be discursive, and this will require deliberative forms that include representatives with different kinds of expertise and diverse perspectives who are not driven by electoral pressures.

Michael K. MacKenzie (Chapter 7) focuses his chapter on future-regarding democratic leadership. Much of the literature in this field neglects the role that leaders can – or might – play in motivating people to think and act in future-regarding ways. Following other democratic theorists, such as Pennock (1979) and Beerbohm (2015), MacKenzie makes a distinction between authoritarian and democratic modes of leadership. Authoritarian leaders act *on* their followers, while democratic leaders act *with* them. MacKenzie argues that democratic leadership has at least three functions that are useful (and probably necessary) for initiating and supporting future-regarding collective actions: (1) aiding thinking (or supporting reflection); (2) forging joint commitments; and (3) mobilising action. He concludes his chapter by arguing that we *will* need future-regarding leaders if we are going to coordinate our actions to achieve long-term goals and objectives, but we will also need to make our democratic systems more deliberative if we are going to create the conditions that are necessary for future-regarding democratic leadership to thrive.

Part Three: Institutional Design

The third part of the book addresses questions of institutional design. Graham Smith (Chapter 8) identifies design principles for future-regarding institutions. His chapter focuses on three types of 'actually-existing' institutions: the Committee for the Future (CF) in the Finnish parliament; Offices of Future Generations (OFGs), such as those in Israel, Hungary and Wales; and deliberative minipublics, such as the recent climate assemblies in France, Scotland and the United Kingdom. The design principles Smith identifies are independence, diversity, deliberation, empowerment and institutionalisation. But he cautions that it may not be possible to realise these goods simultaneously, especially within a single future-regarding institution.

Didier Caluwaerts and Daan Vermassen (Chapter 9) conduct a comparative empirical analysis of future-regarding policies in thirty-six countries over six years (2014–2019). They find that democracies with proportional electoral systems, oversized coalitions and mechanisms for citizen participation are systematically less biased against the future. These findings partly explain why Finland is a front-runner when it comes to long-term policymaking, as discussed in Part Four of this book. Their analysis also shows that certain types of partisan electoral institutions – as opposed to nonpartisan institutions like those discussed by Landwehr (Chapter 6) and Smith (Chapter 8) – can help to mitigate political myopia.

Part Four: Long-Term Policymaking in Finland

The fourth part of the book takes an in-depth look at future-regarding governance in Finland. As explained above, Finland has one of the most advanced and institutionalised foresight systems in the world. Vesa Koskimaa (Chapter 10) describes the various parts of the system, their historical developments, and how they fit together to create a comprehensive foresight network. His chapter highlights the parliamentary context in which the Committee for the Future (CF) was created, and how this institution has secured its unique place within the foresight system. At the same time, Koskimaa emphasises that the CF is only one part of a much larger and more comprehensive foresight system that includes the Prime Minister's Office (PMO), the ministries and many nongovernmental organisations and academic institutions. The Finnish foresight system is therefore much more than the Committee for the Future, even though the CF does, indeed, provide democratic legitimacy for the system as a whole.

Lauri Rapeli (Chapter 11) presents the results of two surveys used to measure political myopia among elites and non-elites in Finland. He shows that while non-elites (both voters and non-voters) are more myopic than political elites (both elected and unelected officials), people in all four of these groups are *more* future-regarding than most people might expect them to be. These results challenge the idea that democracies are short-sighted because voters and elected politicians care only about the present and tend to neglect the future. According to Rapeli's measures, political elites in Finland are *remarkably* future-regarding. This raises the question of whether elites in other political systems that do not have advanced foresight systems would be equally future-regarding. Furthermore, although non-elites in Finland are more myopic than political elites, the former can hardly be described as uniformly or monolithically myopic. Future research is required to determine whether these are unique features of the Finnish political system and culture, or whether similar patterns can be identified elsewhere.

Maija Setälä, Katariina Kulha and Hilma Sormunen (Chapter 12) conduct an analysis of Finland's first deliberative minipublic on climate change policies. This process brought together thirty-three people to deliberate the most controversial components of the Finnish government's climate plan, which will have a direct impact on the lives of many people in Finland. Minipublics – or small deliberative forums – bring diverse and representative groups of people together to deliberate public issues, problems or policies. In this case, the minipublic participants were asked to consider the following question: 'how can climate measures affecting consumers be implemented in a fair yet effective way?' After learning about the issues and deliberating them with each other, the participants expressed a collective willingness to reduce carbon emissions, although they also expressed concerns about the fairness of several measures in the government's plan. They preferred incentives such as subsidies and deductions to tax increases, but they also acknowledged that those who produce more emissions should be taxed at higher rates for those emissions. At the same time, they emphasised the need to address regional differences, and the differential impacts that the government's policies would have on groups such as the elderly, low-income people and the Sami. Setälä, Kulha

and Sormunen argue that minipublics like this one can help governments identify potential problem areas or policies that might
undermine their legitimacy or threaten their ability to make – and
maintain – long-term commitments. Nevertheless, this process
did not fundamentally challenge or alter the elite-driven nature of
long-term decision-making in Finland. It was purely consultative,
and although it may have helped the government to assess its climate action plans, it had no role in formulating those plans.

In the last chapter, Michael K. MacKenzie, Simo Kyllönen and
Maija Setälä (Chapter 13) offer some concluding thoughts on the
study and practice of future-regarding governance. They argue that
societies must learn to navigate a series of tensions if they are going
to act in future-regarding ways and achieve their shared long-term
objectives. There is a fundamental tension between doing what is
right (or needed) for the present and doing what is right for the
future. In some cases, acting in future-regarding ways will also be
good for the present, but in other cases there will be a tension
between these two objectives. As discussed above, there is also
a tension between reversibility (or flexibility) and commitment
(or steadfastness). We must make credible commitments if we are
going to achieve long-term goals, but we must also make appropriate adjustments to meet the demands of changing circumstances.

There is yet another tension between independence and politicisation. We need institutions that can function independently
from the short-term dynamics of electoral politics, as Landwehr
(Chapter 6) argues. But we also need partisan – or politicised –
institutions to ensure that conflicting perspectives, or alternative
visions of desirable futures, are brought into contact with each
other, as Moore (Chapter 3) argues.

Lastly, future-regarding political systems need to balance relatively high levels of trust with effective means for scrutiny and
critique. The Finnish foresight system is predicated more on trust
than critique, but this leaves it open to failure if the trust that the
Finnish people have in their governments and in experts more
generally starts to wane. These tensions are not, then, the sort
that should be resolved or eliminated. Instead, the challenges of
future-regarding governance consist in learning how to strike an
(always-probably-shifting) balance between these – and likely

other – future-regarding goods that may come into tension with each other. MacKenzie, Kyllönen and Setälä argue that despite common assumptions about democratic myopia, democracies are, in fact, quite good at producing these goods and balancing them against each other when they come into tension.

In the second part of the conclusion, MacKenzie, Kyllönen and Setälä outline several research programmes to advance the study of future-regarding governance. There is a lot of conceptual, methodological, practical and political work that needs to be done before we can make our complex modern societies more future-regarding. We are not free to decide *whether* to govern for the future. Whatever we do will affect the future. But we are free to decide *how* we should govern and whether we keep the future in mind when we do so. We *will* govern for the future, and we need to think more carefully about what that involves and how we might do it well rather than inadvertently.

Part One

The Challenges of Long-Term Decision Making

Three Challenges for Long-Term Decision-Making in Democracies: Boundaries, Knowledge and Incentives

Mark E. Warren

Introduction

Can democracies make good long-term decisions? In this chapter, I focus on three general problems, viewed through the lens of democratic theory, and aimed at building out democratic theory so that it might help to specify this question more closely. First, there is the problem of temporal boundaries: how can we include future beings, including our future selves, who cannot participate in decisions that will affect them? Second, if we can find ways of including non-present, non-existing others, how can we know what they might want or choose, so that we might represent them? And, third, what kind of incentives might we have to attend to the interests of future beings, especially if attending to the future is costly in the present?

Long-term problems encompass collective decisions and collective omissions that affect the long-term futures of people who exist today, those who will come into existence, as well as societies, institutions and our environments, both built and natural. The range of such problems is enormous: how can we limit the extraction and burning of fossil fuels so that climates and their supporting environments do not become unliveable? How can we secure nuclear waste that will remain dangerous for tens of thousands of years? How can we ensure that social services and social safety nets will be there for future generations? How can we secure trustworthy institutions that have the capacity to organise and follow through on long-term plans and promises? Some kinds of long-term issues result from intentional decisions, such as building nuclear power plants. Others are the result of collective drift, or they are simply not intended at all, such as climate change. Or they are the result of self-serving and unaccountable elites, particularly, but not only, in authoritarian contexts. Some are the result of perverse practices that despoil environmental commons, such as overfishing, destructive fishing or polluting ocean waters. Still others result from the externalities of market forces. Many are consequences of growing populations that squeeze out natural habitats and result in species extinctions. And still others are the results of insecurities resulting from violence-rationalising ideologies and theologies that will find fertile conditions in poverty, sectarian cultures, injustices and hubris for generations to come. Of course, many long-term issues combine these factors, making them extremely difficult to solve.

From a political standpoint, what these substantive issues have in common is that they are the results of failures of collective action to collective problems, owing to failures of existing institutions, perverse institutions, institutions that are not equipped to deal with new challenges or institutions that are missing altogether. These failures underscore long-term problems of institutions that scale in time and space in ways that can match and pace the collective action problems. Many long-term institutions, such as pension systems that will hold up for lifetimes, can be adjusted and reinvented from time to time. Other problems are less forgiving and will need institutions that can last many centuries, even millennia. Keeping nuclear waste safe, for example, is partly a complicated engineering problem, and partly a problem of devising institutions that can provide security for thousands of years (which is much tougher than the engineering problem). Avoiding catastrophic climate change, if it is still possible, is partly a problem of developing sources of energy, agriculture and building materials that do not produce greenhouse gasses, and partly a problem of inventing forms of global governance that can get us to those goals and keep us there.

Most such problems have been quite clear for many decades. They have been pushed by the security failures that produced two world wars, the tighter integration of economies through global divisions of labour, a keener sense of the ravages of disease, poverty and climate change, as well as the injustices and instabilities of colonial and post-colonial circumstances. The general requirements of institutions that can meet these challenges are also clear. We need institutions that are responsive to the issues and those who are, and will be, affected by them. We need institutions that can deliberatively relate information about those issues to what people need for fulfilling lives. We need institutions with capacities to make collective decisions and collectively act. And we need these capacities within institutions that are trustworthy, stable and intertemporal, as they need to convey commitments and capacities from one generation to the next.

What is relatively new is that we are now thinking of such institutions as *democratic* institutions, particularly those that make space for deliberative approaches to long-term decision-making and do so in ways that generate public conversations (Gundersen 1995; Goodin 2003; Smith 2003; MacKenzie 2018, 2021b). The *prima facie* case that *existing* democracies are better than non-democracies at dealing with long-term issues is strong. The democracies led global institution-building coming out of the Second World War, which aimed at securing long-term peace. Their environmental records, deeply flawed though they are, are relatively better than the non-democratic industrial powers, such as China and the former Soviet Union. They have done relatively better at creating institutions that will provide welfare for future generations (Jacobs 2011). This kind of *prima facie* evidence notwithstanding, the capacities of democracies to make good long-term decisions remains under challenge. Some environmental activists view authoritarian leadership as essential to avert long-term environmental catastrophe (see, e.g., Shahar 2015; Smith 2021: 22–6, for discussions). There is also a resurgence of meritocrats such as Jason Brennan (2017), who likewise view democracy as short-sighted and downward-levelling. These arguments are backed up by the common complaints that electoral mechanisms reinforce short-term thinking and promises among elected leaders (MacKenzie 2016a, 2021b). Moreover, market capitalism, embedded in all developed democracies, comprises agentless structures that are powerful and dynamic, and irresponsible by their very nature, and so require equally powerful state and international regimes to organise and limit their reach (Lindblom 2002).

This said, we also need to recognise that there are almost no examples of non-democratic regimes that are better than democracies at making and enacting good long-term decisions. The number is not zero: Singapore is the best example of a non-democratic polity with high capacities for long-term decision-making. Singapore is notable because it seems to be the only exception. (China, currently the leading emitter of greenhouse gases, has yet to show that its form of authoritarianism can deliver on environmental sustainability.) Looking beyond the Singapore exception, the developed democracies have done better at environmental planning and regulation, developing long-term plans for social safety nets, carrying commitments from one generation over to the next, and generally working to develop stable, clean and trustworthy governments. The simple reason is that democratic institutions are more likely to be responsive and deliberative, and better able to generate legitimacy for long-term planning (MacKenzie 2021b; Smith 2021). If you are worried about your children's future and their children's future, in a democracy you will be better able to translate your worries into collective decisions and actions.

But better does not mean sufficient: democracies have not, on average, treated long-term decision-making as a class of decisions with their own sets of problems. Democratic theorists have not, on average, developed sufficient ways of thinking about long-term decisions (cf. Boston 2016a; MacKenzie 2021b; Smith 2021). Here, I discuss three kinds of theoretical problems that we should integrate into democratic theory. We need to think about: (1) *the temporal boundary problem*: who or what should we include in decision-making?; (2) *the knowledge problem*: how can we know the interests of non-present beings?; and (3) *the incentive problem*: what motivations do we have to take the future into account?

Boundary Problems

Let me turn to the first of the three problems – the boundary problem. Who should count as part of the *demos*, or *demoi*? The most promising approach now emerging within democratic theory is the

All Affected Principle (AAP) (e.g., Warren 2023; Fung 2013; Andrić 2020; Afsahi 2021). The principle that all those affected by a collective decision should be included in the decision is long-standing, dating at least back to the Justinian Code (V,59,5,2) in Roman private law: 'what touches all must be approved by all' (*Quod omnes tangit debet ab omnibus approbari*). Over the last several decades, the idea has migrated into democratic theory, as it expresses a very basic intuition about what democracy is good for: I should want to have a say in decisions that significantly affect my life. With a say, I am part of networks of co-dependants who can collectively self-govern. Without it, I am likely to be subject to forces over which I have little or no control.

The AAP is often in conflict with the standard view of political inclusion dating back to the democratisation of modern nation-states. Entitlements to a say over collective matters – voting in particular – should follow membership, formalised as citizenship. The powers and limitations of citizenship are tied to residence in organised political jurisdictions: nation-states, provinces, municipalities and so on. They are made effective through voting, electoral representation and rights-based protections for advocacy. Within democratic theory, this standard view has been stylised as the 'All Subjected Principle': claims for inclusion, on this view, should be derived from actual or potential subjection to states. In light of their coercive power, the point of democratic inclusions is to limit and guide states, including their capacities for collective action (e.g., Miller 2009; Abizadeh 2012; Song 2012).

This standard view of democratic inclusion has the advantages of familiarity and tractability. But it does not get us very far in thinking about temporal inclusions in democracy. Criticisms of the All Subjected Principle to date have mostly focused on spatial limitations: understanding the boundaries of inclusions in terms of state-based jurisdictions limits our abilities to think about inclusions beyond borders. But the *temporal* features of the All Subjected Principle are equally limiting: those who have claims to inclusion in a *demos* are adult citizens who have residential claims within an organised jurisdiction.

Yet justifications for democratic inclusion based on state membership are increasingly undermined by a combination of changing ethics and developing social and political entanglements. From the standpoint of ethics, we increasingly understand our obligations to others as those of social justice that should extend to every human being, in spite of recent surges in reactive nationalism in most of the developed democracies (Young 2000; Warren n.d.). From the standpoint of social and political development, the impacts of collective decisions reverberate across jurisdictions. People make decisions, often as parts of governments, organisations or firms, that produce effects borne by people in other jurisdictions, in matters of security and war, economic development, trade and environmental externalities including climate change. A decision taken 'democratically' in one polity – that is, inclusive of its members – can be experienced as oppression, domination or tyranny in another. No justification of exclusions based on membership can make such effects democratically acceptable. Stated positively, the normative point of democracy is to underwrite the self-determination and self-development of individuals whose lives are co-dependent with others (Young 2000).

Precisely the same kind of things can be said about temporal inclusions, in the very basic sense that those who are included in the *demos* today make decisions for those who will be affected in the future: our future selves and societies, our children and grand-children who do not yet have democratic powers, and future beings who do not yet exist. The justification for doing so is similar to the spatial justification: the decisions we make today affect those in the future, enabling or constraining their life choices (Goodin 2003; Eckersley 2004; Dobson 2007; Fuji Johnson 2008). Our theoretical challenge will be to develop the AAP in a way that it makes sense temporarily, so the boundaries of the polity extend into the future.

A key problem with using the AAP, however, is that it has not yet been well developed within democratic theory, although it is widely assumed. Indeed, there is no consensus about what it is, what it requires and what kind of work it does within democratic theory – let alone its implications for the future, although there are some proposals now on the table (e.g., Fung 2013; Afsahi 2021). So I will simply propose that we should view the principle in the following way (Warren 2023). Most importantly, the AAP is primarily a democratic principle (or moral norm) of inclusion.

It is a claim about who should, normatively speaking, be entitled to inclusion in collectivities – existing or latent – based on how their life chances are affected by others (Young 2000). That is, it is not a theory about the political organisation of institutions or empowerments. Nor is it a replacement for the ties of memberships. But it is a way of specifying democracy as self-government under conditions of extensive interdependency – and it does so in a way that captures the common-sense normative core of democracy as self-government. The relevant *interests* are those related to the goods of self-development and self-determination. The relevant *affected* interests are those that significantly impact chances and opportunities for self-development and self-determination through (a) relationships of co-dependence and co-vulnerability, and (b) externalities of organised collective entities or structural phenomena such as markets.

Another way of saying the same thing is that the AAP is a principle of social justice, as it is related to democracy. From the perspective of social justice, democracy has value just because it provides individuals with influence over those collective interdependencies necessary to underwrite self-determination and self-development, and to protect against the harms of domination and oppression (Young 2000). Stated in this way, social justice is a description of the goods that justify democracy, in particular, the conditions for self-determination and self-development.

If we follow this kind of social justice logic, we end up with the somewhat surprising observation that inclusion of the interests of future beings should be *proportional* to nature and the extent of affectedness for these essential interests. I am going to develop this point in general, because it bears on how we interpret the AAP for future beings and their interests. On the face of it, the idea of proportional entitlement seems to clash with the basic idea that in a democracy, everyone should have equal empowerments. But the proportional requirements of the AAP make more sense if we distinguish the requirements of *equality* from *equity*. Democracy needs both. If we are talking about current and present human beings, democratic *equality* resides in equal moral worth and equal capacities for collective self-government. It cashes out in those empowerments necessary to exercise influence over collectivities: protective rights to liberty and autonomy, positive rights to vote, speak and organise, as well as welfare rights such as rights to education, a basic income, and so on. Democratic equalities provide *standing* to individuals so they might act as democratic citizens.

We should notice, however, that even when democratic empowerments are equally distributed, they are not equally used, even in an ideal world. No citizen uses powers of association to have a say on every issue; most citizens use their voice and votes quite selectively, according to the issues they prioritise. Ideally, the way people use their *equal* political powers is to exert *proportional* effects on politics and in their uses of welfare entitlements. We should understand this proportionality not through the concept of equality, but rather *equity*. Elaborated as social justice, equity is what we owe to one another by virtue of those co-dependencies and externalities that affect our abilities to self-develop and self-determine. We already practice this difference between equality and equity. In the higher functioning welfare states, citizens are equally and universally entitled to receive state services. Services are delivered, however, in accordance with the AAP. Every citizen has an equal right to schooling for their children. But schooling is distributed not in accordance with the principle of equality, but rather equity, to those who need it – that is, school-aged children. Entitlements to voice are magnified for those most directly affected through institutions like parent–teacher associations.

In an ideal world, equality and equity should be complementary, with equal powers of citizenship underwriting proportional social justice claims. The AAP gives such proportionality its democratic substance by relating it back to self-government. So, turning back to the question of temporal inclusions, what we owe future beings is not equal consideration of their interests, but rather equity, relative to essential interests in self-development and self-determination.

Two important features of the AAP relevant to temporal issues follow. First, the normative claims for inclusion increase *proportionally* to the extent fundamental interests are affected. So 'all affected' does not mean everyone who is potentially affected in any way – a common objection to the viability of the AAP (Goodin 2007) – but rather with respect to fundamental interests in self-determination and self-development (Fung 2013; Afsahi 2021). This social justice interpretation of the AAP is still challenging, but it now accords with democratic ideals: we should want empowered inclusions where they are important for self-determination and self-development. Secondly, the *scope* of the principle is relative to effects that impact individuals' capacities for self-determination and self-development. That is, the AAP should identify just those effects that matter to fundamental interests in self-determination and self-development. If the value of the AAP is that it helps to frame the question of who should, morally speaking, be included in democratic decision-making, then we need to think temporally as well as spatially, about what it would or could mean for non-present, future beings. The specific challenge for long-term decision-making is to figure out how what we do today affects the essential interests of future beings. That is, we should extend social justice into the future – and this is what we need to represent in current decision-making.

There is, of course, a key question that the AAP cannot resolve: decisions today determine whether or not particular future beings come to exist at all, as when (say) a couple decides to bear one or two children rather than four or five. Beyond collective questions about the impact of growing populations on the Earth's carrying capacity, the AAP does not have anything to say about this question. But neither do other principles of democracy, or, indeed, moral theories more generally.

Apart from this existential question, however, we can tailor the AAP to temporal problems a bit more specifically by asking about *who* to include and how, and over *what* domains. With respect to the *who*, all problems of inclusion in long-term decision-making with respect to non-present beings are, of course, problems of representation (MacKenzie 2018). This is a challenging problem, but we do have some conceptual resources in theories of representation that can help to address it. We need to think about representative relationships as vectors of inclusion, in which living individuals, organisations or institutions speak and act for non-present beings. We cannot, of course, follow the standard approach of thinking about democratic representative relationships in principal–agent terms, as the principals do not yet exist. For the same reason, of course, we cannot use our standard conceptualisation of democratic representation, in which agents authorise principals to represent them, and then hold them accountable for doing so, as they can with elected representatives (Castiglione and Warren 2019). Nor, obviously, can we get to any sort of 'democratic representation' for future beings as conceived by analogy to elections.

As many have suggested, however, representing the future is more like existing representative relationships between agents and non-present beings, such as very distant others, animals and their environments, or even young children. The proper analogy would be trustee relationships. If we stand back from election analogies, we can see that democracies are thick with trustee relationships – from the very close ones between parents and children, to the anonymous ones embedded in agencies, ministries, and other institutions structured to uphold and enact 'public trust' (Warren 2017a). When a government sets up a pension system, for example, they usually do so for the long term – not for any specific individual, but for individuals who may not yet be born, and for their yet unknown co-dependents (Jacobs 2011). Norway's sovereign wealth fund is an exemplary case of a trusteeship institution designed to benefit future generations. The Finnish Parliament has a Committee for the Future, tasked with identifying future problems and opportunities (Smith, Chapter 8; Koskimaa, Chapter 10, both this volume). The Israeli Knesset Ombudsman for Future Generations, established in 2001, had a mandate to examine legislation from the perspective of future generations, but it was abolished in 2006, apparently for having too much power to delay decisions. This case, as well as the fact that such commissions remain exceptional, suggests that the political positioning of general-purpose future-regarding institutions needs careful consideration, particularly with respect to political motivations (Smith 2021: ch. 3).

Indeed, the more consistently motivated representatives are often found in single issue organisations outside of political systems, such as Greenpeace (which uses legal and political pressure) or the Natural Resources Defence Fund (which mobilises private resources). The ubiquity of these kinds of organisation suggests that, on average, there are few problems, theoretically or practically, with representing non-present, non-speaking beings, as long as people in democracies view their co-dependencies temporally as well as spatially.

The AAP is also a useful for framing *what* should be represented, establishing boundaries of inclusion. Where there are effects, an implication is that there should be collective agents responsible for them – and hence the target of AAP entitlements. The AAP would expand entitlements for inclusion in several ways: into complexes of effects for which there may not be organised collective agents; beyond nation-states, or within polities with jurisdictions that do not map onto the patterns of affectedness; or as consequences of structural forces such as markets that do not seem to have any responsible collectivity at all (Bohman 2010). These kinds of situation are not an argument against the AAP, but rather an argument for using it as a way of identifying normatively important patterns of effects – latent constituencies (including latent future constituencies) as it were – for which there are no responsible collective entities (Bohman 2010). In such cases, collective agents should be invented and created just so collective responses can exist. In the case of global climate change, for example, the Paris Agreement counts as a step towards creating a collectivity that can coordinate and distribute future-regarding responsibilities.

Knowledge Problems

I now turn to the second problem. Even if we can find ways to include future generations by representing their social justice interests, do we not have a problem with *knowing* what their interests might be so that we can represent them? Part of the idea of democracy is that we get to choose, together with others, our collective futures. If we determine in the present what future individuals might want, does this not violate this fundamental feature of democracy? This question is, of course, simply an extension of the problem of representing those who are not present, with the added difficulty that there is no voice for those beings that do not yet exist. And yet every choice we make now will affect the lives and life-chances of future persons. Because of what we do not know about who and how many will come into existence, we cannot with much certainty represent the interests of future persons – a problem formulated most famously as the 'non-identity problem' by Parfit (2017).

As many scholars have pointed out, the non-identity problem dissolves if we approach it through a common-sense justice lens – either a Rawls' original position (Reiman 2007; Heyward 2008) or the social justice interpretation of the AAP I am suggesting here. We cannot know, of course, what exactly individuals and their collectivities will choose because we do not know who will come into existence. What we *can* know is that they should want social justice and its conditions – that is, conditions that underwrite self-development and self-determination. Thus, whatever we choose and decide today should be oriented towards underwriting social justice for future generations. Substantively, the general conditions for maintaining conditions of choice are not difficult to imagine, because they are the same conditions about which there is broad consensus in the developed democracies today, despite often deep ideological differences about how to achieve them. Thus, we should be maintaining secure environments, sustainable sources of food and energy, clean air and water, education and healthcare, pension systems, systems that provide basic income security, and so on. Maintaining these institutions and systems does not prejudge what future generations will want; rather, it maintains conditions that make the self-development and self-determination of future beings possible.

We can add to these conditions of social justice future democratic institutions themselves, as they provide the political conditions of choice that will be exercised by future beings. The problem of the identity of future beings also dissolves in this instance. Yes, it is true that we cannot know who will exist in the future or what their wants and needs might be. But we can know something about the identities of institutions, just because they have qualities that transcend individual identities. The magic of, say, a constitution, is that it can produce institutions that can make promises, and take on commitments and obligations to future beings (Giddens 1984: 256–62). When current people pass on, they leave their investments under the care of institutions that are, in principle, capable of transferring promises to future people. These kinds of transference are quite clear in the easy cases, such as social security. What we need to create, however, are institutions that can be responsible and build investments over time for emerging legacy problems, such as care for the global environmental commons. We do have a few of these institutions – the Paris Agreement began to establish an institutional responsibility for climate change. But we need them in every area of collective action with a bearing on social justice for future generations – including those issues, like climate change, that transcend nation-state boundaries and require that we invent new collective institutions that can take responsibility for the future.

There is, of course, the problem of specifying the conditions of social justice that should be conferred to future generations, and the related problem of trading off current costs against future benefits. The epistemological part of the problem has two dimensions, both of which call for deliberative democracy. One dimension is, simply, the matter of figuring out how much to invest, what to protect, and what scarce resources to save and support, so that future generations can inherit conditions that support self-development and self-determination. Theoretically, this problem is not difficult: it requires broad integration of expert knowledge and lay values, sorted problem by problem. The other dimension is a bit more difficult: it is not enough that experts should know about the investments and protections that convey conditions of social justice forward. The legitimacy of decisions depends upon broad-based understandings of costs and trade-offs, as well as a broad integration of citizens' values into decisions. For this to occur, knowledge needs to be broadly shared, which in turn suggests that devices of deliberative democracy such as deliberative minipublics need to be sufficiently deployed and used such that they can penetrate populations – at the very least in the form of political bodies that citizens understand as credible and trustworthy (Warren and Gastil 2015; MacKenzie 2018, 2021b).

Incentive Problems

The most difficult issue is that of incentives. Why should human beings today take the social justice interests of future beings into account, especially if they are costly? What incentives do we have to make decisions for the long term? We can refine this question with two contrasting observations.

First, humans are historical animals, aware of time and existentially invested in leaving a better world to successive generations – or, at least, a world that is not worse. There may be some culturally-specific effects in cultures that think of history as linear and progressive, but historical thinking and investment is probably more general, as suggested by the well-known North American indigenous rule that the impacts of decisions should consider the seventh generation (Graham 2008). More than this, we may have a propensity to invest in the present so as to make the future less onerous – from investing in tools to save labour, to investing in knowledge and culture in ways that can be handed down to future generations. Well-designed and trustworthy institutions can function as repositories of investments – they are, in Giddens' term, 'storage containers' of collective capacities (Giddens 1984: ch. 5). We can view these tendencies as resources for long-term decision-making.

But, secondly, these future-regarding incentives are delicate and highly conditional. There are well-known human characteristics that tend to work against decision-making for the long term. We almost universally tend to discount future rewards relative to present rewards. Future discounting is exacerbated by a number of decision contexts. (a) Markets and market capitalism intensify productivity and inventiveness, but also intensify consumerism. They lack inherent mechanisms to protect environmental commons, future scarce resources or attentiveness to the conditions that people or peoples need to thrive (Smith 2021: 17–21). Consumerism feeds on our naturally narcissistic tendencies. (b) Close-knit communities, particularly ethnic, religious and national communities, provide care for members, but often limit the travel of moral concern for others beyond these communities. Strong communities can intensify our natural inclination to care for those who are closest, while rationalising a lack of care for those who do not belong. (c) Contexts of poverty and insecurity will naturally cause people to focus on the present. Even care for their own futures will be swamped by the more immediate concerns of the present. (d) Untrustworthy or low-capacity institutions, particularly state institutions that are predatory, group or class biased, or untrustworthy, will undermine incentives that are future-regarding, simply because investments or trade-offs can be carried forward only by institutions that have the capacity to do so, and also carry forward resources and commitments that will benefit those who present actors intend to benefit (Rothstein 2005). Even well-intentioned people will choose the present over the future if their investments are likely to be stolen or drained by those with power, wasted or despoiled. (f) Finally, democratic elections are often accused of incentivising short-term over long-term thinking and policymaking. This charge is not as weighty as it appears: if constituents have long-term interests, elected politicians should respond to these just as they will to short-term interests. Of far more importance, in my view, is whether voters view the commitments and capacities of institutions as credible and trustworthy.

So good institutions are crucial to capturing the future-regarding interests that people have, and converting them into long-term decisions and policies that can hold up over time. There is no general answer as to which of these tendencies will tend to win out in any given set of future-regarding decisions. But we can sketch general characteristics of institutions that transform short-term, narrowly focused decisions into long-term, broadly focused ones. These characteristics are good, normatively speaking, for many reasons in addition to transforming short-term into long-term incentives, meaning that these reasons build on – rather than compete with – the broad normative consensus that supports them. Institutions for long-term decision-making will have five general characteristics: (a) scope sufficient to the issues; (b) sufficient capacity to address them; (c) trustworthiness sufficient for people to invest in the future; (d) ownership of institutions, so that people experience long-term decisions as their own; and (e) deliberativeness, so that people can understand issues and their commitments to them. Each of these qualities is implied in the discussion so far. None are surprising, as they are all features of good government. Taken together, however, they suggest that capacities for long-term decision-making are integrally related to broader, deeper and better democracy.

First, following guidance from the AAP, we need institutions with sufficient *scope* for the issue. (a) For some kinds of long-term governance – say, in investments in health care systems, or the long-term securing of nuclear wastes, the scope can be relatively narrow. But because of the possibility of externalities – poorly secured nuclear materials, such as with the Fukushima Daiichi accident in 2011 or the Covid-19 pandemic – even issues with relatively narrow governance scopes should be coordinating with international oversight and coordinating institutions, such as the International Atomic Energy Agency or the World Health Organisation. (b) Other kinds of scope problems are presented by the globalisation of markets, particularly those that incentivise current exploitation of scarce resources and despoil environmental commons. Here again, issue-specific international regimes are essential. Trade agreements are especially important, because they link short-term incentives to make money to long-term decisions, particularly in the areas of environment, labour and rights-based securities. Anyone interested in scaling institutions to markets must support the expansion of trade regimes with riders that address a myriad of market externalities. (c) Yet another scope problem – one of the most difficult – is that of scaling norms and cultures in such a way that large or broad-scope regimes will be able to underwrite and uphold them, particularly in the face of assaults by opportunistic nationalists and religious leaders who trade on parochial insecurities. There are no easy institutional fixes, but it is worth noting that globalised cultures can be incentivised by markets, as well as more purposefully, as the European Union has sought to do with its numerous intra-European exchange programmes, or as the United States has sought to do with its Fulbright programmes, and (in still other ways) with the Peace Corps.

Secondly, institutions need to have the *capacity* or power to address long-term issues, so that long-term incentives have a place to land. Collective capacity is largely a function of ownership, trustworthiness and deliberativeness. As Hannah Arendt famously noted, power is something that is gathered from people through democratic processes that coordinate individual or group capacities towards a common purpose (1958: ch. 28). This is why, ultimately, democracies generate the most powerful collective capacities. This is basic stuff in democratic theory, but it is worth noting that capacities in democracies can be limited by a couple of general problems. One is that some kinds of institution, most notably separated power systems like in the United States, tend to gridlock collective capacities. It is much better to have a parliamentary system, like most of those in Europe, that translates winning coalitions much more directly into governance capacity. As important as this kind of political capacity is, most governing capacity ideally resides in professional bureaucracies that are relatively well insulated from everyday politics, with routinised accountability, and combined with economies that generate a surplus sufficient to support administrative capacities. This area of study is basic to comparative politics and public administration, and so I will not discuss it here. But it is worth noting that governing capacities are highly variable across the world – high in the developed democracies and Singapore, increasingly high in China, middling in most of Latin America and other parts of Asia, and weak in much of Africa. Likewise, governance capacities are weak or missing in areas in which the scope of long-term problems flows across borders, such as within the global commons. For these reasons, it is essential that high-capacity states invest in the governance capacities of weaker states and international governance regimes.

Thirdly, and closely related, institutions need to be *trustworthy*, particularly over time (Smith 2021: 15–17). If I put my money in the bank, I need to know that I can withdraw it at some point in the future. If I can trust the bank, then it is able to combine and repurpose the money that I do not need now into long-term investments. Likewise, citizens are more likely to support contributions to a pension system if they believe it will be there for them when they retire, when their children retire and so on. What gets citizens there is the combination of factors that produce trust in institutions: norms that are public and transparent, and incentives by office holders to abide by these norms (Warren 2017a, 2017b). Institutions need to be trustworthy in this sense. It is likely that people are more willing to pay more when they trust that their money will be used wisely for public purposes (Scholz 1998). But when institutions are inefficient, corrupt or otherwise captured by narrow interests, people will prefer lower taxes so they can use their income in ways that allow them to capture the proceeds of their investments. Low trust in institutions thus results in collective underinvestment in the future (Rothstein 2005). Countries like Finland are fortunate to have a relatively solid reservoir of trust in public institutions upon which to draw – something indicated by the very high marks Finland receives on the Transparency International's Corruption Perception Index. The question as to how international institutions might benefit from high trust is something of a frontier, but an important one if long-term issues are to scale onto sites of collective action (Brewer et al. 2018). This is one area in which democratic innovations, particularly deliberative minipublics that can both scale and benefit from high trust, might be especially valuable, assuming such innovations can build on relatively trustworthy traditional institutions (Warren and Gastil 2015).

Fourthly, people need to *own* institutions, to feel like the institutions are theirs, so that their investments are not captured by those who make no investments or, worse, use the investments made by others for their own short-term benefit (Smith 2021: ch. 4). Adam Smith noted that European feudal societies stagnated for a thousand years because incentives and ownership were misaligned (Smith 2010: Book III). Peasants would not invest, because all proceed were captured by lords; lords would not invest, because they could simply capture the proceeds of the labour of others. We can generalise this point to political institutions: if people have and experience ownership over their governments, they will invest in their governments' capacities, understanding that their investments will return to them, or their children or their children's children. This point is basic to democracy, which, described in terms of ownership, is about the institutions that support and enable people to own their governments (Lafont 2019). Problems of ownership become more acute, however, with scale and distance even for democracies with relatively strong representative systems – again, an area in which democratic innovations like deliberative minipublics would likely add to the experience and reality of ownership (MacKenzie 2021b; Smith 2021: 93–9). It is also worth noting that ownership can be increased through the bureaucratic or 'governance' channels of government – and, indeed, many of the important innovations in democracy are driven by administrators and bureaucrats who are seeking new ways of engaging their policy-based constituencies (Warren 2014).

Finally, institutions need to be *deliberative* – something I will not dwell upon, as these features of democratic institutions and innovations are well studied, even if implementation is still in its infancy

(Bächtiger et al. 2018; MacKenzie 2018, 2021b: ch. 4). It is worth noting, however, that the ownership and trust dimensions of the general incentive problem become less difficult to the degree that deliberative processes are in place, because they help align interests between individuals and collectivities (Kulha et al. 2021). They help to relate individual-level reasons to collective reasons, and they help to establish ownership of collective institutions and collective actions. They help to establish the relationships between individual actions and long-term consequences. And, as long established in deliberative democratic theory, individual reasons and reasoning tends to be framed in terms of collective interests when stated to others, within (say) the publics represented by institutions such as deliberative minipublics. Deliberative innovations can help democratic ownership of institutions penetrate to the individual level, altering the ways in which individuals think about, rationalise, express and buy into collective decisions and actions (O'Grady 2020).

Conclusion

Decision-making for the long-term presents three general kinds of challenges. First, there is a *boundary* problem: how can we include in the demos people who are not yet born? Second, even if we can find ways to include future generations, how can we *know* what their interests might be? And, third, even if we could solve these problems, what *incentives* do those of us who are living now have to consider the interests of future people with no voice and no power? We can use recent democratic theory to clarify these challenges. With respect to boundaries, we should be using the All Affected Principle of inclusion, interpreted through a social justice lens. With respect to knowledge of what future people might want or have interests in, we should think about maintaining conditions of self-development and self-determination for future generations – that is, conditions of social justice. With respect to incentives, we need political structures that translate our natural historicity into collective decisions: few people want to leave a world to their children and grandchildren that is worse than the one they inherited. If we can solve these problems, then the long-term interests that people already have as historical beings can be empowered.

TWO

Democratic Weakness of Will

Eerik Lagerspetz

Introduction

Democracy is sometimes defined as a form of collective self-government. For example, according to John Dunn (1993: vi): 'In a democracy, the people . . . its human members, decide what is to be done, and in so deciding they take their destiny firmly into their own hands. The power and appeal of democracy comes from the idea of autonomy – of choosing freely for oneself.' An alternative definition of democracy is that democracy is *responsive rule*, which means that in a democracy there is, or should be, a correspondence between acts of governance and the wishes, with respect to those acts, of the persons who are affected (May 1978). Many people think that these definitions are equivalent (e.g., Lauth 2011: 63). In this chapter, I argue that they are *not* equivalent. While democracy as self-government requires responsiveness, maximally responsive rule does not maximise self-government; it actually precludes self-government.

In the first parts of this chapter, I introduce the idea of self-government as a general ability to make and follow plans and commitments. I discuss the related – and as I argue, partly competing – idea of responsive rule. Then, largely following Philip Pettit's path-breaking studies (preceded, however, by Heckscher 1892), I present the central problem of failures of collective self-government. Finally, I link these issues to the main topic of this book. A maximally responsive rule does not only slavishly reflect the myopic tendencies of the electorate; it may actually be *more* short-sighted than individual voters. Moreover, 'responsive rule' is as such an ambiguous and underspecified idea. It is not possible to be responsive to *all* preferences, not even to all majority preferences. By contrast, the idea of democratic self-government conceptually requires future orientation and long-term planning.

Will and its Weaknesses

When do we say that a being is able to *govern itself*? To be self-governing a being must, at least, possess the abilities to fix its own aims, form coherent plans about how to reach these aims, and execute the plans it has made. As Michael Bratman (e.g., 2009, 2012) explains in his seminal articles, self-government requires that we are able to make and follow structured plans of action. By committing ourselves to a pre-structured plan, we voluntarily and temporarily limit our freedom to deviate from the plan. Our freedom and self-government are valuable only because we can exercise them, and, somewhat paradoxically, we can exercise our freedom and self-government only by limiting them, voluntarily and temporarily.

As Bratman (2009: 413) states, our practical rationality requires that the plans we make are subjected to diachronic as well synchronic rationality requirements. To simplify: (1) our aims and intentions fixed in our plans should be *mutually consistent* in the sense that we should not intend A and intend B if we do not believe that A and B are simultaneously possible (or not mutually exclusive). (2) Plans should satisfy *means–ends coherence*: if we believe that M is a necessary means to E and that M requires that we intend M, then we should intend M if we intend E. Consequently, if we do not intend M, we should not intend E. Bratman (2012) adds that, although stability or constancy of intentions over time is not a categorical requirement but rather a matter of degree, (3) a certain amount of *intertemporal constancy* is necessary for self-government. A creature constantly changing its aims without ever reaching any of them is unable to actually plan its future. For our present topic, requirement (3) is especially relevant.[1]

According to a tradition stretching back at least to Plato's *Republic*, a political community can be an agent, with a will, a reason and an ability to govern itself. Individual self-government and collective self-government can be seen as analogous ideals, subjects of similar rationality requirements (Offe 1996: 91). As such, there is nothing counterintuitive in the idea of collective self-government. Individuals, so we suppose, may be and should be self-governing. When living in a community, individuals and their personal plans unavoidably affect each other. They can reach their personal and shared aims only by coordinating their plans and actions. In order to coordinate, they need a common organisation that can also set aims and make plans. Probably the most famous formulation of this comes from Jean-Jacques Rousseau:

> The body politic, therefore, is also a corporate being possessed of a will; and this general will, which tends always to the preservation and welfare of the whole and of every part, and is the source of the laws, constitutes for all the members of the State, in their relations to one another and to it the rule of what is just and unjust. (Rousseau [1758] 1973: 120–1)

Rousseau emphasises that self-government requires *will*. Some critics have argued that ascribing a will to collectives like political communities or to their decision-making bodies is simply a category mistake, for will requires ability to form intentions and only individuals can have intentions. Intention is a state of mind, a psychological phenomenon. Collective groups have no minds of their own; therefore, they cannot will anything. According to the critics, expressions such as 'legislative will' should be interpreted as metaphors or analogies (e.g., see arguments reviewed in MacCallum 1968; Ekins 2012: chs 1 and 2). However, although metaphors and analogies are not true or false, they may be successful or unsuccessful, illuminating or misleading. Even if we grant that a collective will is in some important sense quite unlike an individual will, we need not conclude that all talk about collective wills and collective self-government is just rhetoric and poetry. We take it as granted that groups and organisations, including political communities are, in some sense, able to *do* things. We admit that they are able to set aims for themselves, to make plans, and to commit themselves by treaties and contracts. We hold them accountable and criticise them for their occasional inability to follow consistent policies. This does not mean that they possess a mystical collective consciousness. Rather, it means that will and intention are not strictly psychological phenomena. A collective will is (except in simple cases of groups consisting of a few people only) an *institutional* construct (Offe 1996: 91).

To take an example, it is reasonable to say that the faculty at my university *does* something. The faculty is, up to a point, a self-governing unit. For example, the faculty may accept a teaching plan for the next year and try to follow it. Although the faculty cannot will or act unless its individual members also will and act, saying that the faculty 'does' something is not just a figurative way to say that, for example, professors A, B, C, etc. do something. The institutional rules determine that the actions of some specific members of the faculty, performed in some specific contexts, are counted as actions of the department. If, for example, I vote for the teaching plan in the council of my faculty, my act, together with similar acts performed by other members of the council, constitutes the 'will' of the faculty. If I then teach according to the plan for the reason that it is our plan, my teaching is part of a (complex) action performed by the faculty. By contrast, if I steal some property from the university, the faculty has not stolen anything. There are constitutive rules and conventions specifying which individual actions, performed in which types of contexts, are actions of the faculty. However, individual actions, even when performed in appropriate contexts, are not always sufficient to constitute a collective action. Individual actions may, for example, be coerced or manipulated.

Let us return, for a moment, to the individual case. Individual people do not always obey Bratman's requirements (1)–(3) of practical rationality. Sometimes they set for themselves mutually incompatible ends, or accept ends without accepting the necessary means (or accept inappropriate means) for those ends. Moreover, it is often argued that human beings have an inbuilt tendency to favour present aims and to ignore long-term concerns. In his *Treatise of Human Nature* (1739), David Hume mentions two reasons for this presentist bias. According to Hume, people

are always much inclin'd to prefer present interest to distant and remote; nor is it easy for them to resist the temptation of any advantage, that they may immediately enjoy, in apprehension of an evil that lies at a distance from them. (Hume [1739] 1948: 101)

Individuals can be *akratic*, suffering from the weakness of will, or they can be *myopic*, unable to evaluate future benefits correctly. The difference between akrasia and myopia is this: akratic decision makers know that B is, according to their own evaluation, better than A, but they still choose A rather than B; myopic decision makers believe – erroneously – that A is better or more important than B because they have a systematic tendency to overestimate the value of earlier benefits at the expense of later ones. Thus, akrasia is a defect in will; myopia is a defect in judgement. Akratic and myopic choices may be described as failures of consistency, of means–ends coherence or of intertemporal constancy and stability, depending on the circumstances. By definition, myopic and akratic decision makers are not fully rational. They would have a good reason to make a different choice, and it is part of the meaning of the notions that akratic and myopic decision makers would themselves agree on this were they able to see their own choices clearly.

In classical political theory, one central task of the political community has been to hold people's myopic and akratic dispositions in check. To take an example, Benedict (Baruch) Spinoza in his *Tractatus theologico-politicus* ([1670] 1951: 73) argues that 'if men were so constituted by nature that they desired nothing but what is designated by true reason, society would obviously have no need of laws'. However, human beings are not reasonable: 'every one, indeed, seeks his own interest, but does not do so in accordance with the dictates of sound reason' (p. 204), for people take no thought beyond the present and the immediate object. 'Therefore, no society can exist without government, and force, and laws to repress men's desires and immoderate impulses' (p. 74). For Spinoza the task of the government is to uphold such a system of general rules that secures public utility by counteracting individual akrasia and myopia. The unexamined and problematic presupposition of the classical account is that political communities are necessarily more far-sighted or strong-willed than individual citizens.

Responsiveness and Democracy

The term 'democracy' has both evaluative and descriptive uses, for democracy is both a political ideal and an institutional arrangement. In order to be called democratic, an institutional system must fulfil some minimum conditions. There are many possible candidates for such a condition but, besides political equality, *responsiveness* is the most popular one. According to Sidney Verba and H. N. Nie (1972: 300), responsiveness is 'what democracy is supposed to be about'. John D. May (1978: 1) defines democracy as 'responsive rule', or, more precisely as a 'necessary correspondence between acts of governance and the wishes with respect to those acts of the persons who are affected'. The key word here is 'necessary'. If democracy were simply a correspondence between popular wishes and executed policies, it would be compatible with government *for people*, not only with government *by people*. May's definition requires that expressed wishes or preferences of the governed are regularly transformed into public actions. Incidentally, this is part of what we mean by will: wishes or preferences make a difference, and they make a difference partly *because* the one who has those wishes or preferences wants them to make a difference. Thus interpreted, May's definition is related to the idea of democracy as collective self-government.

We may agree with the view that a certain amount of responsiveness is a *necessary* element in democracy. One may then take a further step and infer that the more responsive a political system is the better – more democratic – it is in evaluative terms (see Saward 1998: 50, 59, 65 on 'maximal responsiveness'). Thus, Arend Lijphart (1984: 1) states that 'an ideal democratic government would be one whose actions were *always* in *perfect* correspondence with the preferences of *all* its citizens' (emphasis in original). R. A. Dahl (1971: 2) reserves the term 'democracy' for a political system that would be 'completely or almost completely' responsive to the preferences of all its citizens, while imperfectly responsive systems are, for Dahl, just 'polyarchies'.

Ian Budge (2005: 1) states: 'What distinguishes real democracy is an institutional mechanism for ensuring the correspondence [between policies and the preferences].' Alf Ross in his classic *Why*

Democracy? (1952) specifies the nature of the institutional mechanisms in an ideal-typical perfect or pure democracy. For Ross, there are three relevant dimensions: 'intensity' or the relative size of the people entitled to participate; 'effectiveness' or the ability to participate directly; and 'extensiveness' or the extent of popular control. The latter is maximised when 'popular power controls not only legislation but also the executive and the judiciary' (Ross 1952: 89). Numerous possible institutional mechanisms are supposed to increase the responsiveness of a political system. Among the proposed mechanisms are frequent elections, short electoral terms and short term-limits, direct election of officials (including judges), the possibility of recall of representatives, imperative mandates, intra-party democracy and open primaries, the use of popular initiatives and referenda, local participatory institutions and decentralised decision-making. Correspondingly, Richard J. Arneson (2004: 44–5) enumerates institutional arrangements that, according to him, *diminish* the democratic character of a regime. Examples include representation, 'because it lessens the extent to which the present will of a majority of voters controls political outcomes', but also laws that prevent removing 'political officials in any branch of government' from office. Moreover, if there are restrictions 'which are constitutionally specified as the supreme law of the land, and which may not validly be altered by majority vote', then 'the greater the extent of these limits of majority rule, the lesser the extent to which the political system qualifies as democratic'.

Reversibility or revocability of decisions is one general institutional consequence of the responsiveness requirement (e.g., Moore, Chapter 3, this volume). If the wants and preferences of the citizens change, the resulting decisions should change too. A classical formulation that connects democracy and reversibility comes from Jean-Jacques Rousseau:

Now the law of today must not be an act of the general will of yesterday, but that of today. We have engaged ourselves to do not what all *have* wished, but what they all *now* wish. For as the resolutions of the sovereign, as sovereign, regard only itself, it is always free to change them. From which it follows that, when law speaks in the name of the people, it is in the name of the people as it is now and not as it used to be. The laws, although received, only have lasting authority so long as the people, being free to revoke them, nevertheless does not do so. ('Geneva manuscripts', trans. Cole, p. 293)

We have seen that the responsiveness condition, as a descriptive criterion and as a normative requirement, enjoys wide support among the theorists of democracy. Nevertheless, in its standard formulations the condition is ambiguous and underspecified. In large societies, political disagreement is omnipresent. Policies cannot literally be in perfect correspondence with the preferences of *all* citizens. To whose wishes does the system then respond? May's, Lijphart's and Dahl's general formulations do not specify how the – often mutually incompatible – wishes of the citizens are to be compared and aggregated. In their accounts, Saward (1994: 15; 1998) and Ross (1952: 89) simply suppose that 'the preferences of all' could be replaced by 'majority preferences'. In dichotomous cases where only two alternatives ('yea' and 'nay') are involved, there are good arguments for the use of the simple majority rule. However, when there are three or more alternatives, the majority criterion itself is ambiguous (for a discussion of the many problems involved, see Lagerspetz 2016: ch. 3). Even in dichotomous cases, there are problems. First, there is the problem of *permanent* minorities (and majorities). Even if a majority were willing to respect the political rights of minorities (so it is not a tyrannical majority), it might still treat minorities unfairly, ignoring their specific values and interests. If the dominant majority is also permanent in the sense that it is based on some stable pre-political differences (e.g., on ethnic or religious divisions), one may ask what rational reasons those in a permanent minority position have to obey the democratic procedures (Ross 1952). Secondly, there is the classical problem of *intense* minorities (Kendall and Carey 1968; Anckar 1996). In the words of R. A. Dahl (1956): 'What if the minority prefers its alternative much more passionately than the majority prefers a contrary alternative?' As a response to these problems, Lijphart (1984) argues that, instead of being responsive to majority preferences, a democratic system should aim at a wider consensus, to be responsive to the preferences of as many people as possible.

There is a further ambiguity. Majorities may want clean air or to stop climate change, but at the same time, they may also want higher salaries, more consumption goods and faster means of transportation. People have both long-term and short-term preferences, and nothing guarantees that these preferences are mutually compatible. Nothing guarantees that the aggregated wishes, wants or preferences are mutually consistent, means–ends coherent or constant over time. Incompatibilities may sometimes be explained in terms of *individual* akrasia or myopia. However, it is possible that while all or almost all individual preferences are internally consistent and means–ends coherent, the *aggregated* preferences are not. The system may still formally satisfy the responsiveness requirement if its constantly switching, or if internally incoherent decisions are in correspondence with *some* preferences of *some* majorities. However, if the decisions do not satisfy the rationality requirements, no collective will can be constructed, and, consequently, the political community cannot be self-governing. Hence, democratic self-government implies at least some amount of responsiveness, but responsiveness is not sufficient for self-government. The ideal of maximal responsiveness may actually preclude the ideal of collective self-government.

The Judgement Aggregation Problem

Above, we set three conditions for self-government: the ability to fix aims; form coherent plans based on judgements; and execute plans. Many critics have argued that political communities or even assemblies representing them are actually not able to do any of these things. For example, the nineteenth-century French anarchist Pierre-Joseph Proudhon argued against the idea of 'the will of the people' in following terms:

> Does the People, which is sometimes said to have risen like a single man, also think like one man? Reflect? Reason? Make conclusions? . . . Now if the People has, in all historical epochs, thought, expressed, willed and done a multitude of contradictory things; if even today, among so many opinions which divide it, it is impossible for it to choose one without repudiating another and consequently without being self-contradictory – what

do you want me to think of the reason, the morality, the justice, of its acts? (Proudhon 1848)

Let us take a real-life example in which the will of a collective clearly exhibited a contradictory pattern. In her study on the Russian parliament 1990–1993, Josephine Andrews (2002) analyses the voting patterns in the Russian parliament during the constitutional crisis that followed the fall of the Soviet Union. In one case, the task of the parliament was to accept a draft for a new Russian constitution, which would then be sent to the Congress of People's Deputies for ratification. Making a long story short, on 26 March 1992, the parliament accepted nine amendments to Chapter 2 of the draft by majority vote, and then voted against the whole of Chapter 2, including the nine amendments. The shocked Speaker rearranged a new vote, and then a third one, but each time a narrow majority of the deputies rejected Chapter 2, although they had already accepted *all* its parts separately. The same pattern recurred in the next day: the deputies first amended Chapter 3 of the draft five times, and then again rejected the entire chapter. Finally, on 4 April, a majority in the parliament voted to approve the amended version of the draft constitution – including the previously rejected Chapters 2 and 3 – and to submit it to the Congress for ratification (Andrews 2002: ch. 2.)

How was such an anomalous series of voting results possible? This case may be explained as an instance of the logical problem of *judgement aggregation*. This problem has been discussed by Kornhauser and Sager (1986, 1993) as the 'Doctrinal Paradox', and it has been generalised and analysed by Christian List and Philip Pettit in great detail in their numerous works (e.g., List and Pettit 2002; List 2006). In modern presentations, Kornhauser and Sager are usually mentioned as the inventors of the problem. However, the very same problem of collective incoherence was analysed in detail by a forgotten legal theorist, the Danish lawyer Albert Heckscher (1857–1897) in his dissertation *Bidrag till Grundlæggelse af en Afstemningslære* (1892; see Lagerspetz 2014).

The problem of judgement aggregation may be illustrated with the following imaginary example. Suppose that there are three separate decisions that are to be decided in referenda. First, voters are asked whether more money should be spent on defence; in the second referendum, they are asked whether more money should be spent on social services; in the third, they decide whether taxes should be increased. Suppose that if *both* defence costs *and* social services are increased, there is no way to cover the costs of those increases except by rising taxes. In such a series of decisions, groups of rational voters (A, B, C) who vote according to their preferences (or judgements) may produce an irrational *combination* of decisions (see Table 2.1). In the example in Table 2.1, the decision-making body, taken as a collective, accepts both increases to the public budget but rejects the means to finance them. The collective, as a whole behaves like an akratic individual: it sets itself an attractive end, but refuses to accept the available means, thus violating the principle of means–ends coherence. It is important to recognise that this aggregation problem does not presuppose the majority principle; it is more general. Indeed, it can be proven that under some very mild conditions, *no* rule aggregating individual judgements or expressions of will can produce a consistent set of collective judgements on an interconnected set of issues in all possible circumstances (List and Pettit 2002).

The diachronic version of the problem is, from our point of view, more relevant than the synchronic version. While a reduction of the number of options to the dichotomous yes–no format may make synchronically inconsistent voting results less likely or even eliminate them, there seems to be no similar method to reduce the number of interconnected binary decisions arising during the lifetime of a decision-making body. The number of issues, as well as their content and order, is partly exogenous: the issues have to be discussed and decided on when they arise. This would not constitute a problem if a decision-making body could just ignore its past judgements, treating them like the judgements of a different body.

Table 2.1 A problem of aggregation in three referenda

Groups	Increase Defence?	Increase Social Services?	Increase Taxes?
A	N	Y	N
B	Y	N	N
C	Y	Y	Y
Majority	Y	Y	N

However, political bodies are subject to expectations of diachronic as well as synchronic consistency. They are expected to pursue policies consistently over time, and to keep their commitments to their members as well as to outsiders (Pettit 2004b: 98). They are expected to have a 'will'.

The general case of collective means–ends incoherence is depicted in Table 2.2. In the example, a majority (B and C) accepts the commitment to the collective end E. Another majority (A and C) agrees on the essentially factual judgement that if E is accepted as the collective end, M is the best means to it. A third majority, however, rejects M. A rejects it, because they do not accept the end; B rejects it because they do not agree that M is a good means to E. The collective consisting of A, B and C lacks means–ends coherence, hence, it cannot be self-governing.

Prima facie, the possibility of incoherence constitutes a serious argument against all notions of collective will or collective judgement. A more precise version of the argument runs as follows:

1. If a being is self-governing, then the decisions and judgements it makes must be sufficiently consistent, coherent and stable.
2. If a collective being is democratic, then it is responsive, that is, its decisions and judgements correspond to the aggregated preferences and judgements of its members.
3. If the decisions and judgements made by some collective being correspond to the aggregated preferences and judgements of its members, there is no way to guarantee that those decisions (and reasons behind them) are consistent, coherent and stable.
4. Then, there is no way to guarantee that a democratic collective being is self-governing.

Table 2.2 Collective means–end incoherence

Groups	Commit to the End E?	M the Best Means to E?	Accept Means M?
A	N	Y	N
B	Y	N	N
C	Y	Y	Y
Majority	Y	Y	N

Earlier I argued that democratic self-government requires responsiveness. The argument, however, shows that responsiveness may also undermine self-government. Unlike traditional arguments against 'passionate' (i.e., irrational or myopic) majorities, the argument derived from the judgement problem is *not* based on the supposition that individuals are not fully rational.

Limits of Responsiveness

Many authors, inspired by social choice theory, have rejected all notions of collective will, and with it, the ideas of self-government and responsiveness (for the most influential formulation of the argument, see Riker 1982; for a recent version, see Weale 2018). However, for the philosopher Philip Pettit, it is obvious that collectives do at least *sometimes* have intents, ends and plans, and that at least sometimes they *are* able to perform actions and make judgements. The requirements of justifiability of individual decisions and of integrity or coherence of different decisions are meaningful in collective as well as in individual cases. In his work Pettit (2003a, 2003b, 2004a, 2004b, 2006; List and Pettit 2011) has tried to show how the notions of collective will or collective judgement can be reasonable in some institutionally constrained situations, and he argues that this view has important consequences for the design of democratic institutions (Pettit 2003b, 2004a). According to Pettit, collectives can sometimes be like persons with wills of their own that are not reducible to the intentions and actions of individual members of those collectives. For him, the fundamental solution to the problem of interest aggregation is the acceptance of *path-dependence* in collective decision-making. In other words, the content of the final collective judgement or decision is sometimes dependent on the order in which the preceding decisions or judgements are made, and not only on the distribution of opinions. An outcome is justifiable if it results from a path that has an independent justification – even when the outcome is not, as such, supported by a majority of decision makers. Thus, the possibility of collective or social rationality is essentially dependent on the internal organisation of reasoning in decision-making bodies. In our example, one of the three referenda should not be arranged.

Then, the outcome becomes dependent on the chosen path. For example, if people are first allowed to decide that they want more social services and then that they do not want more taxes, the option of spending more on defence would have to be dropped. If, by contrast, people first vote on defence and on social services, then they should not vote on taxes.

Because responsiveness increases the probability of incoherent results, and incoherence precludes collective will, the democratic ideal *does not require maximal responsiveness*. If we insist, *contra* conclusion (4), that democratic bodies may have a will, if premise (1) is a part of the meaning of 'having a will', and if premise (3) is a logical result, then it is the requirement (2) that has to be modified. This means that the strong responsiveness requirement supported by many theorists of democracy from Rousseau to Habermas is potentially incompatible with the requirement of coherence. More specifically, path-dependence is incompatible with the Habermassian requirements that the participants are free 'to call into question any proposal' and 'to introduce any proposal', or the principle that 'in the discursive justification and validation of truth claims no moment is privileged as a given, evidential structure which cannot be further questioned' (Benhabib 1994: 5; cf. Habermas 1996). Although collective deliberation is a part of any solution to the problem of democratic *akrasia*, a reference to deliberation is not sufficient. At any given moment, democratic deliberation has to be constrained by earlier decisions, shared presuppositions and pre-existing rules.

In actual democracies, the responsiveness of democratic mechanisms *is* constrained in numerous ways. A commitment to earlier decisions is an important example. Collectives may be bound by their earlier (substantive as well as procedural) commitments, and those commitments partly determine their subsequent choices. Legislative bodies are bound by constitutions and international agreements that cannot be changed by a simple majority decision. They also face many constraints of a technical nature, which limit the ability of shifting majorities to change policies. A budget, for example, is largely determined by the commitments arising from earlier decisions; the parliament cannot simply refuse to fulfil these commitments without changing the laws that govern those commitments. A change in law, in its turn, is regulated by various procedural rules, committee systems, and other institutional practices and expectations. The representative system forces political groups to negotiate and seek mutually compromises. Once made, the compromises have a binding force. A parliamentary decision cannot simply be revoked when a majority happens to change their mind.

New statutes, accepted by the present parliament, are often interpreted and applied in the light of earlier statutes, unless the earlier statutes are explicitly repealed (on this, see Levenbook 2020). Although parliaments, political coalitions and, in the course of time, entire electorates change, a large mass of older legislation remains in place, and remains authoritative. The authoritative nature of the laws inherited from the past is not based on the acceptance of present majorities. Finally, and perhaps most importantly, the tripartite division of power and the relative independence of judicial and executive powers isolates parts of the political process from majoritarian pressures, and this is likely to increase the means–ends coherence of decision-making.

The rules and practices of constraint that I have identified have two roles. First, they have a constitutive rather than merely regulative role. There cannot be collective self-government without collective will, that is, without the ability to make binding commitments and plans. As noted above, 'collective will' is an institutional creation. It is partly constituted by institutional practices that make collective plans stable and collective commitments binding. Without rules and constraints, the people cannot rule themselves, because they cannot, as a collective, do anything at all. Secondly, constraints do not simply *limit* responsiveness. They may diminish the system's responsiveness to certain immediate changes of preferences, but, at the same time, they may make the system more responsive to citizens' *long-term* preferences. When confronted with conflicting majority preferences, the polity must nevertheless make choices. If it is self-governing over time, it often chooses in favour of those preferences that match with previous democratically accepted long-term plans and commitments (see especially Rubenfeld 2001). If, for example, a firm majority is committed to the general aim of fighting climate change, subsequent temporary majorities should not have a veto over specific policy decisions. If people have opted for less CO_2 emissions, in a self-governing polity, they are no longer free to simply choose higher oil consumption. Thus, while chosen policies cannot correspond to all preferences of all majorities, they should correspond to the preferences of *some* majorities. The majority will may be realised more effectively if the system is less responsive to the preferences of temporary and fleeting majorities. Thus, authors like Ross, Dahl, Lijphart, Arneson and Saward are wrong when they argue that responsiveness may be constrained only because democracy is traded off in favour of other values or principles (e.g., Saward 1994: 14). To repeat, responsiveness alone is an underspecified ideal.

Conclusion

There is no 'will of the people' – or of any larger collective – without concrete institutional rules specifying how individual actions are related to collective actions. In political journalism, every small electoral change is confusingly called an expression of the 'will of the people'. Critics like Riker or Weale are right in that quite often, no collective will can be constructed from voting results. If the Conservative Party wins a majority in a British election, it may make sense to say that 'the people wanted a Conservative government', for obviously getting a Conservative government was at least one reason why many voters voted for the Conservatives. Suppose, however, that no party wins a majority. To say that 'the people wanted to have a hung Parliament' is confusing, for there need not be a single voter in the electorate who wanted (or even expected) that particular result. Every voter simply voted for a party hoping that it would gain a majority.

However, *contra* Riker and Weale, or (even) Pettit, I think the expression 'will of the people' still has its uses. Suppose that clear majorities have, after discussion, freely expressed their support for a long-term political plan or commitment, and later renewed their support. It is plausible to say that the respective community governs itself (at least in these issues), and that the plans and commitments are in accordance with the will of its people. What I have in mind are commitments like the commitment to the welfare state in the Nordic countries, the commitment to human rights in most European states, or the commitment to the common defence policies in the NATO member states. These commitments have remained stable in those countries for some seventy years. They have endured several economic and political crises and innumerable changes in governing coalitions. They are good examples of how 'the will of the people' may guide policies: once democratically accepted they have been confirmed by numerous later decisions and structured the actions of subsequent governments and of courts and bureaucracies.

However, it should be remembered that inter-temporal consistency is only one aspect of rational self-government. We are fallible creatures; hence, we should also have means to change our decisions based on imperfect or erroneous information (Moore, Chapter 3, this volume; cf. Kelsen 1929). Changing circumstances and new information may provide good reasons to revoke past decisions, and an inability to revoke them is another possible sign of irrationality. A being who mechanically executes a pre-established programme is not more self-governing than one that constantly switches its course, and is therefore unable to execute any plan. If a collective body that constantly overrides its past decisions seems to suffer from something analogous to the weakness of will, a body that refuses to change its decisions in new situations behaves like a stubborn or compulsive individual. The latter forms of irrationality can sometimes be as troublesome as the former.[2]

Notes

1. Bratman (2009, 2012) discusses joint planning and self-government over time, but he does not apply his concepts to institutional contexts. Ekins (2013), Richardson (2002: ch. 12) and Shapiro (2011) apply Bratman's concepts to institutional will-formation.
2. I want to thank all the participants of the PALO meetings. I am especially grateful to Michael MacKenzie, Simo Kyllönen, Alfred Moore and Maija Setälä for their comments.

THREE

Reversibility and Democracy: The Epistemic Functions of Political Competition

Alfred Moore

Introduction

Reversibility is essential to democracy, which is often defined by the rotation of officeholders following competitive elections. And those elections are animated by the possibility of reversing the course of laws and policies. Although in practice there is a lot of policy persistence in democratic systems (Coate and Morris 1999, cited in MacKenzie 2021b), a system in which elections did not have the potential to remove officials and change significant policies would be hard to count as a democracy. Thus, German finance minister Wolfgang Schäuble's comment that 'elections cannot be allowed to change an economic programme of a member state', following the election of a left-wing government in Greece in 2015, seems clearly undemocratic in spirit (Varoufakis 2016; cf. Lagerspetz, Chapter 2, this volume). While we often talk of democracy involving the idea that the people, as sovereign, has the 'final say' in decisions, in a wider sense, 'the ongoing series of elections and the possibility of reversal means that *no-one has the final say in the long run*' (Whelan 2019: 559, added emphasis).

Reversibility is widely seen to be a crucial motivation for individuals and groups to support democratic systems even when they lose elections or particular decisions (Przeworski 1999). It is also at the heart of richer normative accounts of democratic legitimacy. Gutmann and Thompson (2004), for instance, emphasise the importance of 'provisionality' in generating democratic legitimacy.

And Urbinati insists that 'democracy is an open game of political decisions and revisions of previously made decisions' (Urbinati 2014: 101). As Albert Hirschman (1986) puts it, 'accepting uncertainty about whether one's own program will be realized is an essential democratic virtue: I must value democracy more highly than the realisation of specific programs and reforms, however fundamental I may judge them to be for further progress, democratic, economic, or otherwise.' Paraphrasing Hirschman, Urbinati notes that 'the only truly essential virtue of democracy is *love of uncertainty*' (Urbinati 2014: 98, italics in original; see also Müller 2021). Reversibility thus seems to be an essential feature of democracy.

Yet reversibility might make governing for the future harder, or even impossible. Acting responsibly in the interests of future generations requires a capacity for action, that is, the capacity for framing, choosing and executing a course of action in the form of policies and programmes. As Eerik Lagerspetz (Chapter 2, this volume) argues, a degree of consistency in action over time is a necessary condition for any individual or collectivity to be said to have a 'will' at all. Thus, whether a democracy can be said to have a will *with regard to long-term issues* would seem to depend on its capacity for consistent and steadfast action over time. For this reason, short electoral cycles are often taken to be one of the causes of democracy's short-sightedness. How can any collectivity make credible long-term commitments if those policies might be abandoned by the next set of officeholders? Why incur short-term costs if those policies might be overturned before they can bear long-term fruit? When Chinese President Xi Jinping told the UN General Assembly on 22 September 2020 that 'China will scale up its Intended Nationally Determined Contributions by adopting more vigorous policies and measures. We aim to have [carbon dioxide] emissions peak before 2030 and achieve carbon neutrality before 2060,' it was taken by one commentator to '*permanently change* the global fight against climate change' (Tooze 2020, added emphasis). By contrast, no sensible commentator would use the words 'permanently change' to describe American commitments on climate change. The commitments made by President Obama in Paris in 2015 under the UN Framework Convention on Climate Change were reversed by a new president after the 2016 election, and then reversed again following the election in 2020.

We thus seem to face a trade-off: democratic legitimacy depends on reversibility, but human survival may depend on steadfast action in the face of long-term threats. The logic of this trade-off has led some commentators to suggest that authoritarian governance is likely to be necessary to effectively combat climate change (Mittiga 2021). One assumption underlying Mittiga's argument – also present in the long tradition of eco-authoritarian thought to which it belongs (e.g., Ophuls and Boyan 1992; Randers 2012) – is that the central problem in responding to climate change is 'democratic Akrasia' or weakness of will. *We know what to do*, goes the argument, *but democratic systems are unable to act on that knowledge because they keep chopping and changing.* However, the decisive objection to this way of framing the democratic challenge of climate change is that *we do not know what to do* – or, more precisely, we might know what the problem is without knowing the best actual solutions or the best ways to realise those solutions. As MacKenzie observes, 'modern societies . . . are impossibly complex. The present is diverse, and the future will be too. As such, it is not clear what we should do now, or how we should respond to any specific public problems with potential long-term effects or consequences' (MacKenzie 2021b: 21). Democracy itself is the source of information not only about the appropriate ends of a society or group of people, but also about the means. Reversibility is thus valuable partly because it is an expression of the human freedom to act otherwise, but also partly because knowledge is provisional. Democracy is, among other things, 'an institution for pooling widely distributed information about problems and policies of public interest by engaging the participation of epistemically diverse knowers' (Anderson 2006: 8). When I use the term 'epistemic' in this chapter, I have in mind this social and technical sense of the epistemic dimension of democracy, and not such things as approximating the truth about justice, invoked in some theories of 'epistemic democracy' (Estlund 2008; see Moore 2017: ch. 1, on these two ways of framing the 'epistemic' dimension of democracy). Rather than a simple trade-off, then, it may be that the features that make democracy good at working out what to do – experimentalism, diversity, criticism, opposition – are also the things that make it difficult to act steadfastly. We then face a question of balance. How can democracies best balance the need for both steadfastness and reversibility? How can the goods of reversibility (both in terms of legitimacy and knowledge) be balanced against its risks?

In this chapter I ask: how, to what extent and under what conditions, might party competition be able to provide this balance of reversibility and steadfastness? Framing the problem of governing for the future around the function of parties, partisanship and political competition constitutes a major departure from existing approaches. Democratic theorists considering the problem of governing for the long term have tended to assume some version of what MacKenzie (2021b) has called the 'democratic myopia thesis': that democracies, in large part because of their reliance on party organisation and regular electoral contests, are structurally unable to govern for the long term. Such theorists have then typically focused on supplementary institutions located above, below or otherwise outside the central institutions of electoral democracy. Examples include Offices for Future Generations (OFGs), councils and committees, randomly selected minipublics and even a 'World Court of Generations' (Boston 2016a; Tonn 2018; MacKenzie 2021a; Smith 2021). This approach echoes a broader trend in democratic theory over the last half-century, which has sought to identify and amplify the democratic potentials of practices and institutions beyond the parties and parliaments of territorially defined democracies. To some extent these theoretical developments track shifts in the location of power to transnational networks of governance (Grewal 2009), and the emergence of issue constituencies and problems of governance that do not necessarily match territorial constituencies (Warren 2009). But these developments also reflect a long-standing neglect by political theorists of the theme of parties and partisanship (Rosenblum 2008).[1] MacKenzie's *Future Publics* (2021b), for instance, details a range of institutional innovations that can contribute to the deliberative balancing of flexibility and steadfastness required for future-regarding governance, and while he proposes to integrate them into a partisan system, he gives little explicit attention to parties and partisan competition. My aim, however, is not to criticise those who focus on supplementary institutions, but to reframe their approach as part of a broader project of finding ways to improve and reform the central institutions of democracy to make them more future-regarding.

I consider three arguments for the broad claim that electoral reversibility can generate epistemic goods that in turn support the necessary balance between flexibility and steadfastness in long-term governance. First, I discuss Hans Kelsen's defence of multi-party coalitions and post-electoral deliberation and compromise, highlighting his emphasis on fallibilism. I then turn to Francis McCall Rosenbluth and Ian Shapiro's defence of two-party systems, in which they argue that these systems help to stabilise and moderate political conflict by motivating responsible, future-regarding governance. And, finally, I consider David Runciman's account of the value of democracy as a system of experimentation. These arguments all challenge the idea that short electoral cycles undermine the ability of democracies to govern for the long term. In various ways they all suggest that party competition can provide both fallibilism and experimentalism, on the one hand, and some measure of stability and steadfastness, on the other. These arguments, I conclude, are not entirely successful, though Kelsen's argument for the merits of proportional representation and multiparty politics is supported empirically by Caluwaerts and Vermassen (Chapter 9, this volume). Governance and governability outside of and across electoral frames – as well as the creation of institutions that embed longer-term perspectives – will be crucial if democracies are to respond to their long-term problems. A careful consideration of arguments for the long-term benefits of party competition opens up space for a more nuanced account of the different ways in which the goods of steadfastness and reversibility can be balanced in democratic systems.

Kelsen and Multiparty Politics

Long celebrated as a legal theorist, Hans Kelsen's democratic theory has recently been rediscovered by political theorists who are interested in parties and partisanship (Baume 2018; Ragazzoni 2018; Wolkenstein 2019a). Kelsen's democratic theory – primarily articulated in *The Essence and Value of Democracy* ([1929] 2013)[2] – places political parties at its heart: a 'democratic state is necessarily and unavoidably a multiparty state' (Kelsen [1929] 2013: 36). The recent wave of attention to Kelsen's work has highlighted a number of key elements of his theory, including his philosophical relativism, defence of proportional representation and theory of compromise. This work continues a long-standing identification of Kelsen with a 'minimalist' tradition in democratic theory (see Przeworski 2010a), and his inclusion in this tradition is understandable: Kelsen clearly rejects the Rousseauean idea of a unitary general will, and treats parliamentary democracy primarily as a device for peacefully managing political conflict in pluralist societies. However, I want to emphasise – contrary to some recent readings – an important thread running through his democratic theory concerning the epistemic function of competition. There is, I suggest, an epistemic dimension to his account of the value of party competition, which links his discussions of relativism, compromise and multiparty politics. He defends party competition in part as a response to the complexity and diversity of modern societies. In short, Kelsen articulates one way of balancing reversibility and steadfastness through political competition.

I will begin where Kelsen ends *The Essence and Value of Democracy*, with a discussion of the connection between democracy and relativism. Democracy, he insists, must be procedural. That is, it must be concerned with *how* norms are created, not *what* those norms should posit. The idea that democratic procedures imply a specific answer to questions of the substantive organisation of society (socialist or capitalist, for instance) rests on a claim that the people have some special insight into the good, and this in turn is a 'religious–metaphysical hypothesis . . . as ridiculous and impossible as a belief in the divine right of kings' (Kelsen [1929] 2013: 83). The rejection of a belief in absolute truth and absolute values is, for Kelsen, at the core of democracy:

> He who views absolute truth and absolute values as inaccessible to the human understanding must deem not only his own, but also the opinion of others at least as feasible . . . He can therefore justify the coercion that a social order inevitably requires in no other way than with the assent of at least the majority of those who are supposed to benefit from the coercive

order. Furthermore, because the minority is not absolutely wrong, the coercive order must be constructed in such a way that the minority will not be rendered entirely without rights and itself can become the majority at any time. (Kelsen [1929] 2013: 84–5)

Some commentators have taken Kelsen's firm rejection of 'absolute truth' and his embrace of 'relativism' as meaning that he offers a non-epistemic account of democracy, treating democracy simply as 'a way of managing conflict and disagreement by giving all competing views and interests within society an equal opportunity to exercise political power, in a provisional and revisable way' (Invernizzi-Accetti, in Moore et al. 2020: 6). Yet this reading neglects the distinction that Kelsen makes between, on the one hand, 'knowledge of absolute truth and insight into absolute values,' and, on the other hand, the 'relative truths and values', which are rooted in experience, and which are 'given and perceptible' to human cognition but 'changeable and constantly in flux' (Kelsen [1929] 2013: 84).

Kelsen, then, is anti-absolutist. But this does not make him anti-epistemic. Rather, Kelsen juxtaposes claims of divine right by way of divine (and unquestionable) knowledge to knowledge produced *fallibly* and *collectively*. As other commentators have observed, Kelsen's conception of relativism is itself underspecified. Across his body of legal and political theory he uses it to mean at least four things: first, moral subjectivism or emotivism, that is, the idea that political convictions have no cognitive content; secondly, anti-foundationalism (Kelsen 1951: 644), the idea that all judgements rest ultimately on presuppositions that cannot themselves be justified; thirdly, the Kantian idea that the subject plays an active role in cognition; and, fourthly, fallibilism, the idea that our judgements rest on imperfect evidence and must always be open to revision (Lagerspetz 2017: 161–2; see also Vinx 2007). I have emphasised his fallibilism, which he articulates most clearly in *The Essence and Value of Democracy*. Carl Schmitt, I think, understood Kelsen correctly in this respect when he associated his thought with a liberal view of parliament as the place 'where a relative truth is achieved through discourse, in the discussion of argument and counterargument' (Schmitt [1923] 1988: 46), and thus with a 'foundational commitment to the principle of government by truth' (Stanton 2016: 42). This commitment itself takes procedural form. Because 'earthly truth' (Kelsen [1929] 2013: 85) is partial, incomplete and ever-changing, democratic politics must resist closure, and remain always provisional and revisable.

Although there is an important epistemic dimension to his theory of democracy, Kelsen's primary argument for multiparty democracy and proportional representation is rooted in the ideal of political equality. At the core of his argument is the idea that political equality implies majority rule. When we find ourselves bound to obey laws we did not vote for, Kelsen thinks we are unfree. He thus firmly rejects Rousseau's claim that we are in some sense free when we obey the majority. For Rousseau, the fact that a majority voted for a law suggests that the majority is *correct*, and that the minority can be said to have made an error. And we cannot be said to be acting freely if we are acting on false premises. This, for Kelsen, is the 'absolutist' conception of truth transposed onto the collective figure of 'the People'. His response is that majority rule is justified not because the majority is likely to be *right* in Rousseau's sense of the term, but simply because it minimises the number of people who find their freedom infringed by laws they did not approve. Kelsen defends majority rule because it reflects the will of *the most*. The proper premise of the principle of majority rule, he writes, is that 'if not all, then at least as many individual wills that are in conflict with the general will of the social order should be minimised' (Kelsen [1929] 2013: 29).

This critique of Rousseau is also manifest in the way Kelsen understands political parties. The 'people' invoked in ideas of democracy is not a substantial or organic unity. The 'people' can be construed only in terms of a plurality of groups, comprising individuals integrated into 'associations based on their various political goals' (Kelsen [1929] 2013: 36), namely, political parties. Parties are necessary for individuals to have influence over the content of law, but they also guard against the illusion of mistaking the majority will for the general will, for its nature as a compromise among competing groups will be written on its face (Kelsen [1929] 2013: 37). In institutional terms, Kelsen's argument implies proportional representation and multiparty democracy.

The problem with Single Member Plurality systems, such as that the UK's 'Westminster model', is that whenever the ruling party has less than 50 per cent support (which is most of the time), the majority has law imposed on it by the minority. Proportional representation reflects the basic commitment to political equality and majority rule. This commitment, however, raises the problem of producing a majority in a multiparty system, and here Kelsen emphasises the importance of *compromise*.

Kelsen imagines a system of multiple parties competing for votes and then engaging in a parliamentary process of post-electoral deliberation which results in the formation of a government that expresses the will of the majority. The process of integrating a majority *as a majority* is one which (in a multiparty state) will typically require compromise and constant shifting and manoeuvring. The majority principle is thus a 'principle of compromise and of the balancing of political differences' (Kelsen [1929] 2013: 60). This process of compromise takes place in parliament, and because the majority emerges from a process in which each party had a share of seats proportional to their votes, it can claim to satisfy the will of *most*. Yet his account of compromise is ambiguous. Some commentators take him to be saying that compromise between parties is essentially a matter of bargaining between conflicting interests, anticipating the somewhat pneumatic theories of interest-group pluralism that became popular in post-Second World War political science. This reading has some plausibility. Kelsen writes, for instance, that 'the determination of the content of the law can only occur in one of two ways: through the dictatorship of only one group interest or through a compromise among several group interests' (Kelsen [1929] 2013: 70). He also seems implicitly to take preferences as pre-formed inputs to the electoral process. Thus, in Przeworski's view, Kelsen replaces deliberation with bargaining and requires only that those 'bargains must be from time to time approved by voters' (Przeworski 2010b: 7051). White and Ypi likewise conclude that Kelsen's notion of compromise reduces ultimately to bargaining between group interests (White and Ypi 2016: 153).

Yet some features of Kelsen's argument clearly push against the idea that he is simply an interest-group pluralist *avant la lettre*.

He views parties, after all, as groups of like-minded people bound by their beliefs and opinions, not simply their interests (Kelsen [1929] 2013: 35). Furthermore, he repeatedly emphasises the importance of argumentation as part of the process of creating parliamentary majorities. The majority becomes a majority only by virtue of compromise issuing from a process of 'speech and counter-speech, argument and counterargument' (Kelsen [1929] 2013: 60). Kelsen's account of post-electoral parliamentary compromise is undermined, as Manin observes, by his recommendation of imperative mandates and the suggestion of recalling representatives who do not show sufficient party loyalty. It seems clear that compromise would be undermined by such practices, for parliamentarians need a measure of autonomy in order to decide which of their positions to soften, which interests to trade-off, which values to compromise, and so on (Manin 1997: 214). Thus, the problem with Kelsen's notion of compromise, then, is not so much that it reduces to mere interest-group bargaining, but that it is ambiguous between bargaining and more principled forms of compromise arising from 'the dialectical process in both the popular assembly and parliament' (Kelsen [1929] 2013: 84; see Knight and Schwartzberg 2020, for a recent survey of bargaining from the point of view of democratic theory).

Kelsen's normative defence of party democracy is often located in the minimalist tradition and taken to be focused exclusively on the management of social conflict through peacefully processing societal conflicts of interest. However, on my reading, Kelsen invokes an epistemic conception of the value of political competition and subsequent processes of partisan compromise, where competition and compromise roughly map onto flexibility and steadfastness. He defends the institutional strengthening of minorities through proportional representation on grounds that political convictions, beliefs and opinions must be balanced, and none adopted fully and without reservation (Kelsen [1929] 2013: 84). Furthermore, this insistence draws on the idea that such beliefs and opinions are rooted in human experience and cognition that is 'changeable and constantly in flux' (Kelsen [1929] 2013: 84). Fallibility is a thread running through his argument, and it suggests an important, though neglected, epistemic dimension to his account of political competition. This epistemic dimension is hinted at by Saffon and Urbinati, who assert that people participate in politics to 'win or contain the winner', but immediately add that '[d]emocracy makes of fallibility a good, by making all decisions open to change, and hence preventing mistakes from becoming permanent' (Saffon and Urbinati 2013: 461). The reference to 'fallibility' and 'mistakes' implicitly recognises an epistemic and future-regarding dimension to practices of political competition. Reversibility – or the possibility of it – can support, rather than hinder, our capacities to engage in future-regarding collective action, precisely because it prevents mistakes becoming permanent. This epistemic dimension of processes of competition and compromise in multiparty democracy is further developed and empirically grounded in Caluwaerts and Vermassen (Chapter 9, this volume).

Shapiro and Two-Party Politics

I now turn to Ian Shapiro, who for many years has given a robust defence of political competition understood in terms of two large parties on the 'Westminster' model. For Shapiro, as for Kelsen, politics is primarily a matter of peacefully reconciling conflicting interests, and party competition serves legitimacy by ensuring that the political system responds to the will of the majority. Yet Shapiro is sharply critical of the case for proportional representation and multiparty democracy. He is also vigorously critical of deliberative democracy, which he interprets as a model of democracy in which participants are supposed to be aiming for consensus, but he invokes a broadly Millian epistemic rationale for political competition. The competition of parties is supposed to drive the adversarial testing of arguments and claims. Shapiro's claim that two-party competition (in its ideal form) produces responsible long-term government rests, at least in part, on this process of adversarial testing and selection.

Shapiro's ideal of political competition is two-party competition. For Shapiro, it is not parliamentary coalitions and compromise that should integrate the majority will, but rather large parties enjoying 'temporary power monopolies' subjected to 'alternating control over time' (Shapiro 2016: 67, 64). The alternation of effective power monopolies between two large parties serves, first, to promote accountability. Well-functioning competition, he argues, serves to institutionalise opposition in the form of a 'potential alternative government' that can hold the government to account and appeal to the interests of those not well-served by that government (Shapiro 2003: 74). Secondly, he suggests, competition between two large parties is a force for moderation. Rosenbluth and Shapiro compare the incentives faced by leaders of political parties at elections as being like the last-best-offer in labour negotiations:

> where the arbitrator is forbidden to craft a compromise between the two sides but must instead pick one of their final offers. This gives both sides powerful incentives to avoid posturing or making demands that will strike the arbitrator as unreasonable. The smart strategy is to take the most robust position that you can for your supporters, but to do it in a way that the arbitrator will find more plausible than the position of your adversary – who you know is trying to do the same thing you are. Not surprisingly, this kind of arbitration generally causes both sides offers to converge. (Rosenbluth and Shapiro 2018: 31)

The end effect is moderation and constraint on both voters and parties: parties are strong enough to make 'tough choices' with a view to their long-term reputation, and voters therefore are not given what they want (which may reflect short-sighted and incoherent preferences), but rather a choice between two relatively coherent options. This moderation, they further claim, yields better long-term decision-making, suggesting a tight coupling between electoral accountability and long-term economic performance (Rosenbluth and Shapiro 2018: 239).

Rosenbluth and Shapiro's argument, in essence, is that two-party systems work, when they work, because competition for the median voter forces parties to craft a fiscally responsible long-term agenda. Voters can be as selfish and short-sighted as they like, but they have no choice but to endorse one of two different but equally credible and responsible policy platforms. To Lagerspetz's problem (Chapter 2, this volume) of willing the ends but not willing the means, Rosenbluth and Shapiro might respond that in idealised two-party systems, party platforms will coherently link means and ends.

The constraint on the escalation of impossible promises is electoral competition between two strong parties. The problem for multi-party systems, on their argument, is that there is no incentive to long-term fiscal responsibility. 'Harmonious coalitions of diverse groups of voters who are willing to compromise for the economy's long-term health' (Rosenbluth and Shapiro 2018: 179) are what we would need, but are extremely hard to create in multiparty systems. Rosenbluth and Shapiro implicitly assume that the sort of fiscal constraints on governments run by a single party (such as financing of government debt on international bond markets) somehow do not also apply to governments formed by a coalition of parties. But their line of argument suggests that they would still have a problem with multiparty governments even if they proved to be every bit as fiscally responsible as their one-party counterparts, and the problem has to do with the visibility and coherence of a policy platform. They point to the risk that policies made through compromise and negotiation between parties will be like those fictional beasts made of the legs of a horse, the arms of a chimpanzee, the tail of a kangaroo and so on – an incoherent and dysfunctional mess (see also Goodin 2008). But this probably overestimates the coherence of policies that emerge from single 'catch-all' parties, and overestimates the degree to which voters vote based on policies or policy platforms. And there is another possibility: although not conceived by a single mind, so to speak, coalition agreements, and the policy packages they produce, might actually make more substantive sense – the process of compromise, haggling and bargaining, while it might produce the crudest of log-rolling, can also have the effect of filtering and checking the worst ideas and the most egregious corruption. After all, a coalition agreement is likely to be based on some common principled ground (see Bellamy 2012), and we would expect the process to reject the most corrupt forms of self-dealing, interest-group payoffs, and so on (at least, if a multiparty system is working well, which is the assumption they generously make on behalf of two-party systems). So the generous argument for *many* strong parties is in part epistemic – they are likely to legislate more responsibly for the long term because they include more perspectives and engage in a process in which the worst parts of every proposal are weeded out (this argument finds empirical support in Caluwaerts and Vermassen, Chapter 9, this volume).

Responsible government on Rosenbluth and Shapiro's model principally means fiscal responsibility. Thus, when they talk of 'policies that might have been better on average' (Rosenbluth and Shapiro 2018: 219), they essentially invoke a utilitarian criterion, referring to broad economic measures of GDP and productivity, as well as gestures to levels of health and education. As Wolkenstein (2019b) notes, this utilitarian definition of better policy is consistent with large minorities being left behind. However, from the point of view of long-term governance, the problem with their approach is somewhat different. There is an empirical sense in which the coupling of electoral accountability and long-term performance is unpersuasive. When they talk about the long-term policy effectiveness of two-party systems, they face the obvious rejoinder: what about Germany? They devote a whole chapter to explaining away the German exception, though their answer amounts to 'wait and see'. And their claim that proportional systems 'too easily reward politicians who cater to intense minorities' appears just pages after noting that then UK prime minister David Cameron, in a first-past-the-post system with a clear parliamentary majority, was bullied into holding a divisive referendum by a party that polled barely 15 per cent nationally (Rosenbluth and Shapiro 2018: 17). The recent experience of the United Kingdom with Brexit and the United States with Donald Trump creates an obvious empirical problem for a theory that two-party systems are more resistant to reactionary populism.

However, Rosenbluth and Shapiro's coupling of accountability and epistemic performance is also theoretically problematic. Parties might try to win elections by making sugar-rush promises that create long-term problems, and by masking trade-offs, but they claim that in well-functioning two-party systems this will not happen, partly because of long-term reputational concerns, and partly due to the constraint of having to aim for the median voter. Yet it is hard to see how – even in the best case – voters are supposed to accurately attribute long-term reputation when they are (on this account) unable to accurately attribute responsibility for short-term policies and their effects. If voters are not capable of attributing causal responsibility in the short term, it is not clear how they will be able to do it in the long term. Thus, on its own terms, it is hard to see how this theory can persuasively link longer-term responsibility to democratic reversibility understood in terms of electoral competition.

Like Kelsen, Shapiro argues that competition generates stability over time while at the same time arguing that competition drives an epistemic process of testing and revising arguments in response to a shifting social environment. While for Kelsen, these dimensions of competition are brought together (in an underspecified way) in parliamentary deliberation and compromise, for Shapiro they are emergent properties of an adversarial and winner-take-all two-party system. Shapiro thus sees competition, on the one hand, as an antagonistic struggle through which order emerges – which is an insight he credits to Schumpeter, who imagined democracy as 'a system [that] could control power by turning it into an object of electoral competition' (Shapiro 2003: 57). Armed with this 'Schumpeterian' model of order emerging through competition, Shapiro thus finds consensus and cooperation not only to be unrealistic aspirations, but also as very real threats to the conditions of competition on which order is based; they are, he argues, forms of 'collusion against democracy' (Shapiro 2017). On the other hand, Shapiro sees competition as generating beneficial externalities in the form of a Millian competition of ideas (Shapiro 2003: 149; 2016: 80). Yet by shifting the centre of this process from parliamentary deliberation and compromise towards electoral campaigning, Shapiro puts higher demands on voters' judgement. I have noted that his own doubts about the capacity of voters to accurately attribute responsibility for policies and their effects make this a less plausible line of argument.

Other theorists have sought to articulate the ways in which parties could (potentially) support and enable the epistemic judgements of voters; partly by reducing the complexity of the field of argument, in the way that a chess player narrows down the range of credible moves so as to focus attention most effectively (Manin 1987: 357); but also, by helping people locate proposals in the 'space of public political reasons' (Rummens 2012: 33). Theorists have also argued that parties can serve as a means of epistemic empowerment. They engage in information-processing about current states of affairs, relevant social and political institutions, and future events, and then they serve as 'epistemic trustees' to party followers – that is, as 'agents of roughly similar beliefs and commitment' (White and Ypi 2016: 90). 'Partisan forums' can function as 'learning platforms for citizens' (White and Ypi 2016: 91), enabling them to 'deepen their knowledge of complex institutional arrangements' (White and Ypi 2016: 91), and promoting 'hermeneutic resilience in the face of dominant discourses that risk suppressing the voices of the marginalised' (White and Ypi 2016: 93). These claims focus on the gain in individual epistemic power that (perhaps) could offset the loss of epistemic independence associated with partisanship. These epistemic dimensions of partisan contestation apply as well to multiparty as to two-party systems, but they also suggest the value of developing more nuanced accounts of the 'earthly' epistemic functions of competitive politics.

Runciman's Electoral Experimentalism

We have so far looked at two stylised accounts of political competition – one involving many parties and post-electoral compromise, another involving two parties and pre-electoral attempts to integrate a majority coalition – each of which suggests at least a possible way in which stability can coexist with argumentative contestation. They suggest schematic ways in which parties and partisan competition can contribute to a deliberative balancing of reversibility and steadfastness. In each case there is a sense in which competition for power is supposed to drive a search for evidence and the evaluation of arguments, and in this way ground a presumption that democracies are likely to find better solutions to complex problems (though, as I noted above, few of these theorists highlight their epistemic ambitions or frame them in those terms). Steadfastness and change are, on these accounts, balanced and combined by the institutions of parties and the procedures of electoral competition. Yet these broadly Millian accounts, in which competition drives the testing of arguments, might be too neat. Put another way, steadfastness and experimentation in a fundamental sense might be harder to combine through electoral and party politics.

To explore this possibility, I turn to David Runciman's argument that it is precisely the *lack* of steadfastness of democracies that gives them their epistemic edge.

In 'The Confidence Trap', Runciman looks at existential crises faced by states in the twentieth century (war, financial collapse, environmental disaster and rival regimes), and argues that the capacity of the democracies to adapt and change course is what enabled them to prevail over seemingly more coherent and decisive forms of government. 'Democracies find it much harder than other systems of government to coordinate their actions in the short term: the haphazard and volatile quality of democratic life makes reaching timely decisions difficult' (Runciman 2013: 20), but they have the 'ability to keep experimenting and adapting to the challenges they encounter, so that no danger becomes overwhelming' (Runciman 2013: 316). All people – voters, experts, statesmen, dictators – make mistakes. What is distinctive about democracies, on Runciman's account, is that they are less likely than authoritarian or technocratic regimes to get locked into their mistakes. The endless repetition of electoral contests and changes of governmental officials and policies means that democracies keep trying new things until they find what works. On this view, electoral democracy is a bit like a Roomba – the automated vacuum cleaner that constantly stops, turns, reverses and goes again, covering the room in a haphazard way. It seems not to be the most rational or efficient way of cleaning a room, but the constant movement is meant to prevent it getting stuck, and eventually it gets the job done. The analogy with democracy is limited because the Roomba has a defined goal – to not get stuck – whereas in democracies we do not have a defined goal, rather we choose various goals to pursue. However, the analogy highlights what Runciman takes to be one of the principal merits of party competition for political office: its ability to generate reversals in policy.

The same qualities that enable democracy to outlast or outperform rivals – 'flexibility . . . variety . . . responsiveness' (Runciman 2013: xv) – also cause democracy to go wrong. Democracies make mistakes and they are not very good at pursuing particular paths with any consistency or resolution. But their constant reversing has the benefit of preventing them from getting stuck. They keep trying different things until they find something that works. This way of looking at democracy does not presume a great deal of wisdom on the part of either the electorate or political leaders. It does not suppose that voters accurately attribute responsibility for effects to particular policies and persons, and reward or punish them at the polls accordingly (which, as Achen and Bartels (2016) claim, they are perhaps not even capable of doing). Rather, elections can have – as Przeworski (2010a) notes – a pretty high degree of randomness. Especially in Single Member Plurality systems, tiny shifts in the distribution of votes can lead to large shifts in the overall composition of the parliament, and routinely turn minority approval across the country as a whole into large parliamentary majorities.

The point here is that even if they are a bit random, democracies can not only still serve to legitimate government – through giving plausibility to the belief that the other side might win next time – but they can serve epistemic ends by trying lots of things and not getting stuck. Of course, this presumes that there is some recognition somewhere in the system that something works at all – some way of knowing what counts as working. Unless good policies are somehow stickier than bad ones, there is no reason to think that chopping and changing will lead to better long-term performance. But the argument does not depend on voters being able to formulate clear policies in response to problems and to evaluate and attribute particular effects to particular decisions. It does not matter – to use Achen and Bartels' (2016) example – if President Wilson did not cause the shark attacks that (supposedly) led him to lose votes in one district in the 1916 election (which he still won, do not forget – for every voter blaming him for a shark attack there was probably another crediting him for a good harvest); what matters is that the system keeps changing things. The capacity to not get trapped, Runciman claims, is a huge epistemic advantage for democracies.

One interesting feature of Runciman's discussion of Tocqueville is the emphasis on the opacity of democracy's strengths. Its weaknesses – that it is 'haphazard, uncoordinated, occasionally ridiculous' – are in plain sight, but its strengths can only be seen over time and at the systemic level. After all, it is not the individual politicians who are characterised by 'flexibility', 'variety' and 'responsiveness', but the political system extended over time. The adaptability of democracy is not a function of anyone actually trying to be adaptable, or of publics or leaders aiming for adaptability. But nor, on Runciman's account, is adaptability simply a side-effect of actors aiming to win power within the rules of the game (though many actors may be doing just that). It is a side-effect of many actors 'groping for a solution, even as they keep making mistakes' (Runciman 2013: xvi).

This, then, is an epistemic argument about the effects of variety and competition on the capacity of a political system to solve problems which threaten its existence. It is cast at a high level of generality and abstraction. Runciman freely admits that he defines democracy in quite general terms, as a political system with regular competitive elections and a free press.[3] But Runciman's theory usefully connects this systems-level analysis to an individual ethos: the 'confidence trap' refers to a sort of complacency that is grounded in a belief in the systemic adaptive capacities of democracies, a belief that is only warranted to the extent that people exhibit a sort of vigilance that is premised on a lack of complacency. The point about the essential opacity of the democratic system, then, is not simply that it is complex, or that power operates through hidden channels and relationships – it is not a thesis about the 'real' location of political power or the deeper 'structures' of power beneath the surface of political contest and electoral spectacle. Rather, it is a claim that democracy works best when its participants think it is not working, and that it works worst when its participants have too much faith it.

On Runciman's argument, the steadfastness that emerges from the process of chopping and changing depends on some recognition within the system that some policies and approaches work better than others. This entails some process of evaluation and feedback in which (1) policies that work sufficiently well are recognised as working, and (2) they then tend to survive subsequent electoral shifts. But long-term issues work on temporal scales that make it hard to see what is 'working'. For this reason, climate change presents a 'potentially fatal version of the confidence trap' (Runciman 2013: 318). The problem with climate change is that by the time it gets really serious, our options for doing anything to stop it may be limited or non-existent. And one of the reasons we do not take it seriously enough is rooted in our faith that experimentation and adaptation will help us sidestep the problem, as happened in the 1890s when it was predicted that New Yorkers would soon be knee-deep in horse manure from all the traffic (Runciman 2013: 317). So:

> democracies have the capacity to deal with climate change. They have the experimental adaptability, and they have the collective resilience under duress. The problem is that they don't know which one they need first. The knowledge that democracies have of their long-term strengths does not tell them how to access those strengths at the right moment. If anything it makes it harder. (Runciman 2013: 318)

On Runciman's account, then, electoral reversibility promotes adaptability in a way that enhances the capacity of the democratic system to cope with a wide range of threats, but meets its limit in the long-term challenge of climate change. Yet there is an underdeveloped aspect of Runciman's account. In order to adapt and solve problems, democracies need to be restless and prone to reverse course, but they also need some capacity for recognising and holding onto the things that turn out to work. Without a way to recognise what works and what does not, the constant changes of course could result in processes of continual change that do not come to rest on good or workable solutions. Implicit in the theory, then, is the idea that democracies have a way to recognise and hold on to things that are working and to think through and call into question things that are not working. This experimentalist argument for competitive politics, in short, depends on a society's capacity to acquire, produce and make sense of knowledge about the effects of policies. It is here that institutions designed to embed and promote longer-term perspectives may be vital to making competitive politics more sensitive to the problem of governing for the future.

Conclusion

In this chapter I have highlighted some of the ways in which parties and electoral competition can be thought to balance the goods of stability and reversibility – of steadfastness and flexibility – which I have taken to be central to future-regarding action. Current arguments in favour of party competition typically downplay their epistemic dimensions, and thus downplay the extent to which their success depends on party competition being embedded within a robust deliberative culture that enables reason-giving to do some of the work of balancing policy stability and change.

By contrast, I have focused on the epistemic dimensions of political competition. The theories explored in this chapter suggest different ways in which adversarialism and competition serve as discovery procedures that underwrite many implicit claims about the long-term performance and sustainability of democratic systems. As I mentioned in the introduction, this approach also marks a departure from those democratic theorists who have approached the problem of governing for the future by emphasising supplementary, non-electoral and non-adversarial institutions. However, the arguments presented here do not stand in opposition to arguments for supplementary institutions. Rather, it seems the case that supplementary institutions might be more productively and consciously conceived of in relation to existing partisan and electoral institutions.

What is crucial, in my view, is to think about supplementary institutions not as alternatives to competitive practices, or as being in opposition to them, but as potentially contributing to the effectiveness and sustainability of those practices. There is a tendency to think of minipublics, for instance, as 'short cuts' to an improved public sphere (e.g., Lafont 2019) – that is, to implicitly frame them as alternatives to, or end-runs around, dysfunctional partisan arenas. It may be more productive to think of them as potentially contributing to the conditions under which adversarial democratic practices can be expected to deliver some of their goods. Institutional innovations designed to embed longer-term perspectives can then be viewed as part of a democratic ecology in which parties can and must play a vital role in organising mass deliberation. This is in tune with what many deliberative democrats have been saying about the importance of 'systemic' views of democracy (Parkinson and Mansbridge 2012), but there is still much work to be done to bring theories of parties and partisanship into a productive conversation with theories of deliberative democracy that focus on new institutional designs.

Notes

1. Nancy Rosenblum's (2008) *On the Side of the Angels: An Appreciation of Parties and Partisanship* did much to reinvigorate interest in this theme, though among deliberative democrats Bernard Manin (1987: 357) has long maintained not only that public deliberation is essential to democratic legitimacy but also that the 'existence of political parties is essential for deliberation'.
2. Kelsen's book was edited and reissued in 2013 with an introductory essay by Nadia Urbinati and Carlo Invernizzi-Accetti.
3. By democracy he means 'any society with regular elections, a relatively free press, and open competition for power'. By autocracy he means 'any society in which leaders do not face open elections and where the free flow of information is subject to political control' (Runciman 2013: xxii).

FOUR

The Covid-19 Pandemic and Global Climate Change: Comparing Two Long-term Dangers

Sven Ove Hansson

Introduction

In recent debates, various connections, similarities and differences between the Covid-19 pandemic and anthropogenic climate change have been discussed. The pandemic delayed international action against climate change, and anti-environmentalists such as Jair Bolsonaro and Donald Trump have used it as a pretext for policies that worsen climate change (Cho 2020). On the other hand, measures against the pandemic temporarily curtailed traffic and industrial activities, with concomitant reductions in greenhouse gas emissions. One writer maintained that the virus 'could sport a silver lining of reduced carbon emissions and in turn lead to a more sustainable economy' (Teale 2020). However, the reduced emissions due to the pandemic are almost negligible in comparison with what is required to curb global warming (Forster et al. 2020; Gates 2020). Furthermore, the reductions needed to mitigate climate change could be much less expensive than the reduced economic activity due to Covid-19 (IPCC 2015: 24).

Worldwide responses to the pandemic have shown that behaviours can be changed abruptly (Vinke et al. 2020: 5), which is a good sign for climate action. The two problems have some common solutions, such as teleconferencing and reduced travelling (Kallbekken and Sælen 2021; Rosner and Schlegelmilch 2020). Some authors have also focused on the scientific evidence showing that climate change increases the risk of pandemics (Rice 2020).

(For pre-Covid-19 discussions of the effects of climate change on the prevalence of epidemics and pandemics, see Shope 1991; Reiner et al. 2015; Meyer 2019. See also Gorji and Gorji 2021; Watts et al. 2021.) Many authors have pointed out that we have important lessons to learn from Covid-19. Jeffrey Frankel, for example, summarised much of this discussion when emphasising that Covid-19 required 'respect for scientific expertise, well-designed public policy, and international cooperation', which must also be applied to climate change (Frankel 2020).

This chapter aims to systematise the comparisons between the pandemic and anthropogenic climate change, and to offer some comments on how democratic decision-making should relate to these types of issues. A major new perspective will be introduced in the comparisons. In the previous literature, the common approach is a comparison between a short-term threat (the pandemic) and a long-term threat (climate change) (see, e.g., Hepburn et al. 2020). This is not an accurate description. We need a strategy against the threat of new pandemics, not just against the current one. Both threats are long term in the sense of involving harms far into the future. They are also both short term, in the sense of requiring immediate action.

In what follows, the major similarities and differences between the threats posed by pandemics and climate change will be discussed. I have divided these threats into four groups, according to whether their main theme is causal, epistemic, temporal or distributional. The final conclusions emphasise the role of science in democratic decision-making on these types of issues.

Causality

There are several similarities but also at least one important difference between the two threats in terms of the cause–effect relationships involved in their creation and potential solutions.

Natural Phenomena Triggered by Human Activities

Both threats are caused by natural phenomena that are triggered by human activities. Therefore, they both have a combined natural and human causality. This may be less obvious for pandemics than for climate change. Humans have suffered from infectious diseases for as long as our species has existed, but pandemics belong to the modern, connected world. A pandemic is a worldwide epidemic, usually also characterised by an almost simultaneous worldwide transmission (Kelly 2011). When humans lived in relatively isolated groups, fast human-to-human transmission of infections over long distances was highly improbable. This changed with the development of farming, with its higher population densities and long-distance trading networks. Diseases such as the plague could then be transmitted over large distances (Rascovan et al. 2019), but the transmission was much slower than today. For example, the Black Death arrived in Europe (Constantinople) in 1347. Its spread over the continent has been described as rapid (Wood et al. 2003), but it arrived in Stockholm only in 1350 and in Moscow in 1351 (Kohn 2008: 32). This can be compared with the global transmission of Covid-19 over the course of a few months in early 2020. Globalisation and international air traffic have dramatically accelerated and extended the spread of infectious diseases (Hollingsworth 2007). In this sense, the threat of pandemics is an effect of human activities, just like global warming.

Solutions Require Government Action and Coordination

Neither climate change nor pandemics can be solved by voluntary action only. A considerable amount of government action and coordination is required. Unfortunately, this insight is a major driving force in the opposition to climate mitigation. Since the 1980s, free-market ideology has been used to attack health, safety and environmental regulations (Glicksman 2010). In a famous 2002 memorandum, Frank Luntz, an American media commentator and political strategist, urged right-wing politicians to employ a free-market strategy to combat climate change policies, which he depicted as 'over-reaching government' leading to 'just another tax on an already overburdened population' (Luntz 2002: 136, 139). According to Dryzek and Lo (2015: 14), this free-market strategy has been implemented on a large scale. Similarly, protests against health measures during the pandemic have been expressed in terms of personal freedom and resistance against government overreach (Agnew 2020; McKelvey 2020; Vieten 2020).

However, neither climate change nor pandemics are problems that can best be solved by leaving markets alone. This was explained by economist Jeffrey Frankel:

> Moreover, contagious disease and environmental damage are both classic examples of what economists call negative externalities: problems that markets cannot handle on their own, because people who sneeze without a mask or who pollute the air do not bear the full consequences of their actions. The growing recognition of public policy's essential role might lead the pendulum to swing away from small-government ideology. (Frankel 2020)

Solutions have to Include Changes in Lifestyles and Daily Habits

Countermeasures against both climate change and pandemics affect our lifestyles and daily habits. To mitigate climate change, we have to modify travel habits, food choices and other consumption patterns (Hoque 2014). Measures against Covid-19, such as curfews and closed workplaces, schools and shops, have given rise to considerable economic suffering and also to social isolation and psychological stress, in particular in vulnerable groups (Maharana et al. 2020; Rossi et al. 2020). These and other psychological issues need to be considered more than they were in previous discussions of possible measures against both pandemics and climate change.

Self-Regarding versus Other-Regarding Actions

Measures against disease dissemination during an acute pandemic can in most cases be justified as both self-regarding and other-regarding. By taking precautions, an individual reduces both the risk of contracting the disease and the risk of spreading it to others.

This is different for individual contributions to climate change mitigation. Those who refrain from flying and avoid buying products produced with CO_2-emitting technology do their part in helping to avert a threat to the whole of humanity, but their own contributions have no specific effect on the climate that they will experience themselves. In other words, the climate-based justification of such actions is entirely other-regarding, which can be a hindrance to climate action. However, some such actions also have positive effects for the individual, although these effects are not climate-related. For instance, reducing one's consumption of ruminant meat helps reduce CO_2, but it also helps promote one's own health (Watts et al. 2021: 130, 152).

Epistemology

Another dimension of these two issues has to do with epistemology. In this chapter I am using this term to cover foundational issues about what is and can be known, as well as social issues concerning the dissemination of knowledge and disinformation.

Predictions by Scientists Long Ago

Both climate change and global pandemics were predicted by scientists long ago. In 1896, Svante Arrhenius showed that higher CO_2 levels in the atmosphere would give rise to higher temperatures (Arrhenius 1896). However, he believed that such an increase would take several thousand years, and he assumed that its consequences would be quite benign. In the 1950s, scientists began to worry that human activities could have severe effects on the climate (Anderson et al. 2016). Two of them warned that humanity was 'carrying out a large-scale geophysical experiment of a kind that could not have happened in the past nor be reproduced in the future' (Revelle and Suess 1957: 19).

When the Intergovernmental Panel on Climate Change (IPCC) was formed in 1988, there was a scientific consensus on the reality of anthropogenic climate change (Oreskes et al. 2008: 115–16, 134–5. Cf. Shwed and Bearman 2010). That consensus is now overwhelming, and it is based on extensive empirical information (IPCC 2015; Cook et al. 2016). Attempts to refute it have all the characteristics of science denial, which is a variant of pseudoscience (Hansson 2017, 2020).

In the 1970s it was commonly believed that the total number of infectious agents affecting humans is 'relatively fixed'

(Rutstein 1974: 29). The discovery of the HIV virus in 1983 made the research community aware that new human pathogens can become threats to human health (Longini et al. 1986). Since the 1990s, this has been a major topic in medical microbiology. Scientists have pointed out the need for improved pandemic preparedness, both in terms of international cooperation and national legislation (Gust et al. 2001; Sands et al. 2016; Madhav et al. 2018). In 2004, the UN High-level Panel on Threats, Challenges and Change emphasised that the international spread of infectious diseases is much more rapid than before. They also called attention to 'the overall deterioration of our global health system, which is ill-equipped to protect us against existing and emerging infectious diseases' (United Nations 2004: viii). Their recommendations included strengthened international cooperation against infectious diseases and the rebuilding of national public health systems in developing countries 'as a means of fighting new emerging infectious disease' (UN 2004: 29).

In an article in 2007 on the risk of future pandemics, a group of researchers noted that:

> Coronaviruses are well known to undergo genetic recombination, which may lead to new genotypes and outbreaks. The presence of a large reservoir of SARS-CoV-like viruses in horseshoe bats, together with the culture of eating exotic mammals in southern China, is a time bomb. (Cheng et al. 2007: 683)

The emergence of a new strain of SARS-CoV virus, capable of human-to-human transmission, is exactly what gave rise to the Covid-19 pandemic that started in late 2019.

Decision-Makers Depend Heavily on Science

Both pandemics and climate change are issues for which the support of science is essential in all phases of decision-making, including problem identification and the construction and evaluation of solutions. Our knowledge of climate change is based on a long series of precise meteorological measurements, as well as scientific analyses of tree rings, ice cores, sediments and other natural objects.

Increasingly, non-scientists around the world, especially people living in close contact with nature, are observing environmental changes that are the effects of a changing climate (Herman-Mercer et al. 2016; Fernández-Llamazares et al. 2017). However, the larger picture, which connects these lay and professional observations with anthropogenic greenhouse gas emissions, could be achieved only with the resources of science.

Diseases caused by microscopic or submicroscopic pathogens can be understood only with the help of technologies and methodologies that have been developed in modern science. A precise understanding of contagion could be obtained only when modern microbiological knowledge of pathogenic organisms became available. Therefore, our basic understanding of pandemics is just as science-dependent as that of climate change. Science provided the tests, vaccines and therapeutic methods that are essential for combatting Covid-19. Science will have an equally important role in programmes for the early detection, containment and treatment of future pandemics.

The Amount of Scientific Uncertainty

In both areas there is a considerable amount of scientific uncertainty. Importantly, scientific uncertainty in an area does not exclude the presence of highly reliable scientific knowledge in the same area. In virtually all fields of science, there is *both* well-supported information that we currently have no reason to question *and* open questions, which science is currently unable to answer (Hansson 2018a). Climate change is a clear example of this. Although there is no reasonable doubt that anthropogenic climate change is real and that it threatens the life conditions of coming generations, there are many open questions concerning its precise effects and possible future trajectories. For instance, there is considerable uncertainty about possible tipping-points, beyond which irreversible and accumulating changes in the climate system will take place (Lontzek et al. 2015; Lenton et al. 2019).

Similarly, in spite of the large body of knowledge about infectious agents and the diseases to which they give rise, when a new type of virus or bacteria turns up, there is always an initial period of considerable uncertainty. This became obvious during the Covid-19 pandemic, not only in its early stages but also later, when new virus variants with largely unknown properties turned up.

Dissemination of Pseudoscience and Misinformation

A considerable amount of science denial and misinformation has been disseminated about climate change and the Covid-19 pandemic. Corporate and right-wing denial of climate science made its appearance in the early 1990s (Boykoff and Boykoff 2004: 129–33), and still has considerable influence, in particular in the United States (Cann and Raymond 2018). Its proponents claim that the existence of anthropogenic climate change is contested within science. According to David Goldston, a former Republican chief of staff for the science committee of the House of Representatives, climate change deniers 'settled on the "science isn't there" argument because they didn't believe they'd be able to convince the public to do nothing if climate change were real' (Begley 2007). The same strategy has been used in previous pseudoscientific and anti-scientific campaigns, not least those instigated by the tobacco and chemical industries (Oreskes and Conway 2010; Hansson 2017).

Throughout the Covid-19 pandemic, a notable amount of denial, misinformation and conspiracy theories about the virus and the disease has been propagated (Atehortua and Patino 2021). Claims have been made that the disease does not exist, that it is not at all serious, that it is disseminated via the 5G mobile network, that it can be cured with bleach, and that the vaccines are ineffective and dangerous. Studies have shown an association between such misconceptions and refusals to adopt behaviours aimed at protecting public health and reducing the spread of Covid-19 (Allington et al. 2020). In the American population, false beliefs about Covid-19 are strongly correlated with right-wing political convictions, just like climate science denial (Calvillo et al. 2020; Motta et al. 2020).

Difficulties in Denying the Existence of the Problem

Attempts have also been made to deny the very existence of important problems related to Covid-19 and climate change – problems that have been confirmed by science. In the case of a widespread deadly disease such as Covid-19, this is usually not easy to get away with. People get sick, and people die. Denying the disease can then be virtually impossible. However, that is no guarantee against misconceptions about the disease. The long history of AIDS/HIV denial shows that even when the presence of a deadly disease cannot be contested, rationally incontrovertible scientific information about its causes and – even more importantly – about efficient treatments can still be denied (Nattrass 2008; Kalichman 2009; Hansson 2020: 19). In the case of Covid-19, a more common form of science denial has been the denial of the severity of the disease. Donald Trump, among others, claimed that Covid-19 is no worse than the common flu (Dale and Subramaniam 2020; Woodward 2020).

Effects of climate change, such as hotter temperatures and higher frequencies of extreme weather events, are increasingly observed in all parts of the world. However, no particular hot period, flooding, drought or forest fire can be attributed to climate change with the same certainty that a particular patient's disease can be diagnosed as Covid-19. In this sense, the deniability of climate change is higher than that of Covid-19 or any other disease for which reliable diagnostic tests are available. There are still contrarians who claim, without evidence, that the observable recent changes in the climate are due to variations in solar activity (Bhatia et al. 2021).

The Amount of Corporate-Driven Science Denial

There are two major sources and drivers of science denial. One is corporate funding. Large companies that can increase their profits by promoting erroneous beliefs among the general public have invested considerable resources in the dissemination of pseudoscience, for instance, about tobacco, toxic chemicals and climate change (Oreskes and Conway 2010). The other major source of science denial is ideology, which can be religious as well as political.

In the case of climate change, both these forces have been highly active. Fossil fuel companies have spent large sums on promoting pseudo- and anti-scientific claims about climate change (Farrell 2016a, 2016b; Brulle 2018). This has been reinforced by an influential ideology, namely, that government non-intervention in the economy is an overarching goal that must be defended against almost any justification that is offered for policies that restrict private profit-making – including the prevention of disasters threatening the basic living conditions of future generations.

As already mentioned, similar ideological convictions have been drivers of science denial concerning Covid-19. However, with rare exceptions (Ward 2020), corporate money and support do not seem to have been involved to any significant extent. The most obvious explanation of this is that there do not seem to be any large companies that have much to gain from disseminating false claims about a pandemic.

Temporal Patterns

The problems of climate change and pandemics have more similar temporal patterns than has usually been recognised, but there is also an important difference.

Long-Term Effects and Need for Immediate Action

As mentioned above, it has often been erroneously assumed that Covid-19 is a short-term problem while climate change is a long-term one. But these notions are both highly ambiguous, since different aspects of a problem can have different time scales (MacKenzie 2021a). It is more useful to discuss the time scales of specific effects of actions (or inactions), or those associated with the need for action.

Climate change and the pandemic both concern effects that will last long into the future. New infectious diseases are sure to emerge, and some of them can develop into pandemics (Holmes et al. 2018; Shaman 2018; Lee et al. 2020). Treating Covid-19 as just a single event is as short-sighted as treating a higher-than-normal number of extreme weather events as a unique occurrence. Pandemic prevention and preparedness (PPP) will be important in the foreseeable future. Furthermore, the two problems both require immediate action. Ulrich Volk, among others, has clarified what this means for climate change:

The next few years are our last chance to avoid catastrophic global warming. It is imperative that the various crisis response measures amount to a transformative policy response. (Volk 2020)

Intermittent versus Accumulating Problems

In spite of these similarities there is also an important difference between the temporal patterns of the two crises: climate change is *cumulative*, growing slowly worse from year to year. Pandemics come *intermittently*. The next pandemic could come after several decades, or it may come while we are still trying to cope with Covid-19. (Viruses do not stand in a queue, waiting for those in front of them to finish.) Therefore, we have already seen the full effects of a pandemic (but not the worst possible pandemic), whereas we only see a small part of the effects that climate change will have in the future.

The intermittent nature of a pandemic may create the impression that it is a unique or once-in-a-lifetime event. This can contribute to explaining one commonly observed difference between public reactions to Covid-19 and climate change policies, namely, that citizens have been much more willing to change their way of life to cope with the pandemic than with climate change (Vinke et al. 2020: 5). But, perhaps not surprisingly, acceptance of Covid-19 restrictions has waned when these restrictions had to be prolonged far beyond the initial 'few months' (Vinke et al. 2020: 4) that were originally projected.

Spatial and Interpersonal Distribution

The last group of comparisons refers to how the harmful effects, the countermeasures and the effects of these countermeasures are distributed around the globe, between and within countries.

Every Person on the Planet is Affected

Both climate change and pandemics are severe dangers that will affect every person on the planet. The best available predictions of the effects of anthropogenic climate change are frightening enough.

The combination of temperature rise, ocean acidification and sea-level rise could lead to large-scale extinctions of terrestrial, fresh-water and marine species. The frequency of extreme weather events will increase, as well that of large wildfires. Risks from infectious diseases will increase globally due to extended infection areas and seasons, and the number of people who lack food security will also increase (IPCC 2015: 8–16, 64–74).

The potential effects of pandemics on human health are well known from history. The mid-fourteenth-century plague reduced the world's population from 450 million to below 350 million, and it killed more than half of the population in many parts of Europe (Huremović 2019). The 1918 influenza outbreak killed around 17 million people (Spreeuwenberg et al. 2018). Around 33 million people have died from AIDS, and around 700,000 still die from this disease each year (UNAIDS 2020). At the time of writing (April 2022), the global death toll from Covid-19 was 6.2 million and still rising. Cases have occurred in every country on the planet, and most of the world's population has been negatively affected by countermeasures against the pandemic.

The Effects are Unequally Distributed

The rich industrialised countries that can afford expensive adaptation measures are the countries expected to be least severely affected by climate change. Sub-Saharan Africa and small island states will be among those worst affected (King and Harrington 2018). In other words, the countries that contributed most to greenhouse gas emissions will be comparatively spared from the consequences, whereas those that contributed least will be much more severely affected. Within countries, the most affected will usually be those with the fewest resources for climate adaptation.

It is still too early to determine the geographical distribution of Covid-19 mortality and the long-term effects of the disease on health and social conditions. However, the delayed and inefficient vaccine distribution to poor countries is in itself a sign of egregious inequities (Loembé and Nkengasong 2021). Within the rich countries, the pandemic has had a much higher death toll in economically disadvantaged groups than in other social strata.

This seems to have been due to factors such as crowded homes, insufficient access to healthcare and working conditions not allowing for social distancing. As Farhana Sultana remarked: 'Thus, in the pandemic, we were actually not all in this together equally' (Sultana 2021: 452). In summary, the distribution of harms from Covid-19 follows the same problematic patterns as that of climate change.

Solutions Require International Cooperation

Both climate change and pandemics can in practice be efficiently dealt with only if national measures are combined with international cooperation and coordination. For climate change, international cooperation is necessary to avoid free-riding, to distribute burdens fairly, and to develop and introduce new technologies that facilitate the defossilisation of our energy systems. International cooperation is equally important in the fight against infectious diseases. No country is safe against an infectious disease that spreads and mutates uncontrolled in other countries. We need an improved early warning system, a fast, open and efficient exchange of information, and cooperation in the development of diagnostic methods, vaccines, drugs and treatments. The remarkably fast development, testing and approval of Covid-19 vaccines in 2020 was not matched by equally efficient mass production and distribution. That problem must be remedied in the preparation for new pandemics. Concerted research efforts to develop new anti-viral drugs, as well as antibiotics, should be equally important parts of any international plan for pandemic preparedness (Sands et al. 2016).

National Problem, International Problem or Mesoproblem

From a geopolitical point of view, we can distinguish between three types of problems. Fully *national problems* can prevail in a country without significantly affecting other countries, and they can be solved within a single affected country. Fully *international problems* are exemplified by climate change. The negative effects of greenhouse gas emissions are distributed over the whole world, and so are the positive effects of mitigation measures. There is no connection between the locality of an emission or a countermeasure and the localities of the effects on the climate that it contributes to.

Finally, *mesoproblems* are characterised by having both international and more concentrated national effects. On the solution side, each country gains most by domestic measures, but it also gains from measures taken in other countries. One example is transnational air pollution. Emissions of particulate matter in a country (e.g., from a coal power plant) usually have their worst effects within the producing country, but such pollution can also be carried to other countries by the wind (Du et al. 2020).

Covid-19 has largely been treated as a national problem, but it is a mesoproblem. Failure to contain the pandemic in a country will usually have its worst effects in that country, but it can also have large effects elsewhere. But the fact that a pandemic is a mesoproblem rather than a fully international problem like climate change provides national leaders with much stronger incentives to act on pandemics as compared with climate change.

Discussion

The comparisons between climate change and Covid-19 are summarised in Table 4.1. In what follows, I discuss the relevance of this analysis for future-regarding collective action.

Differences

Table 4.1 reports more similarities than differences between these two problems. In the *causality* category I identified only one major difference: most measures against infectious disease dissemination that are recommended during a pandemic contribute to protecting the individuals who take these measures. In contrast, those who make individual contributions to measures against climate change will not personally benefit from the specific efforts that they make. This makes it necessary to resort to other-regarding rationales to justify climate change mitigation policies. The lack of self-regarding arguments makes argumentation for climate mitigation more difficult than argumentation for measures against disease dissemination.

Table 4.1 A summary of the comparisons between climate change and pandemics

Type of Comparison	Similarities	Differences
Causality	Natural phenomena triggered by human activities. Solutions require government action and coordination. Solutions must include changes in lifestyles and daily habits.	Self-regarding versus other-regarding actions.
Epistemology	Predictions by scientists long ago. Decision-makers depend heavily on science. The amount of scientific uncertainty. Dissemination of pseudoscience and misinformation.	Difficulties in denying the existence of the problem. The amount of corporate-driven science denial.
Temporal patterns	Long-term effects and need for immediate action.	Intermittent versus cumulative problems.
Spatial and interpersonal distribution	Every person on the planet is affected. The effects are unequally distributed. Solutions require international cooperation.	National problem, international problem or mesoproblem.

In the *epistemological* category I found two important differences. First, it is difficult to deny the existence of a pandemic when we are faced with concrete and easy-to-understand consequences, such as overcrowded hospitals and a large death toll. It is much easier (and more common) to reject or ignore complicated and sophisticated scientific evidence showing that climate change is anthropogenic and accelerating. Secondly, much more corporate money has been invested in denying climate change. Both of these differences make it harder for governments to address the long-term causes and consequences of climate change, as compared with the difficulties they face when trying to mitigate the dissemination of an infectious disease like Covid-19.

In the *temporal* category, I identified one major difference, namely, that pandemics come intermittently, whereas climate change is cumulative and worsens steadily from year to year. Therefore, measures against a pandemic are temporary, whereas measures against climate change include permanent modifications of our ways of life. This makes measures against a pandemic easier to accept than measures against climate change.

Finally, I found one major difference in the *distributional* category: climate change is a fully international problem, which means that the effects of a country's measures against climate change are distributed around the globe. A pandemic is a mesoproblem, which means that measures taken in a country have their largest effects within that country. Therefore, national leaders have stronger incentives to act against a pandemic than against climate change – even though both problems affect people around the world. In conclusion, all the five differences that I have identified pull in the same direction: they tend to make climate policies more difficult to implement than pandemic policies.

Similarities

Many of the similarities between these two problems relate to the fact that decision-making on both issues is highly dependent on science. This analysis therefore provides some insight into how scientific issues can be dealt with in democracies. Democracy is not only a matter of democratic forms and institutions, but also of a democratic ethos, without which democratic systems tend to become unworkable. One of the most important components of a democratic ethos is a broad reliance, across the political spectrum, on non-partisan sources of knowledge such as official statistics and scientific expertise. The dangers to democracy that emerge when political representatives reject science have recently been demonstrated in the United States, with serious negative effects both on climate policies and on the management of Covid-19 (Kerr et al. 2021; Lewandowsky 2021). Based on experiences like this, it has often been pointed out that 'trust in science' is essential for decision-making in our era. However, it is important to clarify what type of trust is desirable.

In political contexts, science tends to be treated as a unique type of knowledge, possessed by a small and smart elite and inaccessible to everybody else. This picture of science makes it into an alien element of democracy and an easy target of populist anti-elitism. A much more useful, and historically more clarifying, approach positions science as one of the many *fact-finding practices* that abound in human societies (Hansson 2018b). Long before modern science, humans developed investigative practices based on empirical observations and critical appraisals of evidence. Members of hunter-gatherer societies obtain sophisticated knowledge about the animal world through reasoning that involves hypothesis-testing and other modes of thinking that we tend to associate with science (Liebenberg 1990). Indigenous farmers have long performed extensive experiments to test different agricultural methods, crops and crop varieties (Hansson 2019). Ancient craftspeople performed experiments in metallurgy and other practical arts (Hansson 2015).

Our own societies use many fact-finding practices that are not officially called 'science' but nevertheless follow the same basic principles for unbiased investigation. Electricians locating the cause of a power outage, mechanics searching for the defect in a malfunctioning machine, journalists investigating corruption, police officers searching for the perpetrators of a crime, and juries determining whether defendants are guilty, all engage in well-established fact-finding practices that have much in common with formal scientific investigations. We have good reasons to rely on the outcomes of these and other systematic fact-finding practices rather than on less well-informed statements on the same topics. We have equally good – and, in fact, largely the same – reasons to make use of scientific information in areas that science has investigated. This observation might appear self-evident, but it frames the problem in a way that is very different from how 'trust in science' is usually discussed.

It is necessary, however, to clarify what it means to rely on expertise in different situations. In some cases, non-experts can make good – and immediate – judgements about the knowledge and skills of experts. For instance, if a park ranger brings you to a place where you can see a pack of wolves, that fact itself is a good reason to believe in the ranger's expertise in animal tracking. But the direct verification of expertise is impossible in many other situations. If you hire a plumber, for example, you will want that person to do quality work that will last for years. But in the absence of your own expertise in plumbing, you will not have any obvious – or easy – means of immediately determining whether the plumber's work will last a long time. The best option in this situation is to trust the judgements of other experts about the skills of that particular individual, or the approaches or materials that person uses. If your plumber recommends the use of materials that most plumbers consider to be unreliable or insufficiently tested, then you had better avoid that particular plumber.

Policy-relevant science is usually more like plumbing than animal tracking. For instance, there is no way to immediately test the accuracy of different long-term climate prognoses. The best we can do as non-experts is to look for the consensus view among experts. The reason why we should listen to the consensus view of climatologists is thus essentially the same as the reason why we should listen to the consensus view among plumbers.

It has often been pointed out that scientific committees should openly report uncertainties and differences in opinion (Moore and MacKenzie 2020). This is necessary to provide the public and other decision makers with accurate information about the state of knowledge in a field. It is, however, important to distinguish between uncertainties and disagreements. For instance, a scientific committee can often reach consensus on the uncertainties pertaining to particular issues, decisions or actions. On the other hand, disagreement about a scientific issue is not a sign of uncertainty if – as is so often the case – one set of views is held by non-experts who neglect the scientific evidence, and contrasting views are held by experts who know the evidence. Once this distinction is made, the identification of scientific uncertainties need not be more controversial than the identification of important topics for further research. In most cases, these two lists have a large overlap.

A defence of science along these lines, emphasising its similarity to other fact-finding practices in our societies, has at least two important advantages. First, it takes the edge off the claim that democracy and science are mutually opposed because the latter relies on elite knowledge while the former is supposed to be responsive to the demands and concerns of non-expert publics and their representatives. Secondly, this approach combines the defence of science with the defence of other fact-finding practices that are important in a democracy, such as the work that is done by independent journalists, statistics agencies and courts of law. What is basically at stake is not only science as a social institution but, much more generally, our willingness to jointly search for the truth in matters that concern us, and to base our deliberations and decisions on what we find.[1]

Note

1. I would like to thank Michael MacKenzie, Simo Kyllönen, Maija Setälä, Anna Wedin and the participants of a PALO seminar for their most useful comments on earlier drafts of this chapter.

Part Two

Thinking and Acting
in Future-Regarding Ways

FIVE

Perspective-Taking, Deliberation and Future Generations

Kaisa Herne

Introduction

Present generations often view future people as an outgroup, and people tend to disregard – or misrepresent – the perspectives of outgroups (Cikara et al. 2011; Bloom 2016). Future generations are an especially vulnerable outgroup because future people are not present in today's public sphere to speak for themselves. So how can democratic processes be designed so that the interests of absent outgroups – such as future generations – are adequately considered when collective decisions are made?

Scholars have shown that perspective-taking exercises, which encourage people to see things from the perspective of an outgroup, can be used to encourage people to think more about the potential interests and concerns of future generations. The problem with such exercises is that they are normally directed towards the perspectives of particular individuals or groups, instead of encouraging people to consider diverse perspectives. Nor do perspective-taking exercises encourage people to engage in deliberation over the conflicts of interest or differences that might exist between different groups.

Deliberative forms – such as minipublics (see, e.g., Setälä et al., Chapter 12, this volume) – are designed to bring groups of people with diverse perspectives into contact with each other. Deliberative forums can, in some circumstances, also encourage participants to consider the perspectives of absent groups, such as future people (Kulha et al. 2021; MacKenzie and Caluwaerts 2021).

Nevertheless, deliberative forums may fail to give due consideration to the potential interests of future people if no one in those
forums acts as a representative of those interests (e.g., Harris 2021).

In this chapter, I argue that this problem can be addressed by
combining inclusive deliberative forums with perspective-taking
methods that are explicitly future-regarding. This approach can be
used to encourage perspective-taking towards future generations
while also ensuring that diverse interests both *within* and *between*
generations are given adequate consideration in decision-making
processes.

What is Perspective-Taking?

Bohman (2003, 2012: 82) defines perspectives as views that people
hold based on their lived experiences in different social positions.
Unlike values or ideologies, knowledge of perspectives is thus
based on individual experiences. When we engage in perspective-
taking, we try to understand other people's needs and interests,
many of which are based on their experiences in specific social
positions, such as what it is like to live as a disabled person, a
woman or a member of a language minority. Perspective-taking
occurs between a subject, who considers someone else's perspective, and a target whose perspective is taken. The subject tries to see
things from the target's point of view and seeks to understand that
person's mental states, feelings and thoughts (Vorauer 2013; Todd
and Galinsky 2014). Perspective-taking is one dimension of empathy, which refers to the response of one person to the experiences
of another (Davis 1980, 1996). Cognitive empathy, a capacity to
understand the emotional states of others, is different than affective
empathy, the capacity to *experience* the feelings of others (Reniers
et al. 2011). Perspective-taking is a cognitive process in which we
try to imagine how another person thinks or feels – but it can also
give rise to affective reactions, affective empathy, empathic concern
or sympathy towards the target.

It is well known that people tend to empathise with people who
are like them, whereas members of outgroups are less likely to
generate empathy (Cikara et al. 2011; Bloom 2016). According
to Bloom (2016), this characteristic of empathy, while useful

in personal relationships, can be harmful in social interactions between groups. The danger is that we will make bad political choices because of our inability to see things from the perspectives of other stakeholders or groups.

When considering intergenerational conflicts, we often put emphasis on the needs and interests of the present generation, whereas we tend to neglect the needs and interests of future generations. Many of our choices will have very long-term consequences and this makes it difficult to have sufficient knowledge about the needs and interests of future generations. But quite often we are *not motivated* to take future generations into account even though we may be aware of the impacts that our decisions will have on them. This raises the question of whether it is possible to induce this kind of motivation. Is it possible to motivate people to more seriously consider – and empathise with – future generations even though they do not yet exist?

People may engage in perspective-taking on their own initiative, but it can also be deliberately prompted. Perspective-taking exercises encourage people to pay closer attention to others who might otherwise have their interests or perspectives neglected (Batson et al. 1997; Bruneau and Saxe 2012; Herne et al. 2022). This can be achieved by reducing the psychological experience of social distance between one set of people and another (Liberman and Trope 2008). The aims of perspective-taking include encouraging people to see some of the similarities between themselves and others (Batson, Polycarpou et al. 1997), inducing empathic concern towards others who are different, and encouraging the development of positive attitudes towards those in outgroups. Effective perspective-taking exercises can sometimes encourage people to act in pro-social ways (Batson et al. 1981). In other words, when subjects are encouraged to take the perspectives of others, they may become more aware of the target's interests and ideally become more sympathetic towards them. In the best-case scenario, perspective-taking methods can encourage people to act on behalf of a target individual or group (Batson et al. 2003).

Perspective-taking methods have been studied extensively, mainly in psychology experiments. In a typical experimental setting, the target individual belongs to a marginalised or a stigmatised group, and the goal is to induce perspective-taking towards the target. A standard method in experimental research involves a description of a target individual's situation (using texts, pictures, videos or audio materials), and a request to the subject to take (or try taking) the target's perspective. Interventions can be made stronger and more impactful by asking subjects to write something about what they think the target's thoughts, needs or interests might be. To encourage people to take the (potential) perspectives of future people into account, participants might be asked to write letters to future others (Shrum 2016). Alternatively, some participants in a perspective-taking exercise might be asked to act as surrogate representatives of future people (Kamijo et al. 2017). To trigger perspective-taking, subjects might be asked to imagine the target individual's mental states (imagine-other), or what their own mental states might be in the target individual's position (imagine-self) (Batson et al. 1997). Batson et al. (2003) found that 'imagine-other' tasks are more effective at inducing empathic emotion and altruistic action. By contrast, 'imagine-self' tasks tend to generate distress along with empathy, which induces egoistic rather than altruistic action (Batson et al. 1997).

Perspective-taking can also be encouraged by asking subjects to imagine not what the target individual might *think* but how that individual might *feel*. There is evidence that imagining the target's feelings is more effective at producing empathic concern and altruistic action (Oswald 1996). But typically, subjects are asked to consider both the thoughts and the feelings of target individuals (Vorauer and Sasaki 2014). While targets of perspective-taking are usually individuals, the goal is to improve attitudes towards a larger group of people and to reduce implicit ingroup biases more generally (Shih et al. 2009; Shih et al. 2013).

Can perspective-taking methods encourage people to see things from the point of view of future people? One challenge has to do with the abstractness of future generations. A lot of imagination is required to consider the needs and interests of future people who cannot articulate their concerns to us. We cannot identify with future individuals or hear stories about their problems or perspectives. Aggregate or statistical information about large numbers of individuals, victims or probabilities, does not tend to move us as much as stories about identified victims (Small et al. 2007; Landwehr, Chapter 6, this volume). In a recent experiment, Wolf and Dron (2020: 1) found that when 'future generations' who will be 'adversely affected' by insufficient or unfair intergenerational resource transfers 'are not identifiable as existing humans, the currently living are less ready to constrain themselves'.

This is where perspective-taking exercises can contribute; they cannot actualise future people, but they can help to make them less abstract, and in so doing help current people better understand their needs and interests. Indeed, research shows that perspective-taking can be used to encourage people to think about abstract or inarticulate entities such as future generations (Pahl and Bauer 2013), or non-human victims of environmental damage, such as animals or trees (Berenguer 2007; Sevillano et al. 2007). These studies show that perspective-taking exercises can increase support for environmental attitudes and behaviours.

Methods that prompt perspective-taking towards future generations have the potential to reduce the degree of abstractness related to future generations. Exercises where people play roles as future people – that is, act as their surrogate representatives – can help to make the needs and interests of future generations more tangible, and thereby enable effective perspective-taking.

Future-regarding perspective-taking has been studied in experimental settings. Kamijo et al. (2017), for example, randomly assigned experimental subjects into different 'generational' groups consisting of three people each. Those in a first 'generation' group had to decide how much of a pot of money to keep and how much to pass on to future 'generations'. Those in subsequent generations had to do the same with whatever money was passed to them from the previous generation. The subjects were told that they would have to decide between two options, one of which would mean less money for their generation but more money for future generations, whereas the other would mean leaving fewer resources to future generations. Kamijo et al. (2017) also included a treatment condition in their experiment in which some participants were randomly assigned to actively represent the interests of future generations in their group's decision-making process. The authors found that the presence of representatives of the future increased the probability that a generational group would choose the option that transferred more money to future generations.

In a similar experiment, Hiromitsu found that representatives of the future 'could activate sympathy towards future generations, through visualising future people who do not have concrete existence' (2019: 166). Saijo (2020) reviewed the extant literature on this topic and concluded that the presence of representatives of the future is a reliable means of encouraging experimental groups to choose sustainable options over unsustainable ones (see Kamijo et al. 2017; Hara et al. 2019; Nakagawa, Kotania et al. 2019; Uwasu et al. 2020).

Nakagawa et al. (Nakagawa, Kotania et al. 2019; Nakagawa, Real et al. 2019) have combined retrospective and imaginary time travel techniques in their experimental studies. In one study, participants were randomly assigned to one of two groups. The control group was asked to consider the issue of forest management from the perspective of the present. The treatment group was encouraged to think about both the past and the future. They were asked to read an article on nuclear power published thirty years ago and to consider what they would have wanted people at that time to do on this issue. Participants wrote down their own thoughts and then discussed the issue with each other. After the retrospection phase of the experiment, participants were asked to consider another topic: forest management. In this case, they were asked to imagine that they had time travelled thirty years into the future. They were then asked to reflect upon how they would have liked the forests to be managed over that period of time, and they then deliberated the issue with each other. Finally, participants in the treatment group were asked to think about the issue from their own perspective in the present. Nakagawa et al. (2019b) found that those in the treatment group (i.e., the group that was encouraged to think about the past and the future) tended to favour policies that challenged and changed the status quo more than those in the control group.

Apart from time travel exercises, techniques such as writing letters to people living in the future (Shrum 2016) have been tested, and new methods could be developed, for example, reading science-fiction novels, watching films or engaging in virtual reality simulations (Davis and Love 2017). Following Morrell's

(2010: 127) suggestion, moderators in deliberative forums could instruct participants to consider the potential interests of future people who may be affected by their decisions.

In the psychology literature, perspective-taking methods are typically aimed at encouraging people to adopt or consider a specific perspective. But this approach may not be sufficient in political contexts where many different, and often conflicting perspectives must be considered. As Smith (2021: 85) argues, it is important to acknowledge that there will be conflicts of interest and divergent perspectives within current *and* future generations, as well as between generations. This suggests that we need to do more than just encourage people to consider the potential interests of specific future people or groups. We also need to bring diverse perspectives regarding the future into contact with each other in deliberative forums.

Perspective-Taking in Deliberation

In ideal terms, deliberation involves unconstrained public reasoning among free and equal participants (Bohman 1998; Cohen 1998). Deliberation is different from ordinary discussion which is not necessarily public and does not always involve reason-giving. In deliberation, participants express their own views and concerns while listening to – and considering – the arguments and concerns of others. In doing so, participants may try to imagine themselves in the shoes of others or try to see things from the perspective of others. This suggests that both perspective-giving (Bruneau and Saxe 2012) and perspective-taking are supposed to happen in effective deliberations. Indeed, many deliberative theorists have emphasised the role of perspective-taking in deliberation. Hannah Arendt ([1954] 1987: 221), for example, talked about representative thinking which involves imagining oneself in the place of others and thinking about how they might act or feel in those positions. She argues that a capacity for representative thinking can be acquired only in public forums where people engage in deliberations with others (d'Entrèves 2006). Other scholars see perspective-taking as an indicator of high-quality deliberation (Bächtiger and Parkinson 2019; Muradova 2020). Theorists have also identified different types of perspective-taking in deliberation, including 'ideal role taking' (Habermas 1996), 'deliberation within' (Goodin 2000) and 'empathy' (Morrell 2010).

Structured deliberative forums, such as minipublics, aim to ensure that all relevant and affected groups are adequately represented in those processes (e.g., Gerber et al. 2018). This is because inclusion is normally thought to be a precondition for groups having their perspectives and concerns addressed in political processes. There is evidence that inclusive deliberative forums can, in fact, encourage people to consider the perspectives of outgroups more seriously (Grönlund et al. 2017; Muradova 2020; Setälä et al. 2020) – but contrasting evidence has also been presented (Mendelberg and Oleske 2000).

What about future generations? Can deliberation encourage participants to consider the interests of future people even though future people cannot be included in those deliberations? Some theorists of deliberative democracy argue that deliberation can give voice to groups or perspectives that are not represented in those processes (Dryzek and Niemeyer 2008; Niemeyer and Jennstål 2016). Diversity and disagreement among participants are likely to be crucial in this respect. A diverse pool of participants increases the likelihood that someone will communicate the interests of those who are not physically present (Goodin 1996).

Politically diverse groups will also be temporally diverse, which means that some participants in an inclusive deliberative forum might decide to actively represent the future in those processes. Those representatives might simply be sympathetic – or empathetic – towards future people, but they might also act as representatives for the future because they see their own near-term or long-term interests as being aligned with future people. In these circumstances, there may be some people who are motivated to actively defend the interests of future people in deliberations (MacKenzie 2021b). When representatives of future people emerge in deliberations, others may be prompted to also consider the potential interests of the future in their reasoning and argumentation. Deliberation should also reduce references to self-serving reasons, because those types of reason are hard to defend in public forums. In a similar manner, arguments that summarily disregard the potential interests of future generations can be easily challenged in public deliberations. To summarise, disagreement among a diverse set of participants in a public deliberation may create dynamics where the potential interests of future generations are considered, at least to some extent, even though future people cannot be included in those deliberations (MacKenzie 2021b: esp. ch. 4).

There is evidence that deliberation can in fact encourage participants to think and act in future-regarding ways. Experimental evidence suggests that deliberation can enhance support for policies with near-term costs and long-term benefits, such as climate action policies (Koirala et al. 2021; MacKenzie and Caluwaerts 2021). It is likely that support for such policies tells us something about whether participants were thinking about future generations, but this is not necessarily the case because future-regarding policies can also be supported for other reasons.

Empirical evidence on deliberation and perspective-taking towards future generations is scarce, but there are a few suggestive studies. Kulha et al. (2021), for example, found that deliberation encouraged participants to consider the perspectives of future generations on the issue of long-term regional planning in Finland. Indeed, my colleagues and I obtained similar results from a deliberative minipublic on traffic planning in the city of Turku, Finland. The process and its main results are described in Grönlund et al. (2020). An interesting observation that is not reported in Grönlund et al. (2020) concerns participants' attitudes about taking the perspectives of future people into account. In pre- and post-deliberation surveys, participants (n = 171) were asked whose point of view should be considered in traffic planning: people living now or people living in the future. We found that 34 per cent of the minipublic participants who had initially said that the views of present people should be considered, changed their opinions in the post-treatment survey to say that the views of future people should be considered (χ^2 = 67.99, p = 0.000). This indicates that deliberation increased orientation towards future people. It is also noteworthy that the minipublic participants were in fact more often oriented towards the perspectives of future generations compared with a random sample (n = 2,385). In the pre-deliberation survey,

61 per cent of the random sample said that the views of future people should be considered in traffic planning, while 73 per cent of the minipublic participants had this opinion. In other words, those who took part in the minipublic were on average already oriented towards future generations, but deliberation also helped many of those participants become *more* future-regarding.

But there is also evidence showing that deliberation does not always encourage participants to consider the interests of future people. In a recent study of the Irish Citizens' Assembly on climate change, Harris (2021) found that the interests of children, young people and future generations were scarcely mentioned in those deliberations. They were, she concludes, at best a whisper in the process.

These studies show that while deliberation can encourage perspective-taking towards future generations, it does not always do so. It may be that some deliberations are not diverse enough to include multiple temporal perspectives. Others may be insufficiently deliberative. Further studies are needed to clarify these issues. But given that deliberation does not always encourage perspective-taking towards future generations, I propose that it could be complemented with perspective-taking methods to increase the chances that participants will take the perspectives of future people into account in their deliberations.

Complementing Deliberative Forums with Perspective-Taking Methods

Combining deliberation and perspective-taking methods can help to ensure that future people are discursively represented in deliberations. This approach can also help to ensure that diverse interests both *within* and *between* generations are given adequate consideration in deliberative processes. These two mechanisms – deliberation and perspective-taking – each contribute something to the process. Perspective-taking exercises encourage participants to consider the needs and interests of future people, but they tend to put emphasis on the perspectives of specific individuals or groups, and they do not normally provide participants with opportunities to bring various perspectives into conversation (or conflict) with each other. Deliberation, on the other hand, can sometimes fail to induce future-regarding perspective-taking, but it provides a mechanism where arguments and counterarguments are presented and tested against each other. The combination of perspective-taking methods and deliberation helps to correct the deficiencies that each approach has when used on its own.

There is empirical evidence that combining perspective-taking methods and deliberation can work. This approach has been adopted by researchers associated with the Japanese 'future design' movement (Saijo 2020). Hara et al. (2019), for example, studied a public engagement process aimed at developing a broad future vision for a municipality in Japan. They designed an experiment that combined perspective-taking methods and deliberation. In their study, participants were randomly assigned to two types of groups. In one group, participants were asked to imagine that they had time travelled to the year 2060 without ageing. They were then asked to address the topic from the standpoint of the future and to represent the interests of those living in 2060. The other group did not engage in a future-regarding perspective-taking exercise. Instead, they were asked to discuss the topic from their own present-day perspective. These two groups first worked separately but were later brought together. Hara et al. (2019) found that combing the two groups helped to ensure that the perspectives of the future were included in the final decisions that the groups made. Hara et al. argue that this method can help people to navigate intergenerational conflicts. In the deliberations involving both groups, those in the 'present generation' group became more aware of future concerns, but those in the 'future generation' group also realised that some of the demands of the 'present generation' group that they had initially opposed were in fact justified. In other words, combining a perspective-taking exercise with deliberation encouraged the participants to consider the potential interests of the future, but it also encouraged them to engage in argumentation about how the interests of the future should be balanced against those of the present.

Hara et al.'s (2019) study is suggestive but empirical evidence on this topic is limited. Future research might be conducted in other geographical or social contexts and focused on different long-term issues and levels of government. Different types of future-regarding perspective-taking methods might also be developed and tested to see which is most effective when combined with deliberation.

Conclusions

My purpose in this chapter has been to consider how the perspectives of future generations might be better represented in democratic processes, thus leading to more future-regarding policies. I have argued that perspective-taking methods can help to encourage people to adopt the perspectives of future generations. But perspective-taking methods, when used alone, do not provide participants with incentives or opportunities to consider or navigate the conflicts of interest that exist between different groups *within* and *between* generations. Inclusive deliberative processes, by contrast, can bring different groups and perspectives into conversation, but deliberative processes sometimes fail to adequately consider the potential interests of those who are not included, such as a future people. In response, I propose that perspective-taking methods and deliberation should be combined to increase the likelihood that the interests and perspectives of both present and future generations will be adequately considered and brought into conversation with each other.

While there is evidence that combining perspective-taking methods and deliberation can help to encourage participants to consider the potential interests of the future more seriously – while also weighing future perspectives against the diverse interests of the present – more research is needed on this topic. At least three issues might be usefully addressed in future research projects. First, perspective-taking methods could be developed to take into account the diversity of future generations. The interests of generations in the near future may be different from those in the far future, and each generation, whether present or future, will have diverse groups with conflicting interests. Perhaps participants of time-travel exercises could be divided into 'near future' and 'far future' groups, and members in each group might be encouraged to adopt the perspectives of different types of future people (the rich or the poor, for example, or people from different parts of the world). These groups could then be brought together in deliberative processes where these diverse perspectives could be considered in relation to each other.

Secondly, future research projects might consider different topics of deliberation. There are some topics where the interests of future generations are widely recognised and considered, such as climate change mitigation or the production of nuclear power and waste. Deliberations on these topics might take the interests of the future into consideration without the use of perspective-taking methods (although see Harris 2021). There are, however, other issues, such as immigration or health care, where the interests of future people may be more likely to go unrecognised. Future-regarding perspective-taking exercises may be especially useful in deliberative forums that address these issues, precisely because (or if) the temporal dimensions of these issues are less likely to be recognised by participants without sufficient prompting. More research is needed to identify topics where future-regarding considerations are – or are not – likely to emerge without perspective-taking methods.

Thirdly, future researchers might consider how different types of people or groups respond to different perspective-taking methods. It is possible that the identities or political attitudes of people will affect how they respond to – or participate in – perspective-taking exercises. The literature on climate change, for example, shows that people with different political orientations and attitudes respond differently to mitigation options and to political communications on these topics (Schuldt et al. 2015; Carmichael et al. 2017). The same may be true for perspective-taking methods. But it may also be the case that deliberation can help to attenuate some of the effects of political attitudes once people with diverse perspectives on these issues are brought into conversation with each other.

As a final point, it is worth emphasising that future generations are not the only group – or relevant set of interests – that may be absent in democratic decision-making processes. Young children, non-human animals and natural systems (such as forests and rivers) are not normally included in our democratic processes because they cannot voice their own concerns. This means that surrogate representatives will be needed if these perspectives are to be taken into consideration. Perspective-taking methods can help to ensure that surrogate representatives of these groups or entities are, in fact, present when decisions affecting their interests are being made. Combining perspective-taking methods and deliberation could be a means of ensuring that 'absent' interests of all types – future generations, but also young people, animals and natural systems – are properly represented and considered in our democratic systems.

SIX

Hearing Silent Voices? Representing Identified and Statistical Policy Victims

Claudia Landwehr

Introduction

Democracy not only promises egalitarian self-government, but also collective decisions that we are less likely to regret than those taken by non-democratic regimes. The two promises associated with the idea of democracy are intricately linked, but the means to fulfil them can be at odds. For example, political equality and self-government seem to require majoritarian procedures (Dahl 1989), while expert decision-making and technocratic forms of government seem to promise more rational decisions. In any case, however, fulfilling the egalitarian and epistemic promises of democracy requires that the interests of all affected groups are adequately considered in the decision-making-process and brought to bear on decisions (e.g., Warren, Chapter 1, this volume). The fact that some groups are notoriously easier to organise and have better access to negotiations and decision-making processes than others therefore constitutes a serious challenge to democracy's promises. In most societies, groups that lack financial resources, are internally heterogeneous and have diffuse rather than concentrated interests, are under-organised and typically under-represented in politics (Olson 1965, 1982). In addition, democratic theory and practice are confronted with intricate boundary problems: it is difficult to give everyone affected by political decisions, in particular future generations, citizen status, and it remains impossible to define the boundaries of the demos democratically (Arrhenius 2005).

This chapter discusses types of groups that systematically lack voice in political decision-making processes and that are therefore likely to become victims of public policy. They become victims either of political programmes that deprive them of opportunities and resources, or they become victims of political failures to prevent damage to their interests and eventually, their lives. While solutions to the under-representation of all these groups are sorely needed, I want to focus on only one of them that is particularly relevant in the context of this volume: statistical victims. These are policy victims that have not yet materialised and therefore have not been negatively affected yet, but will suffer damages in the near or far future due to decisions not to protect their interests. All statistical victims are thus future victims, although some of them are already born and will suffer damages in the near future, while others have not yet been born and will suffer damages only in the more distant future.

In the small body of literature on the topic, the most common example of statistical victims are children who will suffer serious infections preventable by vaccinations. While they are perfectly healthy at the moment, if a decision not to fund a vaccination programme is taken, those who do fall seriously ill or die from that preventable disease must be seen as victims of that decision – even if the overall risk of infection is low. Another, and in this context more salient, example of statistical victims are future generations who will be severely affected by the failures of past and present generations to take decisions to reduce the consumption of natural resources and the emission of greenhouse gases. In the widest sense, all kinds of preventive policy programme, such social investments in education or health promotion, may be viewed through this lens. When decisions not to invest in such interventions are taken, the future statistical victims who will be harmed by those decisions will in most cases lack political voice. Even in cases where future victims are already born, they have not yet been harmed and often do not know that they might be. Thus, they typically cannot speak for themselves and often remain invisible and silent. However, ignoring the interests of these statistical victims may be economically inefficient – as a lack of prevention and social investment – but also morally problematic.

In what follows, I argue that protecting the interests of statistical victims is an important problem for democratic representation, and that reflecting on the problem of statistical victims can shed new light on the question of how to adequately represent future generations. Ensuring that the 'silent voices' of statistical victims and other less vocal groups are heard in decision-making processes may require rethinking our understanding of democratic representation. Thinking about forms of representation that could ensure an adequate consideration of statistical victims' interests gives us reason to explore the potential of institutional innovations. In the second part of this chapter, I discuss possible institutional design strategies for the representation of statistical victims and, in particular, future generations. Each strategy has its own advantages and disadvantages and there is no 'one size fits all' solution for different contexts and political systems. A broader and more inclusive public discussion of the potential of democratic innovations could promote adaptations that enhance the capacity of democratic institutions to successfully address major challenges such as climate change.

Unheard Voices and Under-represented Groups in Politics

When asking which social groups are under-represented in politics, the answer seems obvious: the very groups that are already marginalised and therefore suffer numerous grievances are also the ones less likely to be given adequate voice in democratic decision-making processes. A large body of literature deals with low political participation rates and the inadequate representation of disadvantaged groups and minorities. This literature also highlights the inadequate attention that many policymakers pay to the interests and preferences of these disadvantaged groups (Gilens 2005; Bartels 2009; Elsässer et al. 2018). Why is under-representation a problem? First, it is, even from a purely utilitarian perspective, an epistemic problem. If relevant groups do not participate or are not adequately heard, information that could be used to increase welfare is lost to the system. Secondly, and more importantly, under-representation is a problem of justice. If grievances are not ameliorated or prevented when it would be possible to do so at a reasonable cost, decision makers could be accused of wrongful inaction.

Finally, under-representation is a problem for democracy itself as it undermines the promise of equality that is essential to it.

While some groups' social and economic disadvantages translate into political disadvantage, some vulnerable groups are *targeted* by specific policies, and more or less generous welfare state arrangements protect citizens and avert or ameliorate some grievances. What do societal solidarity and the generosity of protection depend upon? Rehm et al. (2012) have argued that support for the welfare state (and, in consequence, its generosity) will be higher where risks are dispersed rather than concentrated on the poor (i.e., where disadvantage and risk affect various groups). In these cases, more advantaged groups with resources will successfully lobby for insurance programmes which benefit both the middle and lower classes.

The argument presented by Rehm et al. (2012) can also be used to account for differences across areas of social policy. Support for expansionary health and pensions policies is typically higher than support for unemployment and welfare aids. This is because in the former case, the risk of becoming dependent upon social supports is either dispersed and mainly a matter of fate (severe illness such as cancer) or universal (old age), whereas in the latter case, risk is concentrated on already disadvantaged groups (e.g., low-skilled workers or the poor). In addition, patient groups and pensioners tend to be well-organised, 'intense' groups with significant lobbying power.

While groups and individuals depending on societal supports are, to differing degrees, vocal and successful in having their needs met by public policy, there exists another class of potential policy victims which is almost by definition silent, as its members' grievances have not yet materialised. This group of (as of yet) 'statistical' victims have been the subject of discussions in philosophy and medical ethics, but less attention has been paid to them in discussions of public policy.

Statistical Victims: Who Are They?

Imagine the following situation: a given society has only a limited supply of a specific drug available. The drug can be used for two different purposes.[1] Administered in a very high dose, it cures an otherwise fatal disease. Administered in a small dose, it vaccinates against the same disease. The available supply could either be used to save ten people already suffering from the disease who without the drug would certainly die. Or, alternatively, the drug could be used to vaccinate 1,000 people. It is known that without vaccination, 1 per cent of these 1,000 people would contract the disease and consequently die. Should we use the drug to cure ten people imminently facing death? Or should we use it to prevent ten future deaths? How does the situation change if we could save 100 rather than ten lives through vaccinations? Despite the higher number of lives saved under the vaccination solution, many of us would probably still assign more weight to the needs of identified victims already suffering from the disease and allocate the drug to them.

Thomas Schelling (1968: 142) was the first to describe this distinction between identified and statistical victims: 'the death of a particular person evokes anxiety and sentiment, guilt and awe, responsibility and religion, [but] . . . most of this awesomeness disappears when we deal with statistical death'. On the basis of a broad review of psychological literature, Loewenstein et al. (2005) describe the preference for identified over merely statistical victims as a special case of a universal 'identifiable other effect'.

The example above is, of course, entirely hypothetical. No drug can be used alternatively as a cure or for inoculation, and in free markets the supply of drugs usually follows demand.[2] While in low- or middle-income countries, a decision about whether to, for example, invest in a broad vaccination programme or provide haemodialysis for a small number of patients suffering from kidney failure may be a real one, the answer to the above question in wealthy societies would be: 'we must do both!' But even if politicians in most high-income countries are still reluctant to openly discuss setting limits in health-care spending, decisions to allocate resources in one way or another have opportunity costs even in the wealthiest states. The money we spend on health care is money that cannot be spent on other purposes, such as education, culture or security.

One problem with the identification of the statistical victims of political decisions lies with the fact that the causal link between an intervention (or non-intervention) and its effect is rarely as clear and uncontroversial as it is in the hypothetical 'cure versus vaccination' example above. In some cases, statistical victims will later be identified as victims of specific decisions. In other cases, damages cannot be traced back to specific decisions. For example, people suffering from respiratory diseases caused by air pollution may never know the causes behind their problems and thus will not be identified as victims even at a later time.

Moreover, statistical victims are not necessarily fatalities. In many cases, their loss consists merely in a loss of opportunities, income or quality of life. Take the following non-hypothetical example: some years ago, the German Bertelsmann Foundation conducted a survey which found that children who had attended day care under the age of three had higher educational success than those who had not attended day care (Fritschi and Oesch 2008). The effect was particularly strong in families where both parents had only low formal education themselves. In these cases, day care increased a child's probability of achieving a university entrance certificate (*Abitur*) by 83 per cent. While governments in the German states (*Länder*) were struggling to meet increasing demands especially from young professionals to increase the number of places in day care, in 2012, the federal government introduced a payment of €150 per month for parents who cared for their children within the family rather than sending them to day care. The benefit was unattractive to high-income parents, but valuable for poorer families. As a result, some children who might have benefited most from day care stayed at home with their parents who claimed the benefit instead.[3] If the educational success of any one of these children turns out to be low, it will be difficult to say whether or not, and to what degree, day care could have changed the result. The number a variables affecting educational success is much higher than the number of variables affecting disease transmission, especially in cases where effective vaccines are available. Nonetheless, we may view the loss of educational achievement as an efficiency loss for society as a whole, and the loss of opportunities as an injustice to the single child.

To illustrate the fact that statistical victims are a more general problem that affects policymaking in various areas and respects, consider the following cases:

1. elderly people at risk of dying from Covid-19 if insufficient protection measures are taken;
2. criminal offenders backsliding into crime due to insufficient social reintegration programmes;
3. hundreds of road casualties per year due to absent or insufficient speed limits; and
4. future generations suffering as a result of our collective inability to combat climate change.

What these examples have in common is that the victims of policy decisions (or non-decisions) are unidentified at the time these decisions are taken and, therefore, at least in many cases, remain insufficiently considered. However, the cases also differ in important respects. Some of the victims are close to us and their interests clear to us. After the outbreak of Covid-19, groups at high risk were clearly identified. Even young people without pre-existing medical conditions had parents or grandparents in high-risk groups and wanted to protect them.

Future generations, as a particularly relevant group of statistical victims, are more distant and we know less about their interests. Moreover, while some policy victims are affected by domestic policy decisions, and others are victims of foreign policy and supranational decisions, future generations are affected by both types of decisions. In some of the above cases, the damage, even if it has not yet taken place, is nearly certain, whereas in others, it is only a small probability. Therefore, some of the groups may know that they are being wronged by policy decisions, whereas others are unaware of the fact that they will become victims of decisions not to protect their interests. Future generations, of course, will always be unaware of their interests at the moment when decisions relevant to them are taken. Thus, whereas all of these policy victims are by definition less vocal than identified victims, some are still less likely to have their interests considered than others. Where the probability of being heard and represented in politics is concerned, there is one key consideration for both statistical and identified victims: the concentration of risk. Consider Table 6.1 for a classification of different types of policy victim. As mentioned above, those who suffer as a result of the manifestation of a risk that is dispersed

Table 6.1 A typology of policy victims and non-vocal groups

	Statistical Victims	Identified Victims
Risk/loss concentrated on specific societal groups.	Examples: elderly people at risk from Covid-19; young people affected by climate change.	Examples: the poor, disadvantaged and discriminated minorities.
Risk/loss dispersed over society or uncertain.	Examples: road casualties due to lack of speed limit; future generations affected by climate change.	

over societal groups, such as age or illness, are more likely to be included in welfare state programmes and to receive adequate support; they are also less likely to become policy victims than those in groups upon which risks are concentrated. While according to Olson (1965), diffuse interests are difficult to organise in interest groups, empirical evidence suggests that they may actually be well represented in policymaking and likely to be addressed by welfare state programmes (see Rehm et al. 2012). The bottom right cell in Table 6.1 is therefore left empty.

Among statistical victims, by contrast, those in groups upon which risks are concentrated at least know that they are exposed to those risks and might therefore be able to mobilise accordingly. In the Covid-19 crisis, where the risk of infection and possible death was imminent for specific groups, many governments were able to implement containment measures that depended upon a considerable degree of societal solidarity. By contrast, the interests of statistical victims who are dispersed over society and who are subject to smaller or uncertain risks are almost impossible to organise and mobilise, especially where risks are comparatively low. In the climate crisis, people living in low-lying countries or on islands face an imminent threat from rising sea-levels, while people in many other regions, particularly in the global north, have long viewed effects of climate change as small or uncertain – although extreme weather events in many of these countries have already proven them wrong.

Before turning to the question of how these different types of identified and statistical policy victims are politically represented and how their voices are heard in politics, the more general question of how to weigh identified against statistical victims remains to be addressed. Are statistical victims morally significant and if yes, should we factor their interests into our decision-making processes more systematically?

Starting with the weighting of one 'identified life' versus one 'statistical life' – and thus leaving aggregation issues (e.g., one big benefit versus many small benefits) aside – Daniels (2012) assesses consequentialist and non-consequentialist arguments for and against prioritising identified over statistical lives. He concludes that this is ultimately a matter of reasonable disagreement, so that respective decisions can only be legitimised procedurally. The situation may appear different when we weigh a single identified victim against several statistical lives, or mere inconveniences (such as a speed limit) against statistical lives that could potentially be saved. A utilitarian would assign more weight to the (higher) benefits of statistical victims than to the (lower) costs paid by identified persons. However, utilitarianism remains only one among many possible conceptions of justice, and we will still be confronted with reasonable disagreement here.

Nonetheless, it is difficult to make a reasonable argument to entirely disregard statistical lives. I will thus assume that statistical victims are of moral significance and how their interests should be weighed against identified victims is a matter of reasonable disagreement that should be subject to political decisions. But if statistical victims are morally significant, how are they addressed by public policy? How can we make sure that they are adequately considered in democratic decision-making processes?

How Can We Make Silent Voices Heard?

According to Hanna Pitkin (1967: 8–9), political representation may be captured as 're-presentation, a making present again', in which 'something not literally present is considered as present in a non-literal sense'. In modern mass democracies, representation must be seen as 'an intrinsic part of what makes democracy possible' (Urbinati and Warren 2008: 395). This is not only for functional reasons, but also because by ensuring the self-limitation of majority rule and thus dividing popular sovereignty from government, representation enables deliberation and interest reconciliation (Urbinati 2019: 90–3). The traditional model of political representation is a 'promissory' one that combines electoral authorisation with accountability (Mansbridge 2003). However, equal representation in the promissory model depends on all societal groups and interests being equally organisable and able to overcome collective action problems. As argued above, socioeconomically disadvantaged groups tend to be under-represented in many political decision-making processes. They lack resources for participation (Brady et al. 1995) and many experience representative politics as unresponsive to their needs and interests (Gilens 2005).

Democratic reforms and innovations, such as replacing plurality voting with proportional representation or empowering minipublics to make decisions, are often aimed at improving egalitarian participation and voice through descriptive representation. The purpose is to create decision-making bodies that better mirror the citizenry at large. However, where the aim is to ensure that all interests and groups are adequately considered, mere descriptive representation may not be sufficient. Instead, a more explicit 'politics of presence' (Phillips 1995) may be required to make the voices of otherwise marginalised groups heard and thereby ensure that their interests are considered.

The case of statistical victims is different, as their voices are not being marginalised, they are, instead, silent by definition, because statistical victims do not or cannot know that their future interests are being harmed. This is particularly true for future generations who are not yet born. Based on empirical evidence from experimental psychology, Daniels assumes that democratic majorities generally tend to favour identified over statistical victims: 'The issue for public policy is what weight to give to the *views of the majority* in favour of identified victims despite the *power of arguments* against that outcome by others' (Daniels 2012: 43, emphasis added). He thus contrasts the majority will with the 'power of arguments', or a general interest that can only prevail in deliberation, not in mere aggregation of preferences.

The primary problem, however, lies in the challenges associated with conceptualising statistical victims as persons. To begin with, the interest that statistical victims share is often highly diffuse rather than specific, and thus, according to Olson (1965), difficult to organise. If representation and voice through interest groups is unlikely, electoral representation is equally unlikely. People are unlikely to make what they regard as a small risk (e.g., dying in a traffic accident or in a flood caused by extreme weather) a crucial factor in their voting decisions. What is more, many of the potential beneficiaries of policies aimed at preventing harm to statistical victims do not have full citizenship rights: they are, for example, illegal immigrants, minors or disenfranchised convicted criminals (in the United States). Future generations are in many respects a particularly difficult case because all these potential problems apply to them: they do not yet exist and they are therefore by definition silent, they cannot organise and they do not have citizenship rights – even though their living conditions will be dramatically affected by our decisions today.

Given these challenges, how can the interests of statistical victims be better represented in our political systems? In complex modern democracies, there may be room for what Levine and Forrence (1990) call 'Burkean regulation' (i.e., the pursuit of a general interest without explicit majority support). Gerring and Thacker (2008), in their work on the advantages of 'centripetal governance', seem to assume that some kind of Burkean regulation (although they do not use the term) is more likely to occur in systems with broader interest representation in agenda setting, and united sovereign governments – which is why parliamentarism, proportional representation and a unitarian state correlate with higher welfare. If centripetalism is associated with better bureaucracies and better governance more generally, this may be because it enhances the application of what Goodin (1995) calls 'utilitarianism as a public philosophy'. Centripetalism incentivises decision makers to apply a utilitarian calculus rather than give in too easily to electoral pressures or special interest lobbying.

However, the decision-making powers of Burkean regulators ultimately depend upon electoral support as well. As such, they will be unable to completely and permanently ignore majority opinions in favour of their own (perhaps idiosyncratic) ideas of the general interest. Moreover, it remains difficult, if not impossible, to tell whether and where a decision maker engages in Burkean regulation or is captured by special interests. In the end, Burkean regulation differs from captured, special interest regulation only where the motivation of the regulator is concerned, not in its legitimacy or sustainability.

Philip Pettit (2004a) has argued that there are specific types of political decisions that cannot be adequately addressed by majoritarian politics and should therefore be delegated to depoliticised expert bodies. These bodies would, then, be expected to subject their decisions to reason-based deliberation. Pettit's ideal of depoliticised deliberation fits snugly with Daniels' suggestion of establishing decision-making procedures that guarantee 'accountability for reasonableness' (Daniels and Sabin 1997, 2008; Daniels 2012: 42–4). Both Daniels and Pettit position the rationally justifiable, morally adequate decision against the majority opinion, thus assuming that the majority will may be deficient and should not automatically be granted authority. They make arguments for limiting the scope of majority decisions and partly replacing them with expert decisions, thus advancing an argument for (limited) technocracy.[4] Although the idea of a 'majority will' should indeed be treated with caution (e.g., Lagerspetz, Chapter 2, this volume), the very premise of Daniels' reasoning – that majorities *necessarily* give undue weight to identified as compared with statistical victims – is not convincing.

To begin with, people are likely to base their decisions on different reasons depending on whether those decisions are political, that is, whether they are collectively binding and concerning general rules or not. Thus, aggregate survey responses on how to weigh identified versus statistical victims are not necessarily a good predictor for policy preferences based on public deliberation. Many citizens may well find arguments in favour of statistical victims convincing and derive respective policy preferences from them. In the rare cases where a single identified life is weighed against a single statistical life, the more vivid image of the identified victim may induce a preference to save that identified life rather than the statistical one. But things may look different when we weigh a smaller number of identified victims against a larger number of statistical ones, or where we weigh mere inconveniences against statistical lives.

In the case of the Covid-19 crisis, clear majorities in most countries were very willing to accept quite severe restrictions to their liberties and opportunities in order to limit the number of statistical fatalities in vulnerable groups. Taking opinion polls as an indicator, there also seems to be support for other measures that prevent fatalities at the cost of mere inconveniences. In Germany, for example, a majority of 56 per cent is in favour of a speed limit on motorways (Schmidt 2015), which still does not exist. One explanation for why respective legislation has not been implemented is that few people would make this seemingly minor issue decisive in their voting decisions. Moreover, powerful interest groups, such as the car industry, lobby against a speed limit whereas traffic victims are unlikely or unable to organise. Finally, a tendency towards blame avoidance rather than credit claiming makes regulation electorally costly (Weaver 1986). (The loss, in this case, would be the loss of a person's permission to speed.) Similarly, opinion polls tend to show strong support for better environmental protection and in particular, emission control. What impedes public policy in these cases is not so much a majority preference for identified victims; it is, instead, the challenges associated with representing statistical victims in democratic politics.

If the fact that statistical victims are typically silent means that neither traditional, promissory representation, nor a 'politics of presence' are possible, how can we nonetheless ensure that their interests are taken into consideration in decision-making processes? It is difficult or even impossible to represent statistical victims as persons, as they have not yet materialised as victims and in many important cases – such as future generations – do not even exist yet. Instead, their representation must be what Dryzek and Niemeyer (2008) have called 'discursive representation'. That is, the interests of statistical victims have to be brought to bear on the discourses that precede and accompany political decision-making by others.

Table 6.2 identifies different types of representation with different types of policy victims. In general, representation of persons is possible only where individuals can, in fact, be identified. For identified victims, a broad dispersion of needs or losses across society means that traditional, promissory representation by way of electoral authorisation and accountability is likely to ensure adequate

Table 6.2 The political representation of policy victims

	Statistical Victims	Identified Victims
Risk/loss concentrated on specific societal groups.	Surrogate representation.	Descriptive representation (a 'politics of presence').
Risk/loss dispersed over society.	Discursive representation.	Promissory representation (electoral authorisation and accountability).

policy responses. Where loss and suffering are concentrated on specific disadvantaged and marginalised groups, adequate representation is not impossible, but is less likely, and may be improved through institutional innovations that provide descriptive representation or enable a 'special hearing', such as a 'politics of presence' (Phillips 1995).

For statistical victims, by contrast, representation of persons is more difficult, especially where affected individuals do not know that decisions will at a later point harm their interests, or when those who will be affected are not yet born. Representation in these cases can only take the form of a representation of interests and arguments, and must, therefore, be discursive in nature. Where risks are concentrated on specific groups, surrogate representatives may advocate for the interests of people in those groups who will have a high probability of becoming statistical victims. Although these people have not yet been injured, they may expect to be so, and that fact might mobilise non-affected others to raise their voices on their behalf.

However, surrogate representation may in some cases increase inequality and put some statistical victims at an even greater disadvantage, as people may be more likely to organise for some statistical victims (such as poor children) than for others (such as criminal offenders). Those individuals with a high probability of becoming victims may also be more likely to organise themselves. Nonetheless, the *adequate* representation of statistical victims – in particular, when their interests are dispersed over society or through time – seems only possible as some variant of discursive representation. While forms of representation that go beyond the traditional promissory model, such as discursive representation, are often practiced where identified victims are concerned, these forms of representation are indispensable for the adequate representation of statistical victims. The remainder of this chapter will thus discuss how the discursive representation of statistical victims could be institutionalised within a democratic political system.

Institutionalising Discursive Representation

What kind of institutions could offer adequate discursive representation for the interests of statistical victims? Such institutions would clearly have to be deliberative rather than majoritarian (Dryzek and Niemeyer 2008). They would have to conscientiously assess evidence and arguments, offer publicity and transparency, as well as accessible justifications for their recommendations. But these criteria leave open many important questions of institutional design: who should the members of these institutions be and how should they be appointed? Should these institutions be granted some degree of organisational and budgetary independence from governments and legislatures? Should they be empowered to take binding decisions, or should they have only advisory functions? What decision rules should apply in cases when consensus cannot be obtained? While all these questions are important, I will focus on the first one, namely, the membership of an institution designed to represent the interests of statistical victims. There are, I think, three options: expert, corporatist and citizen representation.

Expert Representation

In many cases, the identification of statistical victims' interests will require scientific evidence and specialised expertise. In the case of the Covid-19 pandemic, for example, information on transmission of the virus, its risks to different societal groups, or the effectiveness of containment strategies and vaccines can be provided only by experts. Similarly, climate policy decisions rely on information about the causes, consequences and dynamics of climate change. Even in a seemingly simple case like road safety, information on the number of, say, speeding-related casualties is not easy to gather.

It thus seems that expertise must play a role where the interests of statistical victims are at stake. Moreover, expert bodies often enjoy strong public support, especially when their members are viewed as impartial advocates of the common good.

When it comes to practical decisions that must weigh the interests of different social groups as well as interests of identified and statistical victims against one another, expert representation is neither expedient nor democratically legitimate. While the technocratic temptations behind the call to 'follow the science' of the climate movement are understandable, experts are not in a position to take political decisions (Frinken and Landwehr 2022). Although their judgement remains important in assessing the feasibility and effectiveness of political measures – as, for example, in decisions about whether obligatory masking helps to fight Covid-19 or whether reforestation helps to fight climate change – decisions taken to achieve goals like virus containment or emissions reduction always affect different societal groups (such as the young and the old) differently. Such decisions thus have a strong distributive component that requires processes of democratic will-formation and decision-making. Nevertheless, an expert body that offers assessments of how the under-represented interests of statistical victims will be affected by decisions for political (in)action could provide important inputs into public debates and serve as a corrective to legislative processes that are likely more concerned with the interests of identified victims.

Corporatist Representation

If expert bodies cannot convincingly weigh the competing interests of different social groups, some variant of corporatist representation seems to suggest itself. Traditionally, the term 'corporatism' is used to describe decision-making structures in which labour and capital (or trade unions and employers) negotiate matters of social and economic policy with governments and other decision makers. In the examples discussed here, corporatist representation could mean that societal interests that organise around a topic like climate change would get a say in collective decisions. A corporatist body to address issues of climate policy might include representatives of, for example, airlines, car manufacturers and the coal mining industry, as well as representatives of groups and interests that may be most negatively affected by climate change. The latter could offer some kind of surrogate representation for identifiable victims as well as unidentifiable future victims, while the former would represent the well-organised interests of industry. (See Setälä et al., Chapter 12, this volume, for interest-group representation in Finnish policymaking.)

However, corporatist representation, alone, is not entirely convincing on normative or practical grounds. Normatively, it seems difficult to find criteria to decide which societal interests deserve representation in a corporatist body and who could offer it. Practically, corporatist representation seems unlikely to enable deliberative interaction: members of a corporatist body serve as delegates of their respective organisations. Unlike experts, they are neither impartial nor independent and cannot defer to better arguments without betraying their mandates. In essence, corporatist representation would not only reproduce the representation deficits of democratic politics, but could even increase them.

Citizen Representation

The most popular democratic innovation that has been suggested to overcome representation deficits in contemporary democracies are deliberative citizen forums, or minipublics. While there are different ways to institutionalise citizen deliberation and different types of minipublics (such as deliberative polls, consensus conferences or planning cells), what they have in common is that their membership is based on a random selection of ordinary citizens. Minipublics can provide high-quality deliberation, and they can have a variety of beneficial effects on participants (Dryzek et al. 2019). Minipublics have been employed to address problems involving statistical victims, such as climate policy and Covid-19 containment measures. Some of those in the climate movement argue that citizen forums instead of elected legislatures should be empowered to take decisions on climate policy.

However, Lafont (2019) has offered convincing arguments against empowering minipublics. She argues that expert-guided deliberation will turn citizens into experts themselves, so that after deliberation they are no longer representative of the population at large. Asking non-participants to accept their decisions would be to demand blind deference, which is incompatible with principles of democratic self-government. What is more, while elected representatives enjoy a democratic mandate and can be held accountable, this is not true for the members of deliberative minipublics (Lafont 2019). However, Lafont also identifies three potential functions that minipublics could fulfil even if they are not empowered to actually take binding decisions (Lafont 2019: ch. 5.2): (1) *contestatory uses*, where a minipublic is empowered to criticise both majority opinion and policymaking when relevant interests and arguments have been excluded or disregarded; (2) *vigilant uses*, where minipublics exert pressure to ensure coherence between public opinion and policymaking; and (3) *anticipatory uses*, where a minipublic facilitates and supports public opinion formation on a new issue or challenge. All three uses could be relevant for addressing problems of statistical victims, and future generations, depending on the degree to which the problem is acknowledged by the public and by elected representatives.

Statistical victims could also be represented in forums with a mixed membership of experts and citizens, or experts, citizens and legislators. At the same time, the legitimacy of any non-majoritarian deliberative body with decision-making power will always remain precarious. Even if a minipublic were to be given a mandate by democratically elected governments or legislatures, its members would not themselves be elected and thus they could not be held accountable in elections. Delegation to non-majoritarian bodies or 'institutional de-politicisation' (Wood and Flinders 2014) has therefore, and rightly, been criticised as a strategy employed by governments to shift blame and avoid responsibility for decisions.

The normative legitimacy of a deliberative, non-majoritarian body to represent the interests of statistical victims, can, given pluralism of values and interests, only be procedural (Landwehr 2015). Whether or not procedural legitimacy translates into public acceptance of the body and its recommendations is a further question. In any case, the assumption of deliberative quality is neither normatively nor empirically sufficient to legitimise a decision-making procedure. The delegation of processes of deliberation and decision-making from parliaments to non-elected bodies therefore requires democratic authorisation and accountability (i.e., a democratic mandate). It is worth keeping in mind that institutional design choices will necessarily have consequences for decision-making processes and their outcomes, and design choices therefore have potential strategic implications for political actors (see Böhm et al. 2014; Landwehr and Böhm 2016). Consider, for example, the role of advisory bodies in the Covid-19 crisis. Their recommendations differed significantly depending on whether those bodies were staffed only with virologists and epidemiologists, or whether members included sociologists or citizen experts such as nurses or teachers (Moore and MacKenzie 2020).

Questions about how the interests of statistical victims should be institutionalised must thus be subject to open and inclusive debates, and any institutional design choices should be comprehensively justified, ensuring coherence between societal and institutionally entrenched interests and values (Landwehr 2015). It remains an open question whether meta-deliberative conditions for the democratic establishment of any body to represent interests of statistical victims are empirically fulfilled. However, institutionalising the representation of statistical victims could create an important complement to existing procedures and discourses and could help democracy to meet performance expectations.

Conclusions

Starting from the observation that some groups are more likely than others to have voice in political decisions, this chapter has presented a typology of groups that lack voice and whose interests are therefore under-represented in democratic politics. I have drawn attention to a specific group: statistical victims (i.e., victims who have not yet materialised and are therefore unlikely to have their voices heard in politics). All statistical victims are future victims in that they have not yet been harmed – however, some of them will be harmed in the near term, while others will be harmed in the farther future. Future generations constitute a particularly salient example of statistical victims because *all* the challenges associated with organising and representing different types of statistical victims apply in the case of future generations. While these future – but at present merely statistical – victims have moral significance, and while there may well be majority support for considering their interests, political processes that are driven by electoral pressures are unlikely to do so. The protection of interests of statistical victims is thus a problem that requires us to reconsider our understanding of political representation and explore opportunities for institutional innovations that improve the discursive representation of groups and interests that are difficult to organise politically.

I have argued that even if the moral significance of statistical victims can be assumed, we are still confronted with challenges of institutional design that philosophers often neglect. These challenges must be addressed in democratic processes in order to give democratic innovations legitimate mandates to act. I thus argue that non-elected bodies that improve discursive representation can only be a complement, never a replacement for majoritarian institutions and party democracy. What is more, the establishment and design of these non-elected bodies requires decisions to be made in majoritarian institutions, which both normatively and empirically remain the primary source of democratic legitimacy. I have left open the question of whether these conditions for democratic institutional design are fulfilled in contemporary democracies. Unless they are, the introduction of new non-majoritarian institutions will risk aggravating anti-expert sentiments and undermining trust in governments. However, if democratic societies fail to address the challenges associated with representing statistical victims and other under-represented groups, this may impair the fairness and long-term performance of those democracies.

Notes

1. The situation is an example adapted from Daniels 2012.
2. In situations of acute crisis, such as the Covid-19 pandemic, supply may, of course, not be very elastic in the short term, which is why shortages in protective gear and intensive care beds occurred in several countries.
3. The payment was declared unconstitutional by the German supreme court (*Bundesverfassungsgericht*) in 2015 and can be claimed only in the state of Bavaria now, where it is subject to state (rather than federal) legislation.

4. Daniels and Sabin's (1997, 2008) 'accountability for reasonableness' model was originally devised as a procedure for making the decisions of private health insurers more accountable. They were thus not calling for democratic procedures to be replaced, but for hierarchical decisions to be made more comprehensible and transparent. Moreover, Daniels and Sabin do not envision a body staffed only with experts, but with relevant stakeholders (although they do not specify who these stakeholders should be).

SEVEN

Future-Regarding Democratic Leadership

Michael K. MacKenzie

Introduction

Many scholars have argued that democratic systems are functionally short-sighted because of the myopic preferences of voters and other influential political actors. People have cognitive biases against the future which make them more focused on their own near-term interests and less concerned about their future selves and future others. Democratic systems, it is argued, do little to check or challenge these biases. However plausible this argument might seem, it is predicated on an implausibly narrow conception of democracy, according to which existing preferences are largely unproblematically aggregated to produce collective outcomes. When democracy works that way, collective decisions are often short-sighted. In practice, however, democratic processes typically involve both shaping *and* registering the preferences, opinions and expectations of individuals and groups. We should therefore think more carefully about how democratic processes themselves might be used to encourage voters – and other political actors – to more seriously consider the future when making collective decisions (MacKenzie 2021b).

In this chapter, I argue that democratic leadership has at least three functions that make it useful – indeed, probably necessary – for initiating and supporting future-regarding collective actions: (1) aiding thinking; (2) forging joint commitments; and (3) mobilising action. I argue that each of these functions of democratic leadership helps us to navigate the democratic myopia problem.

The catch is that we will need to make our democratic systems more future-regarding, and more deliberative, if we are going to create the conditions that are necessary for future-regarding democratic leadership to thrive.

It is surprising how little attention has been paid to the concept of future-regarding leadership among scholars of intergenerational justice, environmental politics and democratic theory. For example, Goodin's (1992) major work *Green Political Theory* largely ignores the topic of leadership, and leadership is not mentioned in a recent collection of essays about future-regarding political institutions (González-Ricoy and Gosseries 2016). Robin Eckersley acknowledges the importance of leadership in her book *The Green State*. As she explains, 'visionary political leadership is essential for environmental capacity building (including constitutional reform) and the kind of diplomacy that leads to cooperative solutions to common problems' (Eckersley 2004: 254). But she does not develop a theory of future-regarding democratic leadership or explore why leadership will be needed to help direct societies towards desirable futures and away from undesirable ones. In my own book *Future Publics* (MacKenzie 2021b), I focus on the future-making potentialities of inclusive deliberative democratic processes, but I largely ignore the issue of future-regarding leadership. This lack of attention paid to the concept of leadership in democratic theory and practice should be corrected. We will need visionary democratic leaders who can inspire us to think clearly and act boldly if we are going to solve the many long-term problems that we face.

In this chapter, I briefly discuss the place that leadership occupies in contemporary democratic theory. I then define democratic leadership as conceived by Pennock (1979) and Beerbohm (2015). I use these theories to identify three essential functions of future-regarding democratic leadership. I argue that effective leadership is necessary if we want to make our shared futures together in collectively intentional ways. After that, I examine three challenges to future-regarding democratic leadership. The first involves finding (or nurturing) future-regarding leaders. The second involves creating institutions for future-regarding leaders to act within. The third involves creating the deliberative conditions needed to support effective practices of democratic leadership.

Leadership in Democratic Theory

Leadership is an essential political good. In order for any group of people to act together, some individuals must play leadership roles. Leaderless movements (such as Occupy Wall Street) are the exception not the norm, and movements that are leaderless often fail to maintain their cohesion or achieve their goals (such as Occupy Wall Street).

The study of leadership is, however, often side-lined in democratic theory, in part because leadership appears in opposition – or contradistinction – to other democratic goods, such as equality, non-hierarchical decision-making and self-actualisation. If democracy is about empowering people to create their shared worlds together, leadership would seem to undermine that objective. Leaders get people to do things that they would not otherwise have done. Leaders do not just represent people and their interests, they shape and mould them as well.

These accounts of leadership do not, however, make adequate distinctions between *democratic* forms of leadership and other forms of leadership, such as authoritarianism or demagoguery. All leaders act *above* the publics they seek to lead, and, as such, there is no way to avoid the hierarchical dimensions of leadership. But democratic leaders – if they are, indeed, democratic – seek to act *with* their followers rather than *on* them.

Beerbohm (2015) argues that we should look at leadership from the perspective of the followers rather than the leaders if we want to identify its democratic qualities. Democratic leadership, on his account, is relational. 'Democratic leadership's success condition is the recruitment of citizens as genuine partners in shared political activity' (Beerbohm 2015: 639). Democratic leadership is not about responding to existing preferences or demands, or imposing goals or objectives on otherwise unwilling publics. Democratic leadership involves collaboratively shaping the interests and perspectives of publics (or potential followers) and forging joint commitments with them. Democratic leaders aim to forge constituencies of free and intentional individuals who might otherwise – in the absence of leadership – lack any sense of shared intentionality. The background conditions of democratic leadership are thus freedom and intentionality. Democratic leaders must be free to make the case for their leadership to those they seek to lead, and their potential followers – or fellow actors – must be free to accept or reject those appeals.

On Beerbohm's (2015) account, leadership is undemocratic insofar as the relations between leaders and followers are unauthorised. But democratic leadership does not require formal processes of election or appointment (Beerbohm 2015: 645). Formal processes *may* be used to authorise leaders to act on the joint commitments they have forged with their followers, but democratic leaders might be authorised through informal processes of mutual acknowledgement. The climate activist Greta Thunberg is an example of a democratic leader who has not been elected or authorised in any way other than through her appeals to her followers to act jointly together.[1]

How leaders are selected and authorised will affect which mechanisms they might use to support collective action. Leaders who are authorised in formal processes, such as elections, might legitimately compel people to act in ways that are consistent with collective goals, even if those individuals have not agreed to work jointly with others towards those goals (e.g., Mansbridge 2012). Democratic leaders who have not been authorised in formal processes cannot (legitimately) use coercion to compel others to act with them, but they will have access to other political tools, such as negotiation, persuasion and bargaining, when they seek to forge joint commitments with others and turn those commitments into collective action.

Democratic leaders must be authorised (or acknowledged) by their followers, but their claims to leadership cannot be forged through deception or manipulation because such practices violate the conditions of freedom and intentionality that are required for genuine partnerships to form between leaders and followers (Beerbohm 2015: 646). Instead, democratic leadership involves forging joint commitments between otherwise disparate individuals in conditions of freedom, empowerment and intentionality, such that all those involved (both leaders and followers) recognise themselves to be acting together in pursuit of shared goals.

There will, of course, be more followers and fewer leaders in any context unless we stretch the meaning of leadership beyond all familiar uses of the term. Democratic leadership is also hierarchical like any other form of leadership. But democratic leaders are not authoritative in Arendt's (1961) sense of the term. They do not have the right to issue commands and be obeyed without argument or justification (Arendt 1961: 92). Instead, democratic leaders must actively *persuade* others to grant them some limited authority to act with and on behalf of others. In other words, leaders and followers in a democratic context must be considered equals who have freely and reflectively organised themselves into hierarchical structures to facilitate collective action.

Theorists such as Beerbohm (2015), but also Pennock (1979), have identified at least three essential functions of democratic leadership. These functions can be viewed as chronological steps in a generalised process of democratic leadership. The first step involves aiding the thinking of others. The second involves forging shared intentions and commitments. The third has to do with initiating – or making possible – collective actions to achieve those shared intentions and commitments. In this chapter, I argue that each of these three functions of democratic leadership are needed if we are going to act in collectively intentional, future-regarding ways.

I have argued elsewhere that inclusive deliberative processes can aid or discipline our thinking, help us to forge collective commitments and intentions, and support future-regarding collective action (e.g., MacKenzie 2018, 2021b). In this chapter, I argue that democratic leadership can also play these roles, and that we should not focus our attention only on designing future-regarding political institutions (i.e., institutions that are not biased against the future). In order to act in collectively intentional, future-regarding ways, we will also need future-regarding leaders who can perform the functions of leadership *within* refurbished democratic institutions that are not structurally biased against the future.

Three Functions of Leadership

Aiding Thinking

The first step – or function – in the process of democratic leadership has to do with aiding the thought of others. As Pennock explains:

In part this is simply a matter of identifying and pointing out problems for which political action is appropriate. The problems may already exist in the sense that the public welfare is in some respect suffering, or its improvement is being hampered; or the leader may be anticipating problems. (Pennock 1979: 485)

As Pennock suggests in this quote there is often an anticipatory dimension to democratic leadership. Leaders identify, anticipate and articulate future problems or issues that could (or should) be addressed in the present. Pennock gives an example of anticipatory leadership at the local level: 'Having noted a large influx of young married couples in a particular community, the leader points out that the school facilities, adequate now, will be woefully wanting in a few years' (Pennock 1979: 485).

But effective democratic leaders do not simply anticipate future problems, they aid the thinking of others in more holistic ways that help them to connect their own values and objectives to future potential solutions. As Pennock explains:

Next, but still under the heading of aiding the thought of others, comes the stage of analyzing the problems, of seeking causes, identifying the most likely points and means of attack, of calculating the probable effects of various possible courses of action, of showing what values are involved in each case, and by insightful and dramatic presentation, of helping individuals to weigh these values and to reach judgments that are sound from the standpoint of their own interests. (Pennock 1979: 485)

Each part of this quote – each component of the 'aiding thinking' function of democratic leadership – has a role to play in helping societies, or groups of people, navigate the challenges of acting in future-regarding ways. Let us consider the example that Pennock provides above: that of local leaders anticipating a future influx of school-aged children in their community. In this case, future-regarding leaders must first anticipate and identify the problem. They must recognise that there *will* be a problem in the future if action is not taken now to address it. At this stage they must communicate this to others (i.e., parents, future parents and other community members) who will be affected by this problem.

Secondly, the future-regarding leaders must analyse the problem by seeking causes (e.g., procreation or in-migration) and identifying possible or plausible courses of action. Options might include building more schools, expanding the capacities of existing schools, encouraging alternatives to public schools, hiring more teachers, increasing property taxes or seeking additional sources of funds (such as money from charitable foundations).

Thirdly, future-regarding leaders must help others to calculate and understand the possible effects of alternative courses of action, such as whether increasing property taxes will encourage richer (and more mobile) families to leave the community or exclude poorer families from joining the community.

Fourthly, leaders must help people understand what values to prioritise and which values or trade-offs are involved in the decisions they will have to make. For example, does the community want to prioritise equal access to education or choice in the various education opportunities that may be provided to families?

Fifthly, effective leaders might make insightful or inspiring presentations to help people understand the likely consequences of the decisions or judgements they will make. This function of leadership is particularly important when it comes to future-regarding collective action, precisely because the future is always less tangible than the present.[2]

Sixthly, future-regarding leaders have a role to play in helping communities to 'reach judgements that are sound from the standpoint of their own interests' (Pennock 1979: 485). If the community values equality of access, expanding the number of private schools financed through philanthropy and tuition fees is not going to be the right strategy. But those options might be the right ones if the community decides that they value freedom of choice over equality of access. Leaders help communities to navigate these cognitive tasks together: problem identification, values specification and prioritisation, consideration of alternative options, and reaching collective judgements.

It is difficult to imagine these tasks – tasks which *are* necessary precursors to effective future-regarding collective action – being done *among* collectivities without the guiding and coordinating influence of effective leaders. All the long-term problems that we face – climate change, plastics pollution, rapid technological change, increasing income inequalities, and the generational repro-ductions of racism and other forms of prejudice, just to name a few – will need to be worked through each of these steps if we are going to deal with them effectively. We may be able to do some of this thinking ourselves, as individuals, but we cannot make desir-able futures for ourselves and future others *by ourselves*. If we are going to act in collectively intentional, future-regarding ways, we will need leaders who can aid our thinking *as* collectivities.

There is another function of leadership that Pennock does not mention but is relevant in this context. Most people have cogni-tive biases against the future: we tend to care more about our own present needs and concerns and less about our future needs or the potential interests of future others. Many of our cognitive biases affect how we think about the future, particularly when we are not thinking carefully enough (e.g., Kahneman 2011; Caney 2016). Kahneman (2011) has demonstrated that our cognitive biases are located in the intuitive (or System 1) parts of our brains, and not in the more analytical (or System 2) parts of our brains. Given this, our thinking tends to be most profoundly affected by cognitive biases against the future when we are thinking quickly and effi-ciently rather than slowly and carefully. I have argued elsewhere that participating in public deliberations can help people to recog-nise their cognitive biases, primarily because deliberations encour-age people to slow down their thinking and construct arguments or justifications for their positions and claims that others might plau-sibly accept (MacKenzie 2018, 2021b). Effective deliberations can encourage participants to switch from using their intuitive System 1 brains, to using their more analytical, System 2 brains. If our cog-nitive biases against the future are located primarily in our System 1 brains, as Kahneman argues, then engaging in effective – and cognitively challenging – deliberations should help people come to recognise those biases for what they are, and that is the first step towards challenging and overcoming them.

Democratic leadership can play a similar role in helping people think past – or through – whatever cognitive biases they might have against the future. Effective leaders can challenge people to think about why, for example, it might not make sense to spend now rather than save for the future, or to value the interests and wellbeing of present people more than future ones. Beerbohm mentions a quote from David Foster Wallace that makes this point effectively. 'A real leader', explains Wallace 'can somehow get us to do certain things that deep down we think are good and want to be able to do but usually can't get ourselves to do on our own' (quoted in Beerbohm 2015: 642).

The advantage of leadership in this context is that leaders may be able to influence the thinking of thousands or millions of people, while effective future-regarding deliberations on that scale will be much more difficult to organise and sustain. In practice, a combination of these two approaches – deliberation *and* leadership – may be needed if we want to make our political systems, and our societies, more future-regarding. But it should be acknowledged that democratic leadership rests on deliberative foundations, so these two approaches should not be considered alternatives to one another.

Forging Joint Commitments

Effective leaders 'aid the thinking' of others, but leadership is not just about thinking; it is, ultimately, about acting. It is for this reason that Pennock considers the 'aiding thinking' function of leadership to be 'ancillary rather than central' to the theory and practice of leadership (Pennock 1979: 487). For leaders to *act* as leaders they must perform two other functions. They must forge joint commitments with others to act, and they must mobilise others to act on those joint commitments.

Beerbohm calls the 'forging joint commitments' function of leadership the 'Commitment-Setting Condition'. This involves a Leader or Leaders (L) creating or sustaining a Joint Commitment (J) to act along with Followers (F) (Beerbohm 2015: 642). The function of leadership in this case, is to help collectivities come to understand that they are acting together to achieve specific shared outcomes, goals or states of being. As explained above, the Commitment-Setting Condition helps to distinguish democratic forms of leadership from other, autocratic or demagogic forms of leadership. In seeking to forge shared commitments with followers, democratic leaders do not act *on* their followers but *with* them. Democratic leaders seek to create the conditions necessary for individuals and groups to act together on their own initiatives.

Pennock makes a similar point: 'Although it may be the leader who in the first instance generates the common purpose, the relations between leader and led [in democratic contexts] are thenceforth reciprocal' (Pennock 1979: 472). On this account of democratic leadership, followers must have freedom and intentionality: they must have the ability to contemplate forging shared intentions and joint commitments with others; and they must have real opportunities to accept or reject the overtures made by leaders to forge joint commitments to act. This reciprocal aspect of *democratic* leadership is what helps to resolve the tension between leadership and democracy that Barber (1984) and others have emphasised.

Forging joint commitments to act is precisely what is needed when we are grappling with temporally complex problems such as climate change, plastics pollution, the storage of nuclear waste or the generational reproductions of racism. The first step that future-regarding leaders must take in this sequence is to help people come to understand that a problem such as anthropogenic climate change, for example, exists; why it is a problem; how it threatens things we care about and value; and what the possible options are for dealing with the problem. This is the 'aiding thinking' function of leadership that we have already discussed.

The next step is to forge joint commitments to act among people with different – possibly conflicting – interests at stake, and different reasons for supporting joint commitments to act to help solve the problem of climate change. At this point, the joint commitments that are forged through the efforts of future-regarding leaders may be abstract, general or specific. At its most abstract, a joint commitment to act on climate change might involve committing to 'changing the way we live' without specifying the details. Or we might commit to reducing our reliance on fossil fuels, which would be a general but not abstract commitment. Or we may make specific commitments, such as making it possible for people to heat their homes with geothermal energy and drive their cars less (or not at all). In each case, leadership plays a critical role in bringing people together into share commitments and helping them to understand that they have those shared commitments and intentions.

It is difficult to see how shared commitments might be forged between diverse collections of individuals without someone or some groups playing this leadership role. And leadership is likely to be more important in situations where the individuals and groups that must ultimately act together are more disconnected from each other (either philosophically, culturally or geographically).[3]

The forging joint commitments function of leadership is a crucial step in solving *any* sort of collective action problems, and not just future-regarding ones. But we will need leaders who are self-consciously future-regarding if we are going to make our shared futures together in collectively intentional ways. Leaders who are not future-regarding enough might forge shared commitments to deal with contemporary problems in short-sighted ways. What is needed are leaders who help political communities think in future-regarding ways while helping them forge joint commitments to achieve long-term goals and objectives.

Indeed, joint commitments to act probably *have* to be forged by leaders of some sort or another. Who else is going to do the work of bringing people together? If someone or some group helps to forge joint commitments with others to act, they are, by definition, playing a leadership role. We *will* need joint commitments if we are going to act in future-regarding ways because we cannot make our shared futures on our own: if I decide to, for example, stop driving but no one else does, our futures will not be improved by my action. We must act with others to make the futures we think we might want for our future selves and future others. And leadership is an essential component of making it possible for us to do so.

Mobilisation

The next step is mobilisation. Leadership involves, on Beerbohm's account, not only forging shared commitments to act, but also mobilising – or making it possible – for groups of people *to* act together to achieve those shared commitments. It is not enough to aid thinking by encouraging people to connect their values to specific courses of action (Step 1) and forge shared commitments among people (Step 2). A leader does not lead by changing how people think and forging joint commitments; leaders are leaders because they act with others.

Leaders of all types must figure out how to navigate the politics of collective action; how to get some of what their followers want from collective decisions that must be made with others who disagree or want different things. Within the realm of democratic politics there are numerous political tools, such as persuasion, negotiation, bargaining, aggregation and even coercion in some cases, that might be employed – in various ways – to support collective action. It is the leaders' job to figure out which mix of tools should be used to help groups achieve their joint commitments. As mentioned above, democratic leaders who are authorised in formal processes of election or appointment might legitimately compel people to act in ways that are consistent with the joint commitments they have forged with others. Future-regarding leaders who are authorised through informal processes of mutual acknowledgement, such as Greta Thunberg, must use other mechanisms to motivate and coordinate collective actions aimed at achieving joint commitments. Thunberg has helped to mobilise millions of people to demand more aggressive climate action policies in weekly protests around the globe.

The mobilisation functions of leadership are, as Beerbohm (2015) argues, critical in situations where obligations or options are *underdetermined* with respect to the principles, values or objectives of leaders and followers. Beerbohm gives the example of Buridan's mule to illustrate this point. The mule 'starves when equidistant between two bales of hay, since it can find no rational way to choose among them'. Likewise, Beerbohm's theory of democratic leadership 'predicts that an electorate [or group more generally] that shuns leadership will fail to resolve chronic indeterminacies among political values' (Beerbohm 2015: 643) and thus fail to act.

Unlike the forging of shared commitments, the action-oriented functions of leadership always require or involve specificity: that is, leaders must figure out not only which combination of political tools to use (and how), they must also decide which specific actions should be taken to achieve their shared goals, given existing and probably changing political contexts.

The mobilisation functions of leadership are critically important when it comes to dealing with temporally complex problems. Let us continue with the example of climate change mitigation. Once we have figured out that there is a problem and why it matters to us (Step 1) and forged joint commitments to act on the problem (Step 2), we then must figure out what it is we are going to do about it, and how we are going to do it. But our joint commitments to act on climate change are likely to be underdetermined. Even if we agree on what our obligations to our future selves and future others are, our duties to act will be underspecified. Should we seek to preserve the natural environment as we found it? Or is it permissible to compensate future others for whatever damage we might have done? If compensation is permissible, what sort of compensation should it be? Does it have to be in-kind compensation, or would it be sufficient to provide future others with some other valuable goods?

When deciding which actions should be taken *among contemporaries* to meet our obligations to our future selves and future others (whatever those might be), it is possible (if difficult) to make those decisions in inclusive democratic and deliberative processes. But we cannot *know* which options (e.g., preservation or compensation) will be acceptable to, or preferred by, future others. In these circumstances we must make a choice in the context of underdetermined obligations, incomplete information and insufficient reasons, just like Buridan's mule. And getting groups of people with shared commitments to act in circumstances where there are underdetermined (and, in fact, *undeterminable*) reasons to make one choice or another will require the mobilisation functions of leadership: a choice must be made in either case, and doing nothing is not an option because that will also have long-term consequences.

We need leadership to help us make collective decisions when our commitments to act are clear, but effective leadership is even more important when it is not clear what those commitments should entail in terms of concrete options to act or when people with shared commitments do not agree on the actions that should be taken to meet those commitments. Because of the uncertainties associated with temporally complex issues and problems, future-regarding decisions must always be made in the context of incomplete information. The danger is that groups who have forged joint commitments to act will be unable to do so if they disagree on the actions that need to be taken to meet those joint commitments (e.g., Lagerspetz, Chapter 2, this volume). In such situations, leaders can help collectivities through Buridanian impasses by making decisive decisions while (ideally) bringing people along with them.

When it comes to mitigating the worst effects of anthropogenic climate change, we could, for example, invest in green energy, tax carbon emissions, develop more stringent cap and trade regimes, build carbon capture and storage facilities, use public money to ret-rofit homes and business to make them more energy efficient, and redesign our cities and transportation systems. Which combination of these various options is likely to be most effective and politically manageable? How can our political circumstances and exigencies be altered to make currently unworkable strategies or options more viable? Effective leaders are needed to make these sort of decisions decisively, precisely because it will be difficult (if not impossible) for disparate groups of individuals to make decisive decisions on these issues on their own. There will be reasonable disagreements among people on these issues, even when those people share a commitment to act on climate change. Leaders are needed to support collective action by making decisive decisions in the context of incomplete information, uncertainty, underdetermined obliga-tions and disagreement. But democratic leaders also have a role to play in rendering whatever decisive decisions they make legitimate and acceptable to affected publics.

Three Challenges of Future-Regarding Democratic Leadership

If we want to make our shared futures together in collectively intentional, mutually accommodating ways, we will need to think more carefully about how we can nurture and support future-regarding democratic leadership in our political systems. We need future-regarding leaders to aid our thinking, help us to forge shared commitments to act, and navigate the politics, specificities, uncertainties and indeterminacies of engaging in future-regarding collective actions. There are, however, at least three challenges that we face in this context. The first is finding or nurturing the development of people who are future-regarding *and* capable of performing the three functions of leadership. But future-regarding leaders, once they are found or created, must find themselves in political systems that make future-regarding action possible. Thus, the second challenge has to do with creating political institutions and contexts for future-regarding leaders to work within. These would be institutional environments that do not create insurmountable obstacles to future-regarding action, biases against the future, or myopic political or economic incentives. The third change has to do with creating the deliberative conditions that are required for democratic leadership to thrive.

Challenge No. 1: Finding (or Nurturing) Future-Regarding Leaders

If we want to make our democratic systems more future-regarding we cannot wait for future-regarding leaders to emerge, we must think about how they can be created, nurtured or developed. The challenge is that future-regarding leaders will have the same cognitive biases and myopic tendencies that affect the rest of us. We will need to nurture the development of leaders who are themselves more future-regarding than the people they seek to lead.

There are at least two strategies to encourage the development of future-regarding leaders, both of which would involve educational reforms and cultural or conceptual re-evaluations. The first strategy would focus on training and educating individuals to play future-regarding leadership roles. This could be done in educational institutions such as universities (many of which have leadership programmes that do not focus on the development of *future-regarding* leaders). Another option would be to encourage social movements, activist organisations (such as Greenpeace), charitable foundations, NGOs and political parties to help individuals and groups nurture their future-regarding leadership capacities, and the connections and skills they will need to navigate politics and thereby act on the commitments they share with their followers.

A second strategy would be pitched more broadly and aimed at challenging and changing the myopic assumptions and conceptual orientations that are currently pervasive in our cultural, economic and political lives. There are numerous concepts or ways of thinking that encourage people to approach the world and their lives in temporally limited ways. I have argued elsewhere, for example, that the very idea that there are short-term and long-term issues in public affairs is problematic because it suggests that there is a class of collective actions (or inactions) that will have causes, consequences and potential outcomes that are largely contained within only relatively short periods of time. But this does not appear to be the case: it is remarkably difficult to find any examples of public issues or problems that do not have non-trivial longer-term causes and consequences (MacKenzie 2021a).

Many other concepts encourage people to think more about the present and less about the past or the future. The idea that we can own land or natural resources, for example, implies that we can do what we want with them. By contrast, the concept of usufruct – which involves holding goods in trust rather than owning them outright – would put limits on what we might think we should be allowed to do with land or natural resources.

The idea of 'permanence' in social and political affairs is similarly problematic. We often treat structures within our social, political and economic worlds as if they are permanent (and thus necessary) features of those worlds. We act as if states, for example, are permanent when, in fact, most of the world's states are less than 200 years old. States appear to be permanent from our perspective in time – because they typically live so much longer than any one individual – but thinking of them *as* permanent limits how we might think about our relations with, and obligations to, future others (MacKenzie 2021b). When dealing with issues such as climate change and nuclear waste, for example, we have to think not just about our relations with future members of whatever states (or political communities) we happen to be members of today; we have to think more broadly past the borders of our states; not just because those issues affect humanity as a whole, but also because whatever political communities within which we are now operating will not likely exist in anything like their current forms (or with continuous identities) over very long periods of time.

These two strategies – education reforms and conceptual re-evaluations – are mutually reinforcing not antagonistic. The more we challenge whatever concepts or ways of thinking are likely to induce myopias within existing political, economic and cultural contexts, the better prepared we will be to find and nurture the future-regarding leadership capacities of specific individuals or groups.

This is not, however, a 'great' person theory of future-regarding collective action. We will need future-regarding leaders to aid our thinking, to help us to forge joint commitments and to mobilise our future-regarding collective actions, but this does not mean that we should be looking for a single person or group to step into this role. In the first place, it is unlikely that a single future-regarding leader would be enough to help guide us to desirable futures. In the second place, it is not normatively desirable, from a democratic perspective, to have a single leader or set of leaders. For leadership to be democratic on Beerbohm's model, followers must have real options to accept or reject leaders. Furthermore, as societies we will not agree on what desirable futures should be like, or which future-regarding goals and objectives we should pursue. On this account, then, what is needed is not a single leader or a single set of leaders. What is needed is a diverse set of future-regarding democratic leaders providing different (and potentially) competing visions of desirable futures from which people can choose.

Challenge No. 2: Future-Regarding Institutions

It will not be enough to nurture future-regarding democratic leaders if the political institutions within which they operate are structurally biased against the future, thus inhibiting their opportunities to perform the mobilising functions of future-regarding leadership. This seems to be the position in which many (but not all) leaders of environmental parties have found themselves. They have succeeded in performing the first two functions of future-regarding leadership: they have aided the thinking of their followers (and others) by encouraging them to connect their values to future-regarding green policy options; and they have forged joint commitments with their followers to act in future-regarding ways. Many green parties have, however, thus far failed to successfully navigate the political contexts in which they find themselves to implement sweeping future-regarding green reforms. One problem is that the democratic systems they operate within are not – themselves – future-regarding: they are biased against the future, and they create strong incentives for actors within those institutions to respond to near-term concerns while ignoring or dismissing the potential interests of future others.

A number of scholars have thought about how to make our democratic systems more future-regarding (e.g., González-Ricoy and Gosseries 2016). For the most part, scholars have imagined institutions that are supposed to create future-regarding incentives, such that anyone who operates within them will come to operate in future-regarding ways even if they are not principally committed to doing so (see, e.g., Ekeli 2005, 2009; Tremmel 2015; Caney 2016; MacKenzie 2016b, 2021b; Smith 2021).

Although I am convinced that an institutional approach is the right one – and that we cannot rely on education reforms or conceptual re-evaluations alone if we want to make our political and economic systems more future-regarding – it seems unlikely that we will manage to create such institutions without future-regarding leadership. It is also unlikely that future-regarding institutions will function properly without at least some leaders who are principally committed to acting in future-regarding ways. On this account, future-regarding leadership might be viewed as an umbrella condition: it is both needed if we are going to create future-regarding political institutions and societies, and it is a necessary condition for the maintenance and continued success of those institutions and societies.

Challenge No. 3: The Deliberative Foundations of Democratic Leadership

The third challenge has to do with the deliberative foundations of democratic leadership itself. We will need future-regarding leaders to help us make our shared futures together in collectively intentional ways, but in order to ensure that leadership is (and stays) democratically legitimate, we will need democratic systems that are deliberative in specific ways. As explained above, for leadership to be considered democratic, individuals and groups must have real opportunities to accept or reject potential leaders, but there is a deliberative and an accountability component to such practices.

With respect to the deliberative component, if future-regarding democratic leadership is to retain its legitimacy, there must be robust channels of communication between leaders and followers such that joint commitments can be freely, reflectively and deliberatively forged (and reforged or abandoned if necessary). To forge shared commitments, leaders and followers must engage in deliberations with each other: there is simply no other way. They must be able to talk to each other about what they are doing and where they want to get to in the future. But followers (or potential followers) must also have access to formal or informal (but real) accountability mechanisms, so that they can actively reject leaders who make overtures or decisions that they do not support.

When viewed in these terms, democratic leadership is not a good that can be realised independently from other democratic goods (such as deliberation and accountability) or practiced by 'good' leaders in 'bad' or corrupt political systems. If we want effective and legitimate democratic leaders, we will need to make our democratic systems, as a whole, more robustly deliberative and the leaders themselves more deliberatively accountable to the publics they are meant to serve. If we want to make our democratic systems more future-regarding we will need to nurture the development of future-regarding leaders, but we will also have to ensure that they operate within deliberative democratic systems that do not create insurmountable obstacles to future-regarding collective action.

Conclusion

The challenges of acting together in future-regarding ways are immense. It is difficult to achieve collective goals among contemporary actors who have divergent and conflicting interests. It is even more difficult to navigate conflicting interests and contemporary concerns in ways that also take into consideration the potential interests of our future selves and future others. Acting in future-regarding ways requires making decisive decisions in contexts where our options and obligations are underdetermined or undeterminable. It requires imagination (i.e., the ability to think past what is or what exists now) and inspiration. As Alfred Moore (Chapter 3, this volume) argues, future-regarding action also requires both flexibility and steadfastness. We need to be flexible enough to adjust our strategies and expectations to changing circumstances, but we must nevertheless be steadfast in our joint commitments if we are going to get to where we want to be in the future.

I have argued elsewhere that inclusive deliberative processes are an essential component of effective future-regarding collective action. We need inclusive democratic processes to avoid futures that serve the interests of some types of people while ignoring or trampling upon the interests of others. We need deliberative process so that we can talk to each other about what we are doing and where we want to get to in the future. And we need ongoing processes of public reason-giving so that we can decide when and whether to adjust our strategies, actions and joint commitments to changing circumstances (MacKenzie 2021b: esp. ch. 5). It is difficult for individuals to do all these things when trying to act in future-regarding ways in their private lives. It strains credulity to think that whole societies can do these things together without effective future-regarding leadership. If we want to make our political and economic systems more future-regarding we will have to think about how to correct or counterbalance the myopic incentives that many of our existing political and economic institutions create, but we must also think more carefully about how we might nurture and support the development of effective future-regarding democratic leaders.

Notes

1. Laura Montanaro (2017) makes a similar argument about self-appointed representatives, who may be considered legitimate representatives when those who they seek to represent can actively acknowledge and accept their representation or reject it as they see fit.
2. There is evidence that demonstration – as opposed to merely argumentation – can play a role in helping people to think more clearly about the future. Stephen

Sheppard and his colleagues have shown that using immersive video games, 3D visualisations and other presentation techniques can help people to think more clearly and comprehensively about alternative futures (Sheppard 2012; see also Pahl et al. 2014; Schroth et al. 2014; Dulic et al. 2016). Similarly, Hajer and Pelzer (2018) describe how they used multimedia techniques to help political leaders visualise alternative futures having to do with offshore wind farm developments in the North Sea.

3. I have argued elsewhere (MacKenzie 2021b: esp. ch. 5) that deliberation is necessary to forge future-regarding collective intentions. But leadership is likely needed to facilitate the conditions that make future-regarding deliberations possible, especially when individuals and groups who need to forge collective intentions do not have readily available channels for deliberation or opportunities to talk to each other about what they are doing and where they want to get to in the future.

Part Three

Institutional Design

EIGHT

Democratic Design for Future-Regarding Institutions

Graham Smith

Introduction

When we consider the design of democratic institutions, the criteria we articulate tend not to have future generations in mind. This is understandable, because the institutions and systems that we denote as democratic rarely, if ever, live up to the expectations that we place on them for current generations, let alone future peoples. Democratic theorists tend to focus on the plight of existing people who are excluded or marginalised in some way. When Robert Dahl (1989) presented his five criteria for a well-functioning democracy – (1) effective participation; (2) voting equality at the decisive stage; (3) enlightened understanding; (4) control of the agenda; and (5) inclusiveness – he did so to show that *actually existing* polities functioned more like polyarchies than democracies for *actually existing* peoples. In most of my own work on democratic design, my tendency has been to consider how existing people are impacted by democratic institutions and how the enactment of the goods of inclusiveness, popular control, considered judgement and transparency might better realise democratic expectations across present generations (Smith 2009). The bias of democratic design is generally presentist. If we are to consider future generations within our democratic practices, do we need to think of democratic design in a different way? What criteria, goods or principles need to guide our design thinking.[1]

I approach these questions through the analysis of three institutional forms of varying design that have been integrated into democratic polities in an attempt to engender a long-term orientation: (1) future-regarding parliamentary committees, in particular those in Finland and Germany; (2) offices of future generations (OFGs) in Israel, Hungary and Wales; and (3) deliberative mini-publics (DMPs), such as the recent climate assemblies that have been organised principally across Europe. The aim is to articulate a set of emergent goods or principles for *future-regarding democratic design* from the practices of these institutions.

Future-Regarding Parliamentary Committees

The core defining feature of contemporary democracies – competitive elections – generates institutions that are particularly myopic. The lack of presence of future generations within elected assemblies means that their interests are rarely considered in any systematic manner. Electoral cycles generate incentives for politicians to prioritise short-term returns and make it difficult for the public to have confidence that long-term promises will be delivered across changes in government. Entrenched interest groups are able to shape the agenda to protect their present-day advantage or to sustain those advantages across time. The broader capitalist system reinforces short-term thinking and action. It is as if elected bodies had been designed explicitly to undermine a long-term orientation in democratic politics.

A range of proposals have been proffered to respond to aspects of these myopic tendencies in elected assemblies, including increasing electoral terms, rebalancing the franchise towards the interests of younger voters, creating dedicated seats for designated representatives of future generations, and establishing sub-majority rules to delay bills that would generate significant harm on posterity (Smith 2021: 36–45). All remain proposals.

The Parliamentary Committee for the Future in the Eduskunta, the Finnish parliament, is the best-known example of rare reform within the current structures of a legislature to promote more systematic consideration of the long term (Groombridge 2006; Koskimaa and Raunio 2020). Established in 1993, it has gained international recognition as the first permanent parliamentary committee to have as its core mission consideration of the future across all policy areas. Unlike other committees in the Eduskunta, it has no explicit legislative responsibilities: it has no powers to scrutinise government bills. Its main obligation is to respond to the Government's Report on the Future that is published once every electoral term. While the Report on the Future and the committee's response are rather late in any government's term, it can have an agenda-setting effect on governments that follow. Outside of this statutory function, the committee is free to determine its own agenda and practices. Most of its time is focused on its own inquiries, although it is difficult to trace any sustained impact of these reports on the everyday activity of the Eduskunta. While the policy impact of the committee may be limited, its different way of working and its more strategic orientation ensure continued interest amongst parliamentarians to be members. The committee is recognised as an important training ground for early career politicians. Significant individuals, including prime ministers, credit their time serving on the committee with helping them to learn about and shape their thinking on long-term challenges (for more details, see Koskimaa, Chapter 10, this volume).

What is it about the design of this committee that enables it to take a long-term orientation and has ensured it has remained an institutionalised element of the Eduskunta over time? Its independence from day-to-day legislative politics has created a space in which parliamentarians can work in a non-partisan manner. Because the committee is not required to scrutinise government bills, partisan and electoral dynamics are to a great extent ameliorated. A range of perspectives from across political divides are brought to bear in a context that is more consensual, deliberative and explicitly orientated to the long term. Relative independence and deliberation across party interests are conducive design principles in a legislative arena in which regard for the future is too often lost in partisan positioning. But this set of design characteristics is realised because the committee selects relatively low salience issues for its inquiries and its work offers no threat to the government, political parties and other committees.

A similar story can be told about the Parlamentarischer Beirat für nachhaltige Entwicklung (the Parliamentary Advisory Council for Sustainable Development) that was established by the German Bundestag in 2004 (Kinski and Whiteside 2022). As with its Finnish counterpart, it has no direct legislative role. It has oversight responsibilities for sustainability strategy and plans, but with no powers to affect those activities. The Council seeks consensual positions, creating a space for more collegiate and deliberative engagement typically amongst junior members working across partisan divides. When the idea of a full committee with legislative responsibilities and powers has been considered by the Bundestag, it has been rejected.

In both Finland and Germany, then, parliamentary bodies have been created that enable elected politicians to consider the long term. A diversity of ideological and policy perspectives is brought to bear in a space independent of partisan and electoral dynamics. But in both cases, these spaces are far from empowered: considerations of future generations have little bearing on the day-to-day workings of the legislature.

Offices for Future Generations

OFGs are a relatively rare breed of institution. Three have received a degree of international recognition: (1) the Commission for Future Generations in Israel, established in 2001, but then abolished after its first parliamentary term in 2006; (2) the Hungarian Parliamentary Commissioner for Future Generations, established in 2007 and lasting for four years in its original form before being converted into the weaker Deputy Ombudsman for Future Generations; and (3) the Future Generations Commissioner for Wales, established in 2016 under the Wellbeing of Future Generations (Wales) Act of the previous year (Smith, 2021: 58–82).

The Israeli Commission's work was focused predominantly on the Knesset, the Israeli parliament. The commissioner had extensive rights to obtain information, examine parliamentary bills and secondary legislation and request reasonable time to prepare opinions on proposed legislation where it judged potential harm to future generations. The power to request time was particularly significant because it gave the commission the capacity to delay legislation. At the end of its first full term of office in 2006, the commissioner was not replaced and a bill of annulment for the institution was brought to the Knesset. A Knesset Research and Information Center review suggests that members of the Knesset raised two primary objections that led to its annulment: the Commission's operational costs and the extent of its authority to interfere in their work (Teschner 2013: 3). An institution created by parliament in recognition of its own shortcomings was abolished by the parliament as its influence was felt by elected politicians. Short-term interests of parliamentarians quickly trumped long-term considerations.

The Hungarian Parliamentary Commissioner for Future Generations primarily acted as an ombudsman. The Hungarian constitution establishes that the state and every person is obliged to protect, sustain and preserve the environment for future generations. The commissioner was empowered to conduct investigations on citizens' complaints and to appeal to the Constitutional Court or the Curia of Hungary (supreme court) in cases where national or local legislation may have been in violation of the Fundamental Law. The commissioner had the power to suspend administrative actions that it perceived to be in violation of the Fundamental Law, although it never used that power. As in Israel, Hungary's independent OFG was targeting members of the political class, in this case with the right-wing Fidesz government. In adopting a new constitution in 2011, the government aimed to eradicate many of the state's checks and balances. Agencies with independent powers were particular targets. The Commissioner was vulnerable also because it was targeting financially significant supporters of the governing regime in high-profile actions. While it was not abolished, the institution's powers and resources were significantly downgraded.

While the Israeli and Hungarian OFGs operated differently, both faced the same challenge. As soon as the institution started to bite – to restrict the room for manoeuvre of the government, parliamentarians or powerful social interests – its powers were removed or reduced.

The Future Generations Commissioner for Wales operates in a different way – one step removed from the powers of its Israeli and Hungarian counterparts. The Wellbeing of Future Generations Act places a duty on all government ministries, public authorities and public service boards to establish wellbeing objectives that integrate consideration of future generations into their activities. The commissioner's role is to support these bodies and to monitor the extent to which they achieve their objectives. It is empowered to publicly shame bodies that fail to realise their duty. It is also empowered to publish a Future Generations Report one year before Assembly elections that contains an assessment of the improvements public bodies need to make (Future Generations Commissioner for Wales, 2021). In comparison with the Hungarian and Israeli commissioners, the Welsh commissioner's more limited powers of persuasion mean that its focus is more on shifting the culture and working practices of public sector institutions.

What does the practice of OFGs tell us about designing future-regarding democratic institutions? First, institutionalised independence is critical. Commissioners do not have to fight elections and they operate at a distance from powerful social interests. Their presence over time ameliorates some of the uncertainty and lack of confidence towards long-term policies. For some, the power of these bodies to challenge short-termism is a source of democratic illegitimacy – an independent agency lacking accountability in its exercise of power (e.g., Landwehr, Chapter 6, this volume). Often forgotten though in this criticism of independent status and powers is that these have been granted by law. Such bodies are created by legislatures. Their powers and legitimacy are derived from elected politicians. They can be held accountable by the legislature and their powers revoked, as the cases of Israel and Hungary demonstrate. One of the elements of their political vulnerability is their lack of a strong constituency that will offer political support when they are threatened. Most independent agencies have politically influential lobby groups that provide political capital, placing a brake on government action should it wish to ignore or even abolish the body. As Jonathan Boston (2016a: 331) argues, an OFG 'runs the risk of having few friends and defenders. At the same time, it is bound to generate enemies.'

A consistent critique of OFGs relates to their capacity to speak on behalf of future generations, to act as a surrogate representative. Judgements rest with individual commissioners. The Israeli commissioner, Shlomo Shoham, reports that he was challenged frequently about how he could speak on behalf of future generations:

I have been asked – more than once – if we have the authority to make any kind of decision for future generations, and if so, where it comes from ... How do I allow myself to speak in the name of those who have not yet been born? How do I decide what policy is good or appropriate for them and what is not? (Shoham 2010: 105)

The worry here is that the judgement of a commissioner for future generations will be partial. This could be read as a concern that individual commissioners will use their position to advance their own interests in the name of future generations; or, more charitably, that one person is not the best judge of the interests of future generations.

One response to this concern is to draw on the tradition of collegial panels in France – commissioners as opposed to a single commissioner – or the US practice of bipartisan commissions (Rosanvallon 2011: 88). This was the practice in the now defunct Sustainable Development Commission in the United Kingdom. A number of commissioners with different specialisms were brought together to act as a corporate body. This certainly expands the range of perspectives that are brought to bear on judgements about the interests of the unborn, although such positions are likely to remain relatively restricted to those with particular political allegiances or technical forms of expertise. Social diversity is often lacking. Anja Karnein offers a variation on this approach. If we recognise that different generations may have different interests, then one option is to pluralise representation by employing several commissioners representing different aspects of the future (Karnein 2016: 83–97).

The design of the Hungarian commissioner points in a different direction. Its agenda was established predominantly through its ombudsman function. The first (and only) commissioner, Sándor Fülöp argues that 'we did not want to project our own vision. With over 200 substantive complaints per year, there was no need to invent new problems' (Fülöp 2017). The system ensured a degree of responsiveness to public concerns, although different communities within Hungarian society will have had differential capacities to take such action. The importance of public engagement is also embedded in the principles that guide the operation of the

Welsh Commissioner. 'Involvement' is one of five 'ways of work-ing' articulated in the Welsh Act that all public bodies are expected to embed, including the Commissioner itself. Much is made of the 'Wales We Want' conversation that informed the content of the Act and, even with its limited resources, the Commissioner attempts to engage communities of place and identity – in particular, young people – in its work.

In summary, OFGs indicate the extent to which institutionalised independence and empowerment are critical for ensuring system-atic consideration of future generations. But these examples also show the vulnerability of such empowered institutions to the short-term dynamics of electoral and interest group politics, and to the charge that their perspective on the interests of future generations is partial.

Deliberative Minipublics

In October 2019, La Convention Citoyenne pour le Climat (Citizens' Convention for the Climate) began its work. After seven weekends of learning and deliberating, the 150 French citizens presented their report, laying out proposed legislative, regulative and referendum measures to tackle the climate crisis. The French Convention was the first national-level citizens' assembly dedi-cated purely to climate policy. By the end of 2021, four further national climate assemblies had completed their work in Denmark, Germany, Scotland and the United Kingdom. The following year, climate assemblies in Austria, Luxembourg and Spain began their work. A global climate assembly reported its initial proposals at COP26 in Glasgow in 2021. And a range of local and regional authorities have sponsored climate assemblies. The recommenda-tions emanating from these assemblies are typically far more pro-gressive than the climate action policies of the authorities that have either sponsored or are targets of these institutions.[2]

Citizens' assemblies are the most visible of a family of delibera-tive minipublics (DMPs): institutions in which randomly selected participants learn, reflect and deliberate on often complex and con-troversial areas of public policy before coming to recommenda-tions. DMPs are carefully designed to ensure that the diverse body of participants are exposed to a range of witnesses with different forms of knowledge and insights on the issues at hand. They create the space and time that participants need to work their way through the complexities of the issues and deliberate on them with each other. Aside from citizens' assemblies, examples of DMPs include citizens' juries, consensus conferences, deliberative polls and planning cells (Grönlund et al. 2014; Setälä and Smith 2018).

DMPs have been commissioned to take on a range of tasks with explicit long-term horizons. Consensus conferences, originally developed by the Danish Board of Technology, have provided recommendations on emerging scientific and technological developments, including AI and the use of transgenic animals. Citizens' juries and panels have been established on urban, transport and other forms of planning in Canada, Australia and beyond. Two select committees in the UK parliament employed a citizens' assembly in an attempt to break the political deadlock on the future of social care funding.[3] Deliberative polls on energy provision in Texas provided evidence of informed public support for renewable energy and energy conservation that helped to reshape energy utilities in that state (Fishkin 2018). Beyond climate assemblies, experiments with citizens' juries in Australia, Canada and the United States – as well as the international World Wide Views project – indicate their potential to consider aspects of the climate crisis (Hobson and Niemeyer 2011: 975–71; Rask et al. 2013; Hanson 2018).

More systematic analysis of the temporal orientation of the recommendations of DMPs is needed. The evidence we have suggests that when they are well organised and resourced, given a clear task and adequate time to respond effectively, DMPs outperform more traditional democratic institutions in encouraging participants to consider long-term implications – often on issues where public and political preferences are not well formed (Hobson and Niemeyer 2011; MacKenzie and Warren 2012; Parkhill et al. 2013; Niemeyer and Jennstål 2016: 247–65).

What is it about the structure and practices of DMPs that enables them to adopt a more future-regarding orientation? Like the Eduskunta Parliamentary Committee for the Future and OFGs, the independent standing of DMPs is significant. DMPs are typically organised at arm's-length from commissioning authorities. But it is the method of participant selection that is critical in shaping independence. Recalling ancient Athenian democracy, sortition (or random selection) combined with rapid rotation provides a defence against asymmetries in social and economic power (Dowlen 2008; Owen and Smith 2019: 419–34). Whereas the contemporary use of random selection is typically celebrated for achieving diverse representation (more on this below), its capacity to act as a bulwark against powerful waring families was its main virtue in Athens. Given that one of the drivers for short-termism is the power of entrenched interests, a DMP creates a space in which participants are relatively protected from their influence and actions. Random selection is a protection against strategic action from those with structural power who benefit from current social and economic arrangements that privilege the short term.

A second design principle is realised through random selection: diversity. Whereas parliamentary committees and OFGs are inhabited by actors drawn from relatively limited social backgrounds, the logic of random selection is to create a body of participants that reflect the range of social perspectives across society. Apart from deliberative polls (which bring together hundreds of participants for a weekend of deliberation), most DMPs apply quota sampling to ensure that the selected body broadly reflects the social and cognitive diversity of the population. Common quotas include demographic characteristics such as gender, ethnicity, age, education and social class, and, for some designs, salient political attitudes. For example, the Climate Assembly UK and Scotland's Climate Assembly ensured that participants mirrored the attitudes towards climate change in the wider population. Minority groups are at times over-sampled to ensure a larger presence within the body. This increases the likelihood that disempowered voices are heard and considered and builds confidence amongst politically marginalised groups to articulate their perspectives. The in-built diversity of DMPs is critical to ensure that a variety of perspectives, drawn from different social positions within society, are present amongst participants. DMPs are arguably the most socially and cognitively diverse of any democratic institution within contemporary polities, ensuring a wide range of perspectives on the interests of future generations are brought to bear in deliberations and decision-making.

A third design principle is deliberation. The combination of diversity and protection from strategic action that sortition enables is a critical condition for realising democratic deliberation. But deliberation does not occur naturally. This is particularly the case for the heterogeneous groups of people with very different social perspectives that are removed from their everyday practices and brought together in DMPs. Hence, DMPs are facilitated spaces. Facilitation ensures fairness and equality as participants learn about the issues at hand, hear from and question a cross-section of witnesses, reflect on what they have heard, listen to the views of other participants and then collectively craft recommendations. Facilitation promotes equality of voice and respectful interactions across a diverse group of people who differ significantly in terms of confidence, experience and interests. DMPs approximate the type of communicative rather than strategic motivation celebrated by deliberative democrats. Participants are given the time and space to reflect on the long-term consequences of social choices, informed by the variety of perspectives offered by fellow participants and witnesses.

But DMPs have their weaknesses. First, they tend to be poorly integrated with decision-making processes. The issue here is not simply that future-regarding recommendations can too easily be cherry-picked (Font et al. 2018). While many resources (time, energy, money) have been put into organising citizen participation, much less attention has been given to ensuring that politicians and public administrators are prepared to receive the recommendations that DMP's make, or that the policymaking cycle is at a point where recommendations can make a significant difference. Rare examples of DMPs empowered to make authoritative decisions do exist. Authorities in Ontario and British Columbia committed to holding referendums in the event that the Citizens' Assemblies on Electoral Reform in those provinces recommended alternative voting systems (Smith 2009). Mayors in Poland have committed to implementing the decisions of citizens' panels if those decisions are supported by a specified super-majority of panel members. It is, however, important not to make too stark a distinction between empowered and advisory DMPs: a number of assemblies have begun to institute scrutiny mechanisms whereby, for example, members are re-assembled after the government has made its official response to the assembly's recommendations in order to review and provide their own response to the official narrative. This kind of iterative interaction is likely to have an anticipatory effect: the knowledge that the assembly will be reviewing their response is likely to lead to more accommodation on the part of authorities.

Secondly, DMPs are one-off initiatives. Only rare examples of institutionalised assemblies exist: the permanent *Bürgerdialog* established by the German-speaking parliament in Belgium and *L'Assemblée Citoyenne* in Paris being the most prominent examples. At the time of writing, several European cities are actively exploring the possibility of permanent climate assemblies. The weaknesses of one-off DMPs drives current interest in the idea of sortition legislatures – a proposal of which I am sceptical (Owen and Smith 2019), but which advocates believe would help make legislative processes more future-regarding (MacKenzie 2021b: 173–84).

Democratic Design for Future Generations

Can democratic institutions be designed to safeguard the future? The three institutional forms discussed in this chapter are far from exhaustive in terms of design choice, and they are all fairly marginal political institutions. They do, however, have the virtue of existing and so we can draw lessons from their actual practice. A number of goods can be ascertained to guide future-regarding institutional design. The list below is unlikely to be exhaustive. Rather it gives us some direction as to how we might craft democratic spaces that promote consideration of the long-term and the interests of future generations.

Independence: the creation of institutions that can function independently from partisan, electoral and interest group motivations provides the political space to contest short-termism.

Diversity: where a diversity of voices from across social groups are present in decision-making, different perspectives on long-term policy can be brought to bear. When the vulnerable and politically marginalised are not present within political bodies, their interests are rarely considered systematically, with a detrimental impact on their wellbeing. It also means that their perspectives on the interests of future generations are not considered, increasing the likelihood that inequalities are reproduced across generations.

Deliberation: our tendency is to overlook the long term in our everyday practices as broader social forces and unreflective instincts dominate. Deliberation encourages slow thinking and reflection on the interests of others, including future generations. Deliberation creates political conditions to challenge the status quo and to enable collective political judgement for the long term.

Empowerment: too often bodies that bring forward long-term proposals have only a weak advisory or consultative role in the democratic system and are thus too easily ignored. Bodies that are created to defend and promote the interests of future generations need to have powers to set the agenda, shape working practices and materially affect political decisions in ways that ensure consideration of the impact of policy on those yet unborn. A binary 'advisory-empowered' distinction that valorises singular decision-making power is too simplistic. Modes of empowerment can include powers of delay, veto and scrutiny amongst other forms of action.

Institutionalisation: compliance with political decisions over time requires permanent bodies that are rooted in the political system, promoting long-term thinking. The danger is that temporary spaces are created in which far-sighted recommendations are made, but then the implementation of decisions is left to bodies that are subject to short-term pressures.

We can draw at least four conclusions from this analysis. First, the way in which these goods are realised will vary according to institutional design. Take independence. In the parliamentary committees in Finland and Germany, independence is achieved by creating a non-partisan space where politicians are able to deliberate about future-regarding policy. OFGs are given a legal standing independent from daily control by the executive or parliament. The application of random selection in DMPs generates independence from electoral and interest group dynamics.

Secondly, these cases show us how hard it is to enact all the goods in combination. For example, DMPs realise the first three goods in an impressive fashion, but tend to fall short with regard to empowerment and institutionalisation. OFGs provide a different balance – in this case realising independence, institutionalisation and relative empowerment. Of course, the story of OFGs is that institutionalisation is fragile: they are too easily abolished when they have effects on powerful actors. The Welsh case suggests that empowerment may need to be toned down compared with the earlier Hungarian and Israeli examples if such an independent body is to sustain its position within the institutional ecosystem. The most strongly institutionalised of our cases is the parliamentary committees. In this case, they generate a degree of independence that enhances deliberation across often partisan interests, but at the cost of realising other goods.

Thirdly, the potential for a more robust enactment of goods may be best achieved by combining institutions. We can see an example of this way of thinking in the Wellbeing of Future Generations Bill that has been under consideration in the UK Parliament.[4] While it will not become law – it was proposed by Lord Bird (who established the Big Issue) and was not a government commitment – its ambition to couple the institutional forms discussed in this chapter is instructive. The Bill is influenced by the Welsh legislation of the same name, but looks to embed future-regarding institutions with more diversity and powers. So, for example, it proposes the establishment of a joint Parliamentary Committee for the Future that would include members from both the lower and upper legislative bodies and which would have rights to scrutinise legislation. Whether a more empowered committee will be able to sustain the collaborative, non-partisan practices of its Finnish and German cousins remains an empirical question. Secondly, the Bill proposes a Future Generations Commission with plural membership encompassing both diverse policy expertise and social groups. This Commission would have extensive powers of review. Thirdly, the Bill includes a permanent citizens' assembly that would be institutionalised to work alongside the commission to ensure diverse and deliberative input into its agenda and working practices. This latter proposal aims to counter the limitations of the OFGs in Hungary and Israel. A permanent citizens' assembly could play an important role in both bolstering the perceived legitimacy of OFGs and bringing to bear recommendations that embody a diversity of perspectives on the interests of future generations. The idea here is that an OFG coupled with a permanent citizens' assembly would be more robust both in terms of its defence against strategic action by politicians and in coming to political judgements (Smith 2020, 2021).

Finally, I offer some reflections on the way in which democratic theorists typically consider the principles or goods we associate with democratic institutions and systems. The goods of diversity, deliberation and empowerment that are so key to future-regarding decision-making are easily integrated into Dahl's (1989) five democratic criteria, which are introduced at the beginning of this chapter. They can be clearly articulated within concerns about effective participation, agenda-setting, empowerment, inclusiveness and enlightened understanding. They can also be clearly integrated into my own formulation of the qualities we associate with democratic institutions: inclusiveness, popular control and considered judgement (Smith 2009). The novel insight of the present analysis is to emphasise the importance of *institutionalised independence* for future-regarding democratic institutions: the need to create institutional spaces able to defend themselves against partisan and electoral dynamics, from social interests aiming to protect their short-term advantage in the political system, and from our everyday practices that are moulded by contemporary capitalist dynamics. Critical to this institutionalised independence is the need to ensure that any future-regarding institution – or set of institutions – is embedded. These institutions must be 'rooted' in ways that make them difficult to abolish but nevertheless put them in productive relations with established institutions across the political system (Bussu et al. 2022). Institutionalised independence may well be a categorically different type of design principle from the other goods we have considered. It would appear to be a necessary condition for the other democratic goods of diversity, deliberation and empowerment to be realised effectively in ways that ensure regard for the interests of future generations. The cases explored in this chapter indicate how difficult it is to achieve institutionalised independence, particularly alongside empowerment. For those engaged in crafting future-regarding institutions, the realisation of institution-alised independence and empowerment may be the most signifi-cant design challenge.

Conclusion

This chapter explores three design options for future-regarding insti-tutions: parliamentary committees, offices of future generations and deliberative minipublics. The inductive method employed draws out democratic goods from the practice of actually exist-ing future-regarding institutions, providing important insights into both conceptual and practical design challenges. This has not been an exhaustive analysis of existing design options – for example, the role of constitutional provisions requires further elaboration. Other designs exist too, although many are thought experiments that have yet to leave the drawing board. Such thought experiments are critical for extending our creativity and imagination, although analysis of their potential will always be more speculative. If we are to meet the challenge of embedding long-term thinking into our democratic systems, such creativity and imagination will be key – along with political strategy! Institutional experimentation with future-regarding democratic design is in its early stages. Clarifying relevant design principles and how they might be realised in prac-tice is a critical element of that endeavour.

Notes

1. This chapter develops ideas originally formulated in Smith (2021).
2. The Knowledge Network on Climate Assemblies (KNOCA) provides up-to-date details of current practice of climate assemblies, available at: https://knoca.eu.
3. The Democracy R&D platform provides links to the work of the Danish Board of Technology, Involve (UK), MASS LPB (Canada) and NewDemocracy (Australia) amongst others that have organised DMPs on aspects of long-term policy, avail-able at: https://democracyrd.org.
4. See at: https://www.fdsd.org/ideas/wellbeing-of-future-generations.

NINE

Democratic Institutions and Future Generations

Didier Caluwaerts and Daan Vermassen

Introduction

Modern democracies face many long-term policy challenges, including climate change, public debts, infrastructure maintenance, nuclear waste disposal, social programme management and disaster preparedness. Many authors worry that democratic systems in their current – representative – forms are ill-equipped to deal with such long-term policy challenges (Jacobs 2011; Boston et al. 2014; MacKenzie 2021b). Democracies have an 'appetite for the immediate' (Thompson 2011: 19) in that they experience difficulties in producing policies that take into account the long-term concerns of future generations (Boston 2016b; Jacobs 2016). Because of this intergenerational bias in policymaking, democracies are often considered 'presentist', 'short-termist' or 'myopic'.

Presentism can be caused by many factors, but the institutions of representative democracy are often identified as potential culprits. In representative democracies, elected officials may be insufficiently responsive to the needs of future generations because of the political considerations created by short electoral cycles (Thompson 2011; MacKenzie 2013). A member of parliament seeking re-election thus has incentives to focus on the needs of present-day electors, rather than respond to the needs of posterity, because only the former can make it to the voting booth.

The intuitive claim that democracies, with their short electoral cycles and strategically motivated elites, are geared more towards the short term than the long term has received some empirical support (Healy and Malhotra 2009; Jacobs and Matthews 2012). Students of intergenerational justice have found evidence that democratic policymaking does indeed suffer from an intergenerational equity bias (Vanhuysse 2013, 2014; Krznaric 2020), and that future publics are not given equal consideration to current generations (e.g., Boston 2016a).

However, scholars have also pointed out that the temporal bias in favour of current (or older) generations at the expense of future (or younger) generations does not affect all democracies to the same extent (Vanhuysse 2013, 2014; Krznaric 2020). This makes sense because democracy is not a one-size-fits-all concept. Democracies come in many shapes and sizes (Gerring and Thacker 2008; Lijphart 2012), and there are myriad institutional explanations for intergenerational biases in policymaking (Bernauer et al. 2016; Boston 2016b). For instance, some democracies foster the search for consensus across a wide variety of groups, whereas others empower only those who win the most votes. Some democratic systems are open to all societal interests, whereas others offer fewer opportunities for participation. And some democracies support policy continuity whereas others display more frequent and abrupt alternations of policy priorities. These variations, and many more, in the constitutional and institutional architecture of democracies could impact the way democratic systems deal with intertemporal trade-offs and intergenerational concerns (Bernauer et al. 2016; Boston 2016b).

Despite theoretical claims and empirical support that some of the central institutions of representative democracy favour the near term (Jacobs 2011; Thompson 2011; Boston et al. 2014; Saunders 2014; MacKenzie 2021b; cf. Stoker 2014), 'there are few systematic analyses of how constitutional design affects intertemporal policy choices' (Boston 2016b: 203; see also Ekeli 2005, 2009). Many theoretical claims are made about these causal mechanisms, but the link between the institutions that exist in different democracies and the intergenerational biases in the policies that they produce has not been rigorously tested in cross-national studies.

Taking institutional diversity seriously requires fundamentally reframing the academic debate in this field. After all, the question is no longer whether democratic systems *as such* are presentist, but rather *which types* of democratic institutions are more susceptible to a presentist bias, and which attributes of democratic systems foster short-sightedness. The overarching research question of this chapter is therefore the following: what are the institutional antecedents of the presentist bias in democratic policymaking? Or, put differently: are certain democratic institutions more likely to generate policies characterised by low levels of intergenerational equity?

In answering these questions, this chapter aims to make a theoretical and empirical contribution to the scholarship on democratic myopia. Theoretically, it aims to translate the mostly philosophical literature on intergenerational justice, democratic myopia and policy presentism into empirically testable hypotheses. It therefore goes beyond snapshot case studies, and incorporates a more structural dimension into the analysis. Empirically, it aims to identify the causes of the temporal biases of democratic systems in a large-N comparative analysis over time. The chapter will test for the first time the impact of democratic institutions on future generations by assembling a longitudinal dataset that links intergenerational justice indicators in thirty-six countries to institutional variations over time. To the best of our knowledge, such a combination of longitudinal and comparative data on democratic short-termism has never been tried before.

Based on a comparative analysis of two intergenerational justice indices, we argue that democratic presentism is indeed driven by institutional choices. In particular, we find that executive power-sharing in grand coalitions, proportional electoral systems, unicameralism and the institutional openness to societal participation are associated with future-regarding policies. In what follows, we first discuss which types of institutional variation are more or less conducive to policy myopia. We then discuss the data and methodology, before presenting our results. We conclude with a brief discussion of the relevance of our findings.

Three Institutional Logics for the Long Term

The assumption that democracies, because of their short electoral cycles, produce short-termist policies, does not do justice to the institutional diversity among democracies. After all, democracies exhibit rich institutional variations. Some democracies are characterised by strong executives (congressional systems), whereas others have a more balanced executive–legislative relationship (parliamentary systems) (Lijphart 2012). Some countries allocate seats proportionally according to the percentage of votes each party receives (PR systems), whereas in others, seats are won by the party or candidates with the most votes in each voting district (majoritarian systems). PR systems tend to produce coalition governments, while majoritarian systems tend to produce single-party governments (Newton and Van Deth 2016).

These greatly varying institutional contexts could exacerbate or alleviate the intergenerational equity bias in policymaking (Jacobs 2016). In this chapter, we argue that the tendency for elites (and citizens) to discount intertemporal trade-offs can be mitigated by adopting institutions that follow one or more of the following three logics: (1) the logic of political stability; (2) the logic of political inclusion; and (3) the logic of fragmented authority. We will discuss these three institutional logics below.

The Logic of Political Stability

Democratic presentism has many causes, but it can first of all occur when vote-seeking officials are unwilling to incur short-term costs for potential long-term benefits for fear of not getting re-elected (MacKenzie 2016a). As such, presentism might be overcome by institutions that incentivise political stability and policy continuity (Trappenburg 2005; Boston 2016b: 204). Credibly committing to ensuring the welfare of future generations is much harder when policies can be completely and frequently overturned. Instead, what is required are democracies that can produce coherent policies that transcend four- or five-year electoral cycles, while still remaining sufficiently flexible to changing circumstances, needs and preferences (MacKenzie 2021b).

A first set of institutions which should therefore be considered are those affecting government turnover. 'If governments place a high priority on being re-elected,' Boston argues, '... it is hard to be future-focused. Sacrificing political power for the long-term common good is not a welcome prospect' (Boston 2016b: 66). In other words: institutions which lead to frequent alternations in power could significantly affect the time horizon of politicians. Elites act in short-sighted ways when they fear for their political survival (Nordhaus 1975), so that the lower the chances of incumbents getting re-elected at the next elections, the higher the chances that they will develop short-term policies that will improve their chances of re-election.

Majoritarian institutions that lead to quick and radical turnover in office, and a strong alternation of power between parties from one election to the next (Lijphart 2012), could therefore be hypothesised to foster political myopia (Persson and Svensson 1989). Institutions that stabilise the division of political power between candidates and parties over time – such as PR systems with 'oversized' coalitions that hold more than a majority of the seats and represent all major parties – reduce turnover rates and could therefore incentivise elites to support longer-term policies. After all, if chances are small that elected politicians will be defeated in the next elections, and they expect their parties to remain in the governing coalitions, they may be more willing to stick out their necks for policies that take the potential interests of future people into account. As a logical corollary, the more likely it is that the 'rascals' can be thrown out, the less willing they may be to sacrifice their short-term interests for longer-term political or societal gains.

Whether a politician can be sure of being in government after the next election depends on the design of the political system. Coalitional governments are more common in PR systems than in majoritarian ones (Lijphart 2012). Majoritarian democracies, such as those with Single Member Plurality (SMP) systems with two major parties and single-party governments, lead to frequent alternations in power, with policies shifting from left to right, or vice versa, whenever a new party wins the elections. Such sudden and abrupt shifts in power are not conducive to making credible commitments to long-term policies (Jacobs 2011). In other words, if politicians operating under majoritarian institutions know that their policies might be overturned after the next election, they will be more likely to advocate policies with short-term impacts. This is less likely to occur in consensus democracies with oversized coalitions, multiparty systems and proportional representation. In such democracies, where (almost) all parties have to tie their destinies together, it is much more difficult for voters to vote out all the members of the governing coalition after each election. The chances of each party being re-elected and being part of the next coalition are thus larger in consensus than in majoritarian democracies (Lijphart 2012).

According to the 'institutional logic of political stability', the institutions in consensus democracies – oversized coalitions, multiparty systems and proportional electoral systems – encourage more policy continuity over the long term than majoritarian democracies. As such, these institutions might be more likely to produce policies which take into account the long-term interests of society and future generations.

The Logic of Political Inclusion

A second institutional logic revolves around political inclusion. Presentism is often related to uncertainties (Nair and Howlett 2017). These uncertainties exist because information about the intergenerational consequences of policies is often incomplete or inaccessible. Because future generations do not yet exist, their needs and interests have not yet fully crystallised. As such, it is particularly challenging even for well-intentioned policymakers to identify the interests of future generations and act on their assessments of those interests (e.g., Warren, Chapter 1, this volume).

One way of coping with the uncertainties of long-term policymaking, is to gather diverse viewpoints and make decisions that take into account potential conflicts of interests between diverse groups. The idea that inclusive institutions are conducive to better policies is reminiscent of Lijphart's (2012) arguments in favour of consensus democracy. According to Lijphart, consensus democracies produce policies that foster social consciousness and connectedness between social groups in society. If the processes that engage diverse viewpoints in consensus democracies can help politicians and citizens connect to (and better understand) their contemporaries, they might also encourage politicians and citizens to connect to (and better understand) diverse perspectives on the interests of future generations (e.g., Smith, Chapter 8, this volume). As such, power-sharing institutions may be expected to produce policies that are 'kinder, gentler' not only to contemporary publics but also to future generations.

Power-sharing institutions include those associated with consensus democracies, such as oversized coalitions and proportional electoral systems, but they also include federalism and bicameralism as mechanisms for incorporating the diverse interests of territorially defined groups. These institutions might help encourage long-term policymaking in two ways. First, they allow for careful and inclusive policymaking processes that weigh available information from diverse sources (Trappenburg 2005). In consensus democracies, societal groups are institutionally required to work together and pool their information on policy issues (Deschouwer 2006). Institutions that incentivise decision makers to come to a broad consensus through reflective judgement and thorough argumentative exchange, can help to bring diverse perspectives on the interests of future generations into decision-making processes (Ekeli 2005; Boston 2016b; MacKenzie 2018). This at least partly resolves the information deficit that is at the basis of policy myopia.

Secondly, inclusive decision-making fosters legitimacy and improves implementation (Lijphart 2012). Decisions that receive broad support are also more likely to be carried out in the long run, even if they impose higher costs on current generations to the benefit of future generations. Giving all affected societal groups opportunities to voice their opinions, to participate in decision-making and to weigh all the options, improves procedural legitimacy and facilitates the implementation of difficult decisions (e.g., Setälä et al., Chapter 12, this volume).

There is empirical evidence supporting the theoretical claim that consensus institutions might benefit posterity. After all, social expenditure, which is a crucial variable explaining variations in intergenerational equity (Jacobs 2011; MacKenzie 2013), is higher in non-majoritarian democracies, and Lijphart shows that consensus democracies score significantly higher on one crucial indicator of intergenerational justice, namely, environmental performance (Lijphart 2012: 289). There is thus good reason to assume that consensus democracies might indeed produce more future-regarding policies than their majoritarian counterparts.

In addition, the idea that inclusive institutions lead to better decisions also figures prominently in the literature on democratic innovations (e.g., Smith, Chapter 8, this volume). Inclusive and deliberative democratic innovations have been advanced as a means to incorporate intergenerational concerns into policymaking processes. One idea is that people may come to understand themselves as members of intergenerational communities when they participate in making collective decisions that will have long-term consequences (Ekeli 2005, 2009; MacKenzie 2013). The presence of participatory (or deliberative) institutions in a political system can therefore be expected to correlate positively with the existence of future-regarding policies (Jacobs 2016). After all, democratic innovations are theoretically expected to foster the inclusion of 'other-regarding' and 'future other-regarding' perspectives in decision-making (MacKenzie and O'Doherty 2011). This means that political systems with more democratic innovations (i.e., systems with strongly embedded participatory and deliberative mechanisms) will be more likely to integrate the concerns of future generations into policymaking processes (Fuji Johnson 2007).

Our expectation is therefore the following: inclusive institutions – oversized governments, multiparty systems, proportional electoral systems, federalism, bicameralism and participatory mechanisms – are more likely to produce policies that respect the principles of intergenerational justice.

The Logic of Fragmented Authority

Finally, democratic myopia may be explained by institutional fragmentation. The logic here is not one of policy continuity or inclusion, but rather accountability. Vote-seeking officials might be willing to engage in long-term policymaking as long as they do not have to take (all of) the blame for imposing immediate costs on their electorates. As Jacobs (2016: 444) argues: 'Greater institutional fragmentation of authority . . . should make it easier for governments to invest at low electoral risk by diffusing the blame for short-run costs.' In political systems with fragmented

authority – such as those where the responsibility for costly decisions can be spread over a large number of actors, and where individual accountability is thus low – politicians may be more willing
to impose near-term costs on contemporary publics in exchange for
longer-term benefits.

It is important to acknowledge that authority might be fragmented both horizontally and vertically. Horizontal fragmentation
means that the burden of responsibility for decisions can be shared
within one level of decision-making (i.e., between equals) – as in
a bicameral system in which both chambers have equal powers.
Vertical fragmentation, in contrast, divides authority across different levels of decision-making, such as in a federal system.
Whichever way we define fragmented authority, the consequence
is that (1) accountability is dispersed so that it will be difficult for
voters to assign blame for short-term costs to one single actor, and
(2) that reversing long-term policy commitments will be more difficult because doing so would involve coordinating multiple actors
(Jacobs 2016).

However, fragmented authority can also come at the detriment of
the future. After all, politicians functioning in a system of less direct
accountability can ignore pressing – but long-term – problems, like
climate change, with relative impunity. If voters are more future-
regarding than the politicians they elect, fragmented authority can
lead to short-termism. If publics are less future-regarding than politicians, institutions that insulate politicians from direct accountability might enable them to adopt long-term policies with relative
impunity (MacKenzie 2021b).

Once again, the logic of fragmented authority correlates with different models of democratic design. In majoritarian systems, especially those with one-party governments, it is significantly more
difficult for those in power to shake off the responsibility for imposing short-term costs for potential long-term gains. Moreover, as
Lijphart (2012) argues, majoritarian democracies are often unitary
states with powers being executed at only one level. Where power is
concentrated in a limited number of actors, there is only a limited
possibility to diffuse the blame for unpopular decisions. The unity
of political authority, which some majoritarian democracies have,
thus comes with the burden of political accountability. In contrast,

in consensus democracies that are both horizontally and vertically fragmented, the chain of accountability is more obscured, and this lowers the electoral risks that politicians might face for incurring short-term costs for potential long-term benefits. Our expectation is therefore that democracies with institutions that foster both horizontal and vertical fragmentation will be more future-regarding than those that centralise decision-making power into one (horizontally and vertically defined) unitary actor.

Table 9.1 summarises the causal logics underlying our hypotheses. Our expectations are that democratic institutions that support credible commitments and policy continuity, promote political inclusion, and diffuse and disperse authority and accountability will be more future-regarding.

Data and Methodology

To analyse which democratic institutions are more future-regarding, we take the institutional characteristics of thirty-six countries into account over a period of six years, from 2014 to 2019 ($N = 216$). The countries included in our analysis represent a diverse range of institutions on the spectrum from consensus democracies to majoritarian ones. The countries included are: Australia, Austria, Belgium, Bulgaria, Canada, Croatia, Cyprus, Czech Republic, Denmark, Estonia, Finland, France, Germany, Greece, Hungary,

Table 9.1 Institutional logics and political presentism

Causal Logic	Theoretical Expectation
Logic of political stability	Democratic institutions exhibiting high levels of political stability will be more future-regarding than democratic institutions exhibiting low levels of political stability.
Logic of political inclusion	Democratic institutions exhibiting high levels of political inclusion will be more future-regarding than democratic institutions exhibiting low levels of political inclusion.
Logic of fragmented authority	Democratic institutions exhibiting high levels of fragmented authority (both horizontally and vertically) will be more future-regarding than democratic institutions exhibiting low levels of fragmented authority.

Iceland, Ireland, Italy, Japan, Latvia, Lithuania, Luxembourg, Malta, the Netherlands, New Zealand, Norway, Poland, Portugal, Romania, Slovakia, Slovenia, Spain, Sweden, Switzerland, United Kingdom, and the United States.

To measure the extent to which these democratic states are future-regarding, we use the intergenerational justice component of the Social Justice Index (SJI) which was developed by the Bertelsmann Stiftung (2019). This component of the SJI corresponds to a previously validated measure, namely, the Intergenerational Justice Index (Vanhuysse 2013; 2014; Gál et al. 2018; Vanhuysse and Tremmel 2018), which measures the extent to which public policies adhere to the principles of intergenerational justice.

The SJI measures three dimensions of intergenerational justice: (1) policy support for both younger and older generations; (2) environmental sustainability; and (3) economic and fiscal sustainability (Bertelsmann Stiftung 2019). The first dimension comprises expert assessments of each country's family and pension policies, as well as a measure of each country's old-age dependency ratio. The second dimension combines expert assessments of each country's environmental policies with four quantitative indicators: greenhouse gas emissions per capita; share of renewable energy in gross final energy consumption; ecological footprint; and the consumption of non-renewable resources. The third dimension includes indicators of public and private R&D spending as a percentage of GDP, national debt levels overall and national debt levels per child. In the following analyses each of the nine quantitative indicators is transformed to have values between 1 and 10, with higher values indicating higher levels of intergenerational justice. The three qualitative measures, from the expert assessments, also run from 1 to 10. Our intergenerational justice index is calculated by taking the means of all twelve individual indicators and adding them together. Hence, every indicator is given equal weight in the index.

This measure of intergenerational justice derived from the SJI will support our main analyses because the data are available for thirty-six countries over a period of six years. However, to further validate our findings, and to check their robustness, we run comparable analyses on the Intergenerational Solidarity Index (ISI)

(McQuilkin 2019), which aggregates complementary environmental, economic and social indicators. The ISI averages indicator scores over a five-year period ending in 2018, thus producing only a single score for each country. The number of data points in the ISI is consequently much lower, which is why we conduct only robustness checks using this measure.

Intergenerational justice is conceptually complex. Our actions today will affect future generations in innumerable ways, and since we do not know what the various interests of future generations will be, whatever indicators are used to measure intergenerational justice will be contested. Neither the SJI nor the ISI takes into account measures of biodiversity, investments in education, policies to help advance science or preserve culture, or the robustness of democratic systems, all of which may also be considered important dimensions of intergenerational justice. Nevertheless, both the SJI and the ISI provide solid and comparable starting points because they include measures of multiple policy domains in which our actions might affect the lives of future generations.

We include seven independent variables in our analyses that are linked to the three institutional logics above, namely, the logics of political stability, political inclusion and fragmented authority. The first three independent variables – cabinet composition, the electoral system and the party system – are derived from the Comparative Political Data Set (Armingeon et al. 2020). Minimal winning cabinets (in which no party is redundant to have a majority) and one-party cabinets represent majoritarian characteristics. The mean of these two indicators was the largest coefficient in Lijphart's (2012) factor analysis representing the executive-parties dimension of democratic systems. As majoritarian democracies lead to more alternations in power, cabinet composition can also be used to measure the degree of the political stability within a country. In our analyses, we use the mean of these two types of cabinets averaged over a period of ten years to measure cabinet composition.

For the proportionality of the electoral system, we use the Gallagher index, which represents the relative *dis*proportionality between the percentage of votes and seats each party receives (Gallagher 1991). High scores on the Gallagher index, therefore, equate to low levels of proportionality. Finally, we also look at the effective number of parties in the legislature to assess the political stability of our thirty-six democracies (see Laakso and Taagepera 1979).

For federalism and bicameralism, we use the Comparative Political Data Set, while the values for participatory and deliberative institutions are taken from the Varieties of Democracy (V-DEM) project (Coppedge et al. 2020a). For federalism, we divide our set of countries in two categories, namely, 'no or weak federalism' versus 'strong federalism' (see Huber et al. 2004). Bicameralism is also dichotomised, with unicameral and weak bicameral systems coded as 0, and medium and strong bicameral systems coded as 1 (see Lijphart 2012). Weak bicameral systems (e.g., Belgium and Canada) are thus treated as unicameral systems because they have one chamber with considerably more power than the other.

Our V-DEM measure for participation is a continuous scale that focuses on the active participation by citizens in all political processes – taking engagement in civil society organisations, direct democracy and subnational elected bodies into account. The variable for deliberation is also continuous and focuses on the processes by which decisions are made. More specifically, it looks at whether politicians offer public justifications for their decisions, whether these justifications rely on public good claims, whether they acknowledge and respect counterarguments, and whether public consultations are regularly conducted on a wide range of issues (for more information on these variables, see Coppedge et al. 2020b). We test our hypotheses by looking at the main effects of these independent variables on the SJI intergenerational justice index using an OLS regression.

Analysis

Our dataset contains values for thirty-six countries over six years ($N = 216$). Values on the SJI intergenerational justice index lie between 3.95 and 6.95, with a mean of 5.49 out of 10, and a standard deviation of 0.69. These values are normally distributed, with a skewness of 0.05 and a kurtosis of -0.24. There is, however, a rather large variation between countries. If we look at the means over six years for all countries (Figure 9.1), the top five positions

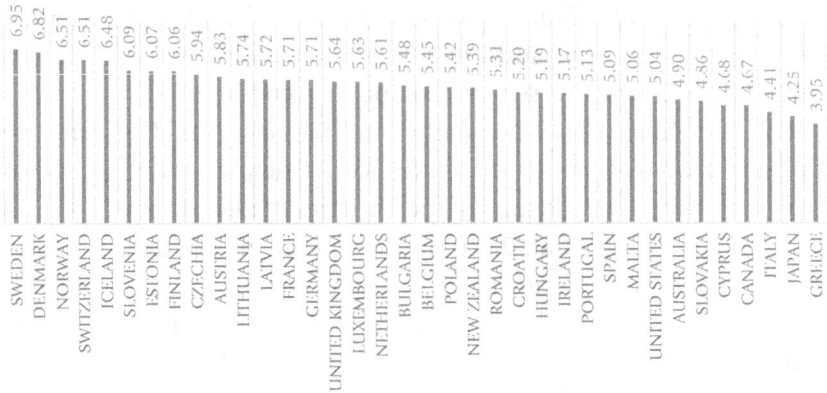

Figure 9.1 Scores on the SJI intergenerational justice index (mean score per country 2014–2019)

are occupied by four northern European countries: Sweden (6.95), Denmark (6.82), Norway (6.51), Iceland (6.09) and Switzerland (6.48). These countries also have high scores on Lijphart's (2012) executive-parties dimension, with their multiparty and proportional electoral systems and oversized cabinets. Figure 9.1 gives us a first indication that these countries also tend to adopt policies that take into account the interests of future generations. At the other end, the figure displays countries such as Greece (3.95), Cyprus (4.68) and Canada (4.67), which are generally considered to be more majoritarian on the executive-parties dimension (Lijphart 2012). This lends some preliminary support to the claim that the institutional set-up of a democracy matters for the future-regarding qualities of the policies it produces. To test our hypotheses that political stability, political inclusion and fragmented authority are positively correlated with future-regarding policy we ran multivariate analyses. Our seven independent variables were entered into two OLS regressions using the SJI intergenerational justice index and the Intergenerational Solidarity Index (ISI) as dependent variables. Model 1 uses the SJI index and includes thirty-six countries at five points in time (N = 216). Model 2 uses the ISI and includes thirty-four countries at one point in time.[1]

Table 9.2 shows that the model does a good job explaining variation in both the SJI intergenerational justice index and ISI (*Adj. R*^{2} = 39.8% and 37.7%, respectively). Given that we ran a very

Table 9.2 OLS regression predicting intergenerational justice scores of the SJI (with clustered robust SE)

	Model 1 IJI (Bertelsmann 2019) (0–10 scale)			Model 2 ISI (McQuilkin 2019) (0–10 scale)		
	B	SE	Sign.	B	SE	Sign.
Constant	4.833	.630	.000	5.149	1.801	.008
Cabinet composition (mean minimal winning and one-party cabinets over last 10 years).	−.941	.174	.000	−1.432	.520	.011
Disproportionality of electoral system (Gallaghar index).	−.037	.009	.000	.044	.027	.113
Effective number of parties.	.057	.032	.078	.146	.084	.095
Federalism (ref = strong).	.034	.131	.793	.371	.389	.348
Bicameralism (ref = medium or strong).	−.199	.097	.042	−.501	.286	.092
Participation (participatory component index).	1.462	.711	.041	3.259	2.275	.164
Deliberation (deliberative component index).	.209	.336	.535	−.748	.850	.387
	N = 216; adjusted R^2 = .398.[a]			N = 34; adjusted R^2 = .376.[b]		

Notes:
[a] Unit of analysis is country–year; [b] unit of analysis is country.

parsimonious statistical model with only seven institutional variables, the explained variance is high. This indicates – in line with our theoretical expectations – that even the most basic institutional (and constitutional) variations in a democracy play a significant role in explaining variations in future-regarding policy.

Our analysis shows that institutions matter for long-term policymaking, but it also shows that some institutions matter more than others. Based on the three institutional logics outlined above, we would expect a negative relationship between the intergenerational justice indices and the percentage of time that minimal winning and one-party cabinets were in power (i.e., cabinet composition). We would also expect a negative relationship between intergenerational justice and the Gallagher index, with higher scores denoting a high level of disproportionality of the electoral system. And we would expect the relationship between intergenerational justice and the effective number of parties to be positive (i.e., party system). The results largely confirm these expectations. Regarding cabinet composition, we find a statistically significant effect in both models, which is moreover negative. In short, majoritarian democracies produce policies that are less future-regarding and consensus democracies produce policies that are more future-regarding. Moreover, cabinet composition is the strongest predictor in our model. The composition of a cabinet, with either a minimal or an oversized coalition, thus determines to a large extent whether the needs and interests of the future are taken into account when governments make policies.

In Model 1, the electoral system is the second strongest predictor. The negative slope (B = −.037) indicates that disproportional electoral systems are associated with lower scores on the SJI intergenerational justice index. Or, in other words: politicians functioning under proportional electoral systems are more likely to develop policies that take into account the interests and concerns of future (and younger) generations. PR systems with high levels of political inclusion and fragmented authority are thus associated with policies that have short-term costs and longer-term benefits. Interestingly, the proportionality of the electoral system is not significant in the second model (which, as we explain above, is included here as a robustness check). We should thus be cautious when interpreting these results.

The effective number of parties variable is positive in both models and statistically significant (albeit at the 10 per cent level). This means that democracies with more parties are associated with policies that are more future-regarding. Multicollinearity tests did not reveal any modelling problems, but proportionality is, of course, positively correlated with the effective number of parties. Nevertheless, these results are very much in line with each other.

Both sets of results show that political systems that are more inclusive are more future-regarding.

The federalism variable is insignificant in both models. The vertical fragmentation of authority does not seem to affect the future-regarding character of the policies that a democracy produces. In contrast, the effect of bicameralism is significant, but the relationship is the opposite of what we expected. The negative slope indicates that strong bicameral systems are less future-regarding when compared with weak bicameral or unicameral systems. We had expected the opposite result since bicameral systems promote political inclusion and fragmented authority. We cannot conclusively explain this finding, but it could be that decision-making in strong bicameral systems, characterised by a power symmetry between both chambers, creates coordination problems because both legislative chambers have to agree on policy before they can act. This in turn creates institutional veto-players who can delay or inhibit policies that have short-term costs (Jacobs 2011).

The participation indicator positively correlates with the dependent variable in Model 1. Democracies that are more participatory (i.e., those in which citizens and civil society organisations are more actively included in policymaking processes) tend to do better on intergenerational justice. As argued above, the inclusion of diverse societal actors in policymaking may increase legitimacy and thereby facilitate the implementation of policies, even when they are controversial or have short-term costs. In addition, when all (or many) societal actors are invested in a decision, it may be more difficult for political actors to renege on previous commitments.

Finally, political systems that are more deliberative do not appear to be more future-regarding than those with lower levels of systemic deliberation. We should, however, be careful when interpreting results using the V-DEM measures of deliberativeness. First, these indicators do not measure actual levels of deliberation among or between citizens and politicians in a political system. Secondly, practices that involve politicians publicly justifying their policies are not two-way processes of deliberation. This finding contradicts Jacobs' (2016) assumption that deliberative political institutions produce more future-regarding policies, and MacKenzie and

Caluwaerts' (2021) findings that deliberation can increase support for climate action policies with near-term costs and future potential benefits.

Discussion and Conclusion

The underlying assumption in many studies is that democracies with their short electoral cycles, strategically motivated elites and myopic voters, are fundamentally short-sighted. Our analysis shows that this assumption is a simplification. Democracies are characterised by strong institutional diversity, and this diversity matters. Our results show that democracies with coalition governments, proportional electoral systems, multiparty systems and high levels of public participation among diverse societal groups, are more future-regarding than those built on majoritarian foundations. These findings challenge Thompson's (2011: 19) claim that democracies have an 'appetite for the immediate'. Some have a bigger appetite for the immediate than others.

Our study shows that a democracy's most basic institutional structures matter when it comes to future-regarding policymaking. Recent literature has formulated many institutional cures for democratic myopia, such as parliamentary commissions for the future, the representation of future generations by proxies, youth quotas and future-regarding constitutional provisions (Dobson 1996; Ekeli 2005, 2009; Bidadanure 2016; Boston 2016a; MacKenzie 2016b; Smith, Chapter 8, this volume). However desirable or necessary these institutional or constitutional 'patches' may seem, we should not neglect the fact that the most basic institutional design choices can affect whether, and to what extent, the potential interests of future generations are considered in policymaking processes. If the aim is to make our democracies more future-regarding, we should dare to question fundamental design decisions (such as whether a PR system or a majoritarian one is used) alongside any considerations of promising but largely untested institutional innovations. Any efforts to redesign foundational democratic institutions are likely to face myriad political challenges, but so will any proposals for new constitutional clauses or innovative democratic institutions aimed at protecting the rights of future generations.

Our analysis also shows that some institutional arrangements have little or no effect on whether a democracy is short-sighted or future-regarding. Federalism and bicameralism are mechanisms for including diverse territorially defined groups in decision-making processes. We hypothesised that such inclusion might lead to more future-regarding policies. Our results show that federalism has no impact on future-regarding policies, while bicameralism might actually reinforce short-sightedness (although this result is inconclusive). These results defy our expectations, but they are in line with Lijphart's (2012) finding that the federal–unitary dimension of consensus democracies has little impact on socioeconomic indicators.

The results of this study are substantively significant and suggestive, but they are not without limitations. One limitation is that we are unable to adjudicate between the three institutional logics outlined above. We have argued that political institutions may be more or less future-regarding depending on whether, and to what extent, they foster political continuity, political inclusion or fragmented authority. Based on our analysis, we cannot definitively conclude whether one logic outperforms the others. More research will be needed to determine which institutional logics play the most significant role in motivating policy makers to pursue long-term objectives. These questions may be most effectively addressed in detailed, qualitative studies. Nevertheless, we can conclude from our study that the three strongest drivers of long-term decision-making (i.e., government composition, proportionality and civic participation) all contribute to inclusion and fragmentation, and that additional indicators of inclusion (i.e., federalism, bicameralism and deliberation) did not yield any conclusive results.

Another limitation is our focus on the SJI and the ISI as composite indices. However, both indices incorporate multiple substantive indicators, ranging from R&D investments to climate policies, and from pension policies to the consumption of non-renewable resources. Within the scope of this chapter, it was not possible to run separate analyses on the different dimensions of these two indices, but future research might adopt this empirical strategy to determine whether specific institutions affect long-term decisions in different policy areas. This approach might also shed light on which institutional logic underlies our findings.

Overall, our analysis demonstrates a strong link between the type of democratic institutions a country has and the temporal biases in the policies it produces. Institutions that foster regular alternations of power and exclude rather than include, are less likely to produce future-regarding policies when compared with institutions that foster policy stability and inclusion. In other words, the institutions that produce 'kinder, gentler' policies – as Lijphart (2012) has said – also seem to be those that are kinder and gentler towards future generations.

Note

1. These are the same thirty-six countries we analyse for the SJI, without Malta and Lithuania for which no data were available.

Part Four

Long-Term Policymaking in Finland

TEN

The Finnish National Foresight System

Vesa Koskimaa

Introduction

The Finnish Committee for the Future (CF) is the world's first and only permanent parliamentary committee dedicated to the future. It has inspired others around the globe to establish parliamentary future committees (Koskimaa and Raunio 2022), and it has become a standard 'benchmark' for those innovations (e.g., Caney 2016). While some scholarly attention has been paid to the Committee for the Future (Arter 2000; Boston 2016a; Koskimaa and Raunio 2020, 2022; Smith, Chapter 8, this volume), this chapter will provide a more comprehensive account of the Finnish foresight system by providing an overview of the other parts of the system and an analysis of the CF in this broader context.

By doing this, the chapter also aims to make a more general contribution to the literature on the 'democratic myopia thesis' (e.g., MacKenzie 2021b). Without denying the basic logic of the thesis, this chapter starts from two observations that justify new directions for the study of future-regarding policymaking. First, the democratic myopia thesis overemphasises the voter–politician nexus as an explanation for why policy outcomes are often myopic. In practice, voters have less influence over specific policy agendas and elected politicians have less discretion in the day-to-day governance of their societies than is often assumed. In contemporary complex societies the activities of policymakers largely concern the managing of *existing* policy programmes (Pierson 2004), and the piecemeal development of capacities to address *emerging* challenges (Pollitt 2008). The essence of technocratic, expert-driven policy-making is to act independently – at least in some respects – from the demands of voters and the fray of electoral politics. The purpose is to make policies that are based on expert insight rather than political considerations (Caramani 2020).

Secondly, empirical studies show that the discretion of policy-makers varies across political systems. Some institutional config-urations give politicians and other policymakers more freedom to make decisions – and long-term policy investments – in ways that are not directly constrained or inhibited by short-term electoral considerations (Jacobs 2011). Power-sharing institutions, such as coalition governments and corporatist systems, which also facili-tate deliberation among diverse groups of elite actors, can enhance a political system's capacity for making and maintaining long-term commitments (Boston 2016a, 2021; Jacobs 2016; Caluwaerts and Vermassen, Chapter 9, this volume). Taken together, these observa-tions suggest that there are features of existing democratic systems that can help to address the democratic myopia problem.

Power-sharing institutions exist in all Nordic democracies, but even among them Finland can be regarded as a frontrunner in future-regarding governance. During the past three decades, the country has developed a permanent foresight system that connects state institutions and other foresight actors into a joint exercise that seeks to lengthen the time perspectives of Finnish policymaking. This 'deliberate and concerted endeavour by policy makers to pre-pare for surprises . . . and foster an innovative, forward-thinking and adaptive learning culture' emerged in the early 1990s around the 'Future Dialogue', an ongoing formal communication proce-dure between the government and the parliament (Boston 2016a). In the early 2000s, the foresight activities of government ministries and organised non-state actors were integrated into the broader foresight system, which today is unique in its scope and capacity (Boston 2016a; Koskimaa and Raunio 2020, 2022).

This chapter describes the various parts of the Finnish national foresight system, its historical development and how the parts of the system fit together. Particular attention is paid to the role that public servants and experts (i.e., non-elected political actors) play in the system. I discuss three main components of the system: (1) the Future Dialogue; (2) intra- and inter-ministerial foresight activities; and (3) the National Foresight Network that integrates non-state actors into the system. I describe the key tasks and roles of these institutions and evaluate their capacity to 'bend' the time horizons of Finnish politics. The chapter reviews the emergence of these institutions and the role-searching processes that they went through as they became established components of the foresight system. I also explore why and how different actors and institutions got involved, which helps to explain how strategic foresight has become integrated into the Finnish political system. Indeed, the institutionalised nature of the Finnish foresight system is widely regarded as one of its greatest strengths (e.g., Boston 2016a).

In what follows, the analyses of the Future Dialogue – and the role that the Committee for the Future plays in that dialogue – draw on research previously conducted and reported by Koskimaa and Raunio (2020, 2022). The other analyses rely on numerous sources of information, including government assessment reports and five in-depth interviews with leading foresight officials in three ministries (the Prime Minister's Office (PMO), the Ministry of the Environment and the Ministry of Foreign Affairs); the Committee for the Future; and Sitra, which is a state-funded think tank that is involved in developing the Finnish political system, including governmental foresight activities. In total, over 7 hours of interviews were conducted. The analyses presented here are supported by other materials collected during the Participation in Long-Term Decision-Making (PALO) project, especially the dozens of interviews conducted with other experts in the Finnish foresight system.

The Components of the Finnish Foresight System

Today, the Finnish foresight system is an institutionalised structure for future-regarding governance. It is a 'network of networks' that combines the foresight needs and efforts of various executive, parliamentary and non-governmental organisations and actors. However, the system has evolved gradually, over decades, through the amalgamation of separate actors and networks, slowly broadening and clarifying the system's functional scope and base of legitimacy.

This chapter examines the development, operation and impact of three components of the Finnish foresight system, which can be regarded as its constituent units. These components of the system are summarised in Table 10.1. With their distinct roles and tasks, they make various contributions to the overall functioning of the system. In what follows, I describe the key participants in each part of the system, the evolution of its parts, and the purpose or function of each part within the contemporary structure of the system. The last part of the chapter outlines recent developments that have enhanced coordination between the different components of the Finnish foresight system.

The Future Dialogue and Committee for the Future

The establishment of the Committee for the Future (CF) in the Eduskunta – the Finnish parliament – in the early 1990s was a

Table 10.1 The constituent units of the Finnish national foresight system

	Key Participants	Main Tasks and Outputs	Primary Role in the System
1. The Future Dialogue	The government (through the PMO) and the parliament (through the CF).	Future reports and supporting material (assessment reports); the CF's 'own projects'.	Formal institutional 'backbone': combining strategic foresight and parliamentary legitimacy.
2. Intra- and Inter-ministerial Foresight Activities	Ministries; PMO (as a coordinator).	Detailed policy-relevant strategic foresight, ministerial future reviews, ministry strategies and joint reviews.	Informational steering and issue-specific input; coordination of state-related foresight activities.
3. The National Foresight Network	Organised non-governmental foresight actors.	Foresight information for CF and ministries.	Connecting non-state actors with state foresight activities.

major development in parliamentary foresight activities, even from a global perspective. Within Finland, the CF acts as an institutional 'backbone' for the larger foresight system, and is a source of democratic legitimacy. The CF's primary function is to engage the parliament in a dialogue on the future with the government, represented by the PMO. The details of the 'Future Dialogue' will be explained below.

The CF's development has been exceptional in two ways. First, the Future Dialogue started on the explicit request of independent Members of Parliament (MPs). Secondly, the Dialogue has been institutionalised into a procedure that is controlled by the MPs. The fact that the CF was initiated and developed by parliamentarians has had a crucial impact on the form and longevity of the Future Dialogue, as well as the emergence and consolidation of the broader foresight system. The most important features of the process are the central role that individual MPs play in the Dialogue and the implicit commitment by the CF to work in a non-partisan manner (see below). This level of independence is rather exceptional in the Finnish political system, where parliamentary work is normally characterised by a strict government–opposition divide.

In 1983, MP Martti Tiuri of the National Coalition Party became the chair of the parliamentary Association of Researchers and Members of Parliament (Tutkas), which started to advocate for a parliamentary foresight unit. In 1986, a group of future-minded scholars, journalists and politicians issued a citizen initiative to establish a parliamentary foresight unit. A parliamentary motion in support of the initiative was later signed by 136 out of 200 MPs, but this process did not ultimately lead to any concrete actions. A major turning point in the process occurred in 1987, when MP Eero Paloheimo of the Green League initiated a parliamentary motion that would require governments to issue a comprehensive report on the future at least once during their term in office. By 1992, Paloheimo's initiative gained the support of 167 out of 200 MPs. In response, the first Government Report on the Future (*tulevaisuuse-lonteko*) was issued to the Eduskunta in 1993. The CF was created at this time – on an ad hoc basis – to act as the body that would prepare the parliament's official response to the government's Report on the Future. This was the beginning of the Future Dialogue.

Initially, the formation of the CF was opposed by established Eduskunta bodies, including the Constitutional Law Committee (CLC). However, the CF's broad-ranging and visionary work created enthusiasm among MPs and the government, and it was re-instituted for two subsequent terms (in 1995 and 1999) as a temporary committee. The CF was made permanent in the constitutional reform process of 2000 – again, against the wishes of the CLC, but with broad cross-party support (Arter 2000; Wilenius 2005; Aalto-Lassila 2008; Tapio and Heinonen 2018).

Today, the CF is a permanent standing committee in the Finnish parliament that has a similar basis of membership and organisation as the 'normal' standing committees. It has seventeen members who are appointed by party groups in proportion to the relative strength of the parties in the parliament. The typical term of each member lasts for the duration of one four-year electoral cycle. Four clerks assist the CF, one of whom is a permanent representative of the Finland Futures Research Centre (FFRC), a special academic institution that was also established in the early 1990s partly in order to assist the CF in methodological questions concerning its own foresight activities.

Officially, the principal task of the CF involves representing the parliament in the Future Dialogue. Formally, the first stage of the Future Dialogue is the Government Report on the Future (*tulevaisuusselonteko*). The report is a broad and detailed assessment of the government's perspective on a specific future-regarding topic or issue. The subject of the report is announced at the beginning of each government's term. Even though the government chooses the topic of the report, the CF can influence the choice of themes through the ongoing interactions that happen between the CF and the PMO. Past reports have dealt with various topics, including Finland's place in the world, changing demographics and working conditions, and environmental issues (Arter 2000; Boston 2016a; Koskimaa and Raunio 2020). Overall, the chosen topics have reflected the major political issues of each era.

Once a theme is chosen, the government examines the issue and writes its report before the end of the parliamentary term. The PMO is responsible for preparing the government's Report on the Future, but because of its many responsibilities associated with governing, the PMO relies on the expertise of others, especially those working in relevant ministries, and non-governmental organisations (including academic institutions). Overall, the functioning of the national foresight system is intertwined with the work of various policy and foresight experts.

After the government's Report on the Future is submitted to the parliament, the CF assesses it and issues a formal reply. The CF conducts its own thorough review process, which also involves consulting with various experts, including academic experts (Seo 2017). Due to the relatively open form of the Dialogue, the CF can 'expand' the dialogue in its own report and raise new or related points that are not addressed in the government's report. The two extensive reports – one from the government and another from the CF – average around 100 pages each. Together they provide a detailed and thorough assessment of any future-regarding concerns related to the topic of inquiry. An important attribute of these reports is that they are heavily influenced by expert opinions, analyses and recommendations. The documents produced by the Dialogue have a distinctly 'academic' and non-partisan nature.

Unlike other Eduskunta committees, which primarily scrutinise bills prepared by a corresponding ministry, the CF is not generally directly involved in the legislative process. However, it may issue evaluative statements on bills for other committees when requested to do so. While the CF has no formal powers to influence policy directly, it is empowered to issue resolutions (*toimenpidealoite*) which instruct the government. These resolutions become active after the Eduskunta has voted to accept the CF's report on the future. The resolutions oblige current and future governments to consider the issues or concerns raised by the CF and provide a response on how the resolution has been dealt with. The resolutions are considered active until the CF is satisfied with the government's response.

If rigorously enforced, the resolution mechanism would be a powerful instrument for future-regarding policymaking. It does not empower the CF to directly influence government policies, but it does provide the members of the committee with a formal means of ensuring that certain future-regarding issues remain on the government's policy agenda. In practice, reflecting the voluntary nature of the Dialogue, the resolution mechanism is more cooperative than contentious. The resolutions typically provide only broad thematic suggestions that are too general and cross-sectorial to be executed and monitored effectively (Koskimaa and Raunio 2020).

The CF also has some other formal roles and tasks. Since 1998, it has conducted technology assessments (TA), which, over time, have broadened into more general assessments of various futures issues. Today, these projects are called the CF's 'own projects' to distinguish them from the committee's responses to the government's Reports on the Future. The CF's own projects begin with agenda-setting discussions between members of the CF and various external experts. Once the themes for projects have been identified, the CF divides into working groups, each of which addresses one project. When working on these projects, the CF operates like a scientific seminar. Experts are consulted and they deliberate the issues amongst themselves and with the members of the committee. 'Own projects' are conducted in a largely non-partisan manner, even though the members of the CF represent different political parties. Each project produces a broad but detailed report, which can be over 100 pages long (Boston 2016a; Koskimaa and Raunio 2020).

In principle, members of the CF can select any relevant topic for extensive study. In practice, the themes of the CF's own projects typically reflect issues addressed by the PMO in its Report on the Future, subjects addressed in the CF's active resolutions, or issues of particular concern to the public. Past reports from the CF's 'own projects' have addressed topics such as nanotechnology, ethical issues related to information and communications technology (ICT), municipal democracy and aging. The CF's reports have been praised for their thoroughness, but their impact on political agendas or public perceptions remains debatable. Reflecting the CF's commitment to operate in a deliberative, scientific and non-partisan fashion, the extensive and complex reports rarely make explicit political recommendations and seldom raise much public interest. However, the interviews conducted for this chapter indicate that the reports are generally well-regarded within relevant ministries, and therefore they may have indirect impacts.

The CF primarily operates outside the formal legislative process, and it thus has no direct impact on legislation unlike 'normal' committees. Nevertheless, the Future Dialogue and the CF's 'own projects' have institutionalised formal and ongoing deliberations between the parliament and the government which help to keep future issues on the policy agenda – and that alone is more than what happens in most other legislative systems. Many of those interviewed for this chapter said that the institutionalisation of the Future Dialogue – with the CF at the centre of the process – has been the most important accomplishment of the Finnish national foresight system.

It can be argued that the influence of the CF has increased in the 2010s because ministries – where most policies are formulated – have become more involved in foresight activities (see below), and their engagement with the CF and the Future Dialogue has consequently deepened. In addition, the CF may have other indirect and diffuse forms of influence. Many former members of the CF have gone on to occupy powerful positions in the government, including former CF chair Jyrki Katainen, who was prime minister from 2011 to 2014, and former CF member, Juha Sipilä, who was prime minister from 2015 to 2019. As PMs, both politicians continued to advance themes that they had learned about in the CF. Finally, in 2017, the CF was given a significant new task: it will issue the parliament's formal response to the government's Agenda 2030 report on sustainable development (Koskimaa and Raunio 2020: 173).

The CF does not have any direct or formal role in making public policies, but it does support ongoing dialogues on future issues that happen right at the centre of the legislative process. These dialogues engage the government, the ministries, the parliament and non-governmental foresight actors. There is no other legislative system in which elected politicians are regularly required to engage in future-regarding deliberations with other elected officials, experts and policy analysts in a formalised process. The fact that the CF has no formal role in policymaking – apart from statements that may influence considerations of other committees – may seem inadequate to those who believe that we will need empowered future-regarding institutions to deal with long-term problems like climate change. The Future Dialogue, however, is designed to encourage elected representatives and other policymakers to consider the future when they are making decisions. This approach, which relies on persuasion rather than authorative power, is one means of encouraging and supporting future-regarding governance that does not challenge or undermine the basic structure and legitimacy of a representative system.

Ministerial Foresight Activities

Finnish government ministries were conducting long-term policy assessments long before such activities were called strategic foresight. Around the mid-1990s, when national foresight activities became more organised, these assessments were especially common in policy fields such as education, human geography, labour and economics more generally. These issues were salient in the aftermath of the great recession in Finland in the 1990s, and they were thus prominent themes in the government's Reports on the Future during that era (Boston 2016a).

As mentioned above, the ministries have provided expert advice to the PMO and the CF since the beginning of the Future Dialogue in 1993. At the turn of the millennium, however, their foresight activities were becoming more institutionalised. In 2002, a group of the highest-ranking elected officials and public servants encouraged the ministries to publish 'future reviews' in their specialised policy areas. These reviews summarise the ministries' long-term insights, describe relevant policy developments in future-regarding terms, outline the most significant future problems in those policy areas, and sketch alternative solutions to these problems. The future reviews are published once each electoral cycle in advance of the election in order to provide evidence-based information and insights that can be used by parties during coalition negotiations (Bergman 2011).

The 'future reviews' have the potential to significantly impact policymaking in Finland. Evidence-based policymaking has real currency among public officials in Finland, and policy experts in the ministries play key roles in shaping public policies more generally (Koskimaa et al. 2021). Ministry officials also write the future reviews. The permanent secretaries of ministries are the highest-ranking public officials in Finland, and they often have considerable influence on the policies advanced by their ministries.

Permanent secretaries often have more direct influence on policies than elected ministers, because ministers are rarely policy experts in their fields, and they are also regularly replaced by new ministers as governments and cabinets change (Murto 2014).

According to those interviewed for this chapter, ministry officials have near-exclusive control over what is written in the future reviews. The review process is run by a designated foresight body which collects information and policy recommendations from other ministry officials, external experts, such as scientists, and public stakeholders. Ministry officials process and condense relevant foresight information, guarding their right to interpret their findings in ways that are in line with their ministries' general objectives (as they understand them). They value the right to present *their* insights to politicians because providing neutral information on key policy issues is a central obligation of tenured ministry experts. This form of influence is significant because coalition negotiations are by far the most important political events in Finland when it comes to the substance of governmental policies. The government programmes that are produced during these negotiations are long and detailed lists of policy objectives and compromises which are rigorously followed while those governments are in power (e.g., Arter 2015). In addition to providing evidence-based information to politicians and other stakeholders, the future reviews enhance transparency by providing the public with insight into policy processes, a sense of the challenges that elected politicians are facing, and the alternatives that they have for addressing them (Bergman 2011).

The interviews conducted for this study revealed two justifications for the influential role of unelected officials in the future review processes. First, ministry officials see themselves as policy experts who are not – and should not – be limited to simply preparing and implementing public policies. In their view they have, and should have, a more active role in assessing developments in their policy fields and keeping politicians informed about them. In this case, their influence on policymaking may be seen as legitimate because elected representatives have the final say over policy decisions and they retain the right to reject the suggestions of the ministry experts.

Secondly, as indicated above, the future review processes are designed as a means of defending the system – and the public interest – against the excessive influence of partisan interests and lobbyists. If the selection of relevant information about long-term challenges is open to political influence, especially before elections, powerful organised interests might use these opportunities to skew policy decisions in their favour. In the Finnish system, ministry officials, as knowledge-producers, have a dual vanguard role: they are expected to provide elected politicians with the best possible information while trying to prevent overtly partisan considerations from impacting policy decisions.

In addition to the foresight work being done *within* ministries, the government has made increasing efforts to coordinate foresight work *between* ministries. In the early 2000s, the ministries developed their own foresight practices, which reflected the varying importance different ministries gave to the task. In 2004, after the first ministerial 'future reviews' were issued, government officials created a Government Foresight Network to coordinate the work being done in different ministries, and to develop synergies and foresight expertise within the state administration more broadly (PMO 2007). Formally, the Government Foresight Network was designed as an instrument of 'soft coordination', a loose and largely informal network for facilitating interactions and collaborations between ministry experts doing foresight work in different policy fields. From the beginning, however, the network organisers have reported to the joint meeting of the ministries' permanent secretaries who also played a key role in the creation of the Government Foresight Network (Bergman 2011).

With the establishment of the Government Foresight Network, the future review processes assumed a more cooperative and coordinated structure. From 2005 to 2014, the Network produced extensive summary reports based on the foresight work done in different ministries. In 2007, the PMO started coordinating the Foresight Network to more effectively integrate the ministerial reviews into its own Report on the Future and to enhance the connection between strategic foresight and policymaking more generally. In the 2010s, the foresight activities of the ministries were officially consolidated into a process known as the 'Ministries Joint Foresight Activities'.

Today, the foresight work being conducted in the ministries follows an established procedure that is outlined and coordinated by the PMO (see below for details).

Although the Finnish foresight system has been regularly amended and reshaped over the last thirty years, the ministries' policy experts – non-elected and tenured public officials – have always played a central role in the system. In addition, it appears that the influence of the ministries has strengthened over time, and the relative impact of other foresight actors, such as those in non-governmental organisations, think tanks and academic institutions has decreased. The PMO and the CF have also increasingly come to rely on the input and expertise of the ministries, and this has further strengthened, and institutionalised, the influence of the ministries in the foresight system. According to the experts interviewed for this chapter, the ministries have also come to recognise the increasing importance of foresight work in the broader Finnish governance system, and they have positioned themselves closer to foresight activities to maintain their role in policymaking processes.

As Jonathan Boston (2016a: 412) has observed, 'evaluating the contribution of foresight to policymaking poses formidable methodological challenges'. It is difficult to determine whether – or to what extent – any specific idea might have influenced or persuaded policymakers to consider the future more seriously, especially during complex foresight processes that often take several years to complete. Given these constraints, foresight work is often evaluated indirectly through assessments of the actors who have taken part in those processes.

Evaluations show that the future review processes have helped the ministries to detect future challenges, identify possible solutions and engage in strategic planning, but their foresight work has not had much direct influence on policymaking (PMO 2007, 2014). Pouru et al. (2020) have noted that the visions articulated by the ministries in their future reviews are often one-sided, limited in scope and sometimes based on faulty or inadequately applied scenario models (Pouru et al. 2020: 53–4). Nevertheless, Pouru et al. (2020) conclude that the ministries are the most important actors in the Finnish foresight system.

The ministries have developed their foresight capacities and they have helped lengthen the time perspectives of those working in their policy areas. The interviewees acknowledged that ministries' policy experts working on highly technical issues could, in practice, have too much influence on elected officials who are not in a position to make informed and independent judgements about the policy recommendations made by those experts. But they also noted that this is precisely the reason that 'semi-autonomous' ministerial policy experts are needed in governance systems: they are there to help advise elected politicians who cannot be expected to have both broad and detailed expertise in all potentially relevant policy areas.

Ministries' officials seem to have taken on a more assertive role in the Finnish system in recent years. One event illustrating this was highlighted by several of the people interviewed for this chapter. Before the parliamentary elections in 2019, the permanent secretaries from every government ministry published a joint policy statement titled 'Opportunities for Finland'. The central message of the document, which stemmed from the ministries' foresight activities, was that 'the future of the welfare society will require significant reforms in the 2020s' (PMO 2019a). The report identifies climate change, government debt and an aging population as key challenges that will need to be addressed in the near future, and it articulates policy options for dealing with them. The report, however, is not overly stipulative: it leaves room for parties to adopt various positions in their coalition negotiations. Nevertheless, the report communicates a clear overall message that includes many specific and unambiguous policy proposals, such as a recommendation to quickly increase work-based immigration to address labour shortages (PMO 2019a). The publication of this document is a notable development because ministry officials have not traditionally played such a public role in Finnish long-term policymaking. The people interviewed for this chapter emphasised the report's explicit and straightforward style. It is also worth noting that the report did not give rise to widespread public criticism, likely because it was framed as a timely reminder of the 'hard realities' that politicians should acknowledge.

Non-State Foresight Actors and Networks

The contemporary Finnish foresight system also involves foresight actors working outside the government. Networks of non-state foresight actors, representing many different parts of society, including research institutions, third sector associations and business organisations, existed before the development and institutionalisation of the Future Dialogue. Indeed, these non-state actors have played a crucial role in the establishment and development of the foresight system (Tapio and Heinonen 2018; Koskimaa and Raunio 2022). In the 1990s, the CF regularly interacted with various non-state actors, especially when working on technology assessments (Arter 2000). During this time, the ministries also worked with foresight actors operating outside the government (Wilenius 2005). These interactions intensified when the CF's role in the foresight system was institutionalised and when the foresight activities of the ministries were consolidated.

In 2005, the involvement of non-state foresight actors was institutionalised with the creation of the National Foresight Network (Wilenius 2005; PMO 2011). The Finnish Innovation Fund Sitra, which is a publicly funded think tank, was given a mandate to coordinate the National Foresight Network (PMO 2007: 28–31). The stated purpose of this network is to enhance the 'agility' of the government's foresight activities by giving policymakers access to high-quality foresight information from a diverse range of actors. The inclusion of diverse experts and their perspectives was valued for its own sake, and the National Foresight Network can be seen as a source of legitimacy for the foresight system because it (ideally) empowers a diverse range of non-state actors to both critique and contribute to foresight activities.

The reality is more complicated. The problem is that policymakers wanted detailed and coherent foresight information, which is rarely provided by a diverse network of analysts with different types of information and contrasting perspectives on the issues. As futures researchers have noted, foresight information is seldom objective, clear and unambiguous, because it is inherently value-laden, partial and uncertain (Dufva and Ahlqvist 2015; Ahvenharju et al. 2020; Pouru et al. 2020). These challenges have meant that the CF and the ministries must spend considerable time and expertise in 'sieving' the information that they receive from the non-state actors in the National Foresight Network, a task that has proved to be overly demanding (PMO 2007, 2011; Dufva and Ahlqvist 2015).

According to the experts interviewed for this chapter, the National Foresight Network – which one interviewee called a 'hotpot-style ecosystem' – has produced massive amounts of information but little in the way of clear guidance for policymakers. Many policymakers feel that they have not benefited from the eclectic output that has been produced by the National Foresight Network. This feeling appears to be mutual. In a recent survey of non-state foresight actors, 92 per cent of the respondents agreed that the system gives them only very limited potential to impact government policies. In their view – and as demonstrated above – the ministries are the only actors within the Finnish foresight system that have any genuine influence over policymaking processes (Pouru et al. 2020).

Recent Developments: Towards More Coordinated and Professional Foresight

The Finnish foresight system has been reformed over the last dozen years, primarily on the initiative of the PMO. Official analyses revealed that the system suffered from fragmented, unfocused and poorly coordinated information flows. In response, a more hierarchical and coordinated approach has been adopted to enhance the system's impact on policy.

The PMO, which already controlled other major foresight projects, such as the government's Report on the Future, became the foresight system's lead coordinator. It strengthened its ties with the ministries and started to play a more significant role in the coordination of the National Foresight Network. These efforts have created more direct channels of communication between the PMO and the ministries, on the one hand, and between the PMO and non-state foresight actors, on the other. The PMO's capacity to perform these coordination functions has been enhanced by the creation of a new unit within the organisation – the 'Government Foresight Group' – which comprises a permanent secretary, a professional secretariat and a council of experts.

During Juha Sipilä's term in office (2015–19), the government's Report on the Future was organised in a new way: it was divided into two complementary parts. The first part presented an overview of the theme of the report, along with an assessment of the associated challenges and problems. The second part described potential solutions to those problems. In its reply to the first part, the CF demanded that the Future Dialogue should be enhanced by giving the ministries a formal and more influential role, especially when it comes to framing the challenges and problems. According to those who were interviewed for this chapter, the purpose of this would be to use the foresight expertise of the ministries to identify the most important futures issues, so that politicians could more effectively focus their attention on those. The 'Opportunities for Finland' report that was issued by the ministries in 2019 is in line with this approach.

Overall, recent developments in the Finnish foresight system have decreased the influence of non-state actors and strengthened the roles played by the ministry officials. In a recent report, the PMO recommended that ministerial foresight activities should also be given a more prominent role in the ordinary policy preparation processes at ministry and government levels (PMO 2019b: 39). Obviously, this new 'strategic', forward-looking role, which includes comprehensive ministry strategies alongside the more focused future reviews, allows ministry policy experts to expand their role beyond traditional policy planning and implementation.

The foresight work that is being done in the ministries has become increasingly important – and valued by the PMO – in the 2010s. This change has been initiated by the transformation of the Finnish governmental system over the last thirty years, from a traditional, more reactive system, to one that emphasises long-term strategic planning and coordination across governments over time. Ministry officials often remain in their jobs longer than elected cabinet ministers, and this means that the ministries can provide a degree of continuity within an ever-changing political system – which is precisely what is needed if long-term objectives are to be achieved.

Ministry officials, who are generally recognised as leading experts in their fields, thus have the potential to develop – and maintain – large-scale, future-regarding, political initiatives.

Discussion and Conclusions

This chapter begins by criticising the 'democratic myopic thesis' for adopting an overly simplified view of policymaking in democratic systems. Scholars who work in this field often assume that the most important and influential actors within a democratic system are the voters and the politicians they elect. This chapter, by contrast, emphasises the diverse roles played by other actors within the Finnish foresight system, including policy and foresight experts operating both inside and outside the government bureaucracy. Elected politicians have a central role to play in the Finnish foresight system, but they are not the only influential actors within that system because they rely on foresight information produced and distributed by various expert groups.

This chapter has outlined efforts that have been made to enhance the foresight capacities of the Finnish political system over the last thirty years. Over this period, the Finnish foresight system has evolved to be become the most advanced and institutionalised system of its kind. It facilitates regular and formalised discussions between elected representatives in the government and the parliament, and non-elected policy and foresight experts in government ministries and non-governmental organisations. The system's capacity to 'bend' the time horizons of elected policymakers relies on persuasion, and high-quality foresight information, as opposed to more direct forms of political power. The influence that foresight actors have within the system depends almost entirely on the quality of the information they produce and whether they can use it to influence the decisions of elected officials.

In summary, the Finnish national foresight system consists of three primary parts: (1) the Future Dialogue, which involves the PMO and the CF; (2) the foresight activities being conducted by policy experts in government ministries; and (3) the National Foresight Network, which aims to integrate non-state actors into the system. Each of these components plays a complementary role within the system, even though some parts of the system are more important and influential than others. The Future Dialogue was the first part of the system to be developed and institutionalised. The Dialogue engages elected representatives in foresight work and thereby provides democratic legitimacy to the system as a whole. But the Dialogue does not operate independently of the other parts of the foresight system. The PMO and the CF engage with experts in ministries and non-state organisations when they are preparing their reports on the future. In particular, the foresight work done by the ministries provides continuity in an ever-shifting system of governmental power.

At the present time, the Finnish foresight system stands firmly in its place: it has evolved over time to respond to the changing demands of the system itself, but in the process, it has been consolidated and institutionalised. The institutionalisation of the system is a major accomplishment because it means that future-regarding issues and problems are regularly addressed in formal political processes in Finland. Nevertheless, the official reports that are produced in the system are often too broad and abstract to influence specific policy decisions – in part because they aim at being both scientifically rigorous and non-partisan, and policy decisions are always partisan (at least in some respects). The CF could exert more power over the government if its resolutions were more rigorously enforced, but up to this point the CF has been reluctant to do anything more than offer the government general advice on futures issues.

In the early 2000s, the National Foresight Network was created to coordinate the foresight activities of non-state actors. This system has managed to include a diverse range of stakeholders, but it has failed to produce specific, coherent and coordinate foresight information for policymakers. This failing may point to a more general challenge in future-regarding governance. It may be difficult to have foresight processes that are simultaneously inclusive and policy relevant. This is a problem because future-regarding governance needs to be broadly inclusive to address all the diverse needs and concerns of different types of people both now and in the future. At the same time, detailed and coherent expertise will be needed to guide public decisions on issues that are technically and temporally complex. As the Finnish case demonstrates, these two goals may be difficult to achieve simultaneously within a single foresight system.

Despite this difficulty, the Finnish foresight system seems to be working quite well. While government executives around the world have developed sophisticated foresight mechanisms and research capacities, Finland is the only country that has created a formal and strongly institutionalised role for parliament in its foresight system (Koskimaa and Raunio 2022). This is what makes the Finnish foresight system both unique and democratically legitimate.

This conclusion should, however, be tempered by consideration of two potential problems that might result from the current form of the Finnish foresight system. First, despite the fact that the CF extends state-level foresight to parliament, it is primarily an expert-based system. This is not necessarily a problem because experts have a legitimate role to play in democratic systems. Policy experts should help to ensure that policy outputs reflect the wishes and intentions of elected governments and the societies they serve, while providing informed and rigorous analyses about the possible consequences of alternative courses of action. However, if policy outputs begin to reflect the personal views of policy experts, there is a risk that the system will become disconnected from the intentions of elected officials and their publics. In this case, an expert-driven foresight system, like the Finnish system, might lose its democratic legitimacy, even if it retains its grounding in the parliamentary system. Secondly, and relatedly, there is a danger that an elite-driven foresight system will eventually lose the support of ordinary people, especially if it makes recommendations that challenge their near-term preferences or material interests. This may aggravate the risks of a hostile, populist surge, especially when dealing with future-regarding issues, like climate change mitigation, that may impose significant costs on contemporary publics.

ELEVEN

Voter Myopia Reassessed

Lauri Rapeli

Introduction

According to a common scholarly understanding, democratic institutions (at least in their current forms) are biased towards making short-sighted decisions (Nordhaus 1975; Bechtel and Hainmuller 2011; Jacobs 2011; MacKenzie 2021b). These biases are particularly problematic in the contemporary world, where many of the most pressing problems, such as climate change, immigration and aging populations, require policy responses that must be enacted over several electoral cycles. Policy responses to long-term problems typically require paying costs in the short term in order to produce benefits in the future.

'Long-term policy investments', as Jacobs (2011) calls them, are difficult for democracies to make for many reasons. Politicians seeking re-election may be reluctant to promote policies that impose costs on voters today, even if substantial benefits could be expected later. Decision makers may also face fierce opposition from organised interest groups worried about carrying significant costs associated with long-term policy initiatives. The future is also uncertain and complex. From the viewpoint of voters, who typically try to minimise informational costs, the uncertainties associated with future policy benefits are likely to make short-term options more attractive (Jacobs 2016: 439). Many scholars have called for more authoritarianism in the handling of long-term political issues, precisely because future uncertainty requires unusual competence and wisdom, which is possessed, it is argued, only by the few (e.g., Shearman and Smith 2007). Indeed, voters are typically not very well-informed about politics (e.g., Delli Carpini and Keeter 1996), which could further contribute to voter myopia.

In representative democracies voters are nevertheless in a key position. Politicians cannot act only on their own initiatives but must consider the preferences of voters when they make policy. If voters are biased against the future, elected officials may be incentivised to make myopic policy choices, even when they know better than to do so. Despite the prevalence of this argument, the empirical evidence for voter myopia is rather thin. Only a handful of studies directly measure the temporal component in voters' policy preferences and these studies do not find strong evidence of voter myopia (e.g., Jacobs and Matthews 2012, 2017).

One problem, which partly explains this lacuna in the literature, is the lack of a yardstick. There is no obvious, let alone commonly accepted, way of measuring political myopia. Most existing studies have used survey experiments to measure support for specific long-term policy options. In this chapter, I adopt a different approach. In the absence of an absolute measure of policy myopia, I use comparative measures that examine democratic myopia in four different groups: voters, non-voters, elected politicians and unelected public officials. This approach corresponds with the idea that there are different political strata in a democratic society, with varying degrees of political attachment and influence in decision-making processes (Dahl 1961; Koskimaa, Chapter 10, this volume). By comparing voters with other groups, this analysis helps to contextualise – and problematise – familiar claims about voter myopia.

In what follows, I utilise two surveys conducted in Finland in 2018 and 2019. One survey uses a representative sample ($n = 1,906$) of the voting age population in Finland (hereafter CS for 'citizen survey'). The other uses a sample ($n = 675$) of decision makers at the national level (hereafter DS for 'decision maker survey'). Both surveys used the same items to measure political myopia. My results show that in the Finnish context, decision makers are less myopic than voters and non-voters. Indeed, the vast majority of decision makers are both future-regarding and willing to acknowledge that near-term costs must be paid to solve future problems.

Although voters and non-voters are significantly more myopic than decision makers (and less likely to say that the present should pay costs to solve future problems), these groups are not as myopic as many democratic theorists expect them to be (e.g., Thompson 2010). A large majority of voters and non-voters think that governments should act to solve future problems, and a smaller majority (but still a majority) acknowledge that near-term costs must be paid to solve these problems. Overall, my analysis shows that voters and elites are not straightforwardly opposed to acting in future-regarding ways in Finland. This analysis also sheds light on who is more future-regarding: members of left-wing parties, those with more education, those who have high levels of trust in political institutions, and those with higher levels of empathy for others are significantly more future-regarding.

The Myopic Voter Argument

The myopic voter argument suggests that voters, or citizens more broadly, exert pressure on elected officials to adopt policies with benefits in the short term, although politicians might themselves prefer more future-regarding policies. The core of the argument, as presented by Thompson (2010), assumes there is a natural human tendency to prefer what is temporally closer to what is farther away. This tendency, it is argued, is also the root cause of democratic myopia – as a democratic system is supposed to be responsive to the (myopic) demands of the people.

Empirical evidence supporting the myopic voter argument comes mainly from studies by psychologists, political economists and political scientists. Psychologists have convincingly established that people are usually biased towards short-term solutions. When given the opportunity to choose, most of the time people favour immediate rewards instead of delayed benefits (Kahneman and Tversky 2000). Furthermore, people tend to emphasise avoiding risks rather than maximising gains (Kahneman et al. 1991), which often results in bias towards the present, because the more distant future is, in many respects, less certain than the nearer future. Political economists have a long tradition of discussing the same phenomena by referring to positive time preferences. But they have also extensively examined the prevalence of future discounting, which refers to situations where individuals have (good) reasons to prefer immediate benefits to future ones. In an extensive literature review, Frederick et al. (2002) conclude that positive time preferences lack conclusive empirical support, thus casting some doubt on the idea that individuals are generally myopic.

While some studies in political science do indeed suggest that people are myopic, the evidence is not overwhelming. In studies of political behaviour, people tend to prefer risk-minimising options that will avoid significant losses over more risky options associated with bigger potential gains. Many elected representatives, for example, are more interested in 'avoiding blame' than getting credit for big policy wins that would require a certain amount of risk-taking (Weaver 1986). This dynamic has often been attributed to pressure from voters, who prefer risk-minimising policy options. Furthermore, students of retrospective voting often interpret their findings in terms of myopia even though they do not, typically, have direct measures of the temporal preferences of voters. People tend to be more retrospective rather than prospective in their voting habits and this is often interpreted as indirect evidence in support for the myopic voter argument (e.g., Nannestad and Paldam 2000).

Addressing voter myopia more directly, a handful of studies have examined public preferences and voter behaviour on specific, temporally complex issues. Healy and Malhotra (2009), for example, examined whether voters are more inclined to reward politicians for providing relief aid during natural disasters, or, alternatively, for making investments in preventative measures to reduce the dangers and damages associated with future natural disasters. They found that voters – in the aggregate – were more likely to reward politicians for providing relief aid and less likely to reward them for making long-term investments in disaster prevention and mitigation, even though long-term investments in prevention can be less costly and more effective overall. As Healy and Malhotra summarise:

> Voters are, in a word, myopic. They are not, as we have shown, myopic
> in the sense that they respond more to spending just before an election
> than to spending a year or two earlier; rather, they are myopic in the sense

that they are unwilling to spend on natural disasters before the disasters have occurred. An ounce of prevention would be far more efficient than a pound of cure, but voters seem interested only in the cure. (Healy and Malhotra 2009: 402)

Healy and Malhotra's study is certainly suggestive, but it only provides evidence that voters are myopic, on this specific issue, at the aggregate level. The study does not tell us whether – or when – individual voters might be willing to choose longer-term policies over myopic ones.

In two survey experiments, Jacobs and Matthews (2012, 2017) have shown that US voters are not radically myopic. Instead, voters tend to favour short-term policies when they have low levels of trust in politicians and thus do not believe that those politicians will – or can – produce the long-term benefits they promise. These findings suggest that it is not myopia, per se, but a lack of trust that drives short-termism in electoral politics (Jacobs and Matthews 2012). In another survey experiment, Jacobs and Matthews (2017) examined levels of support for long-term policymaking in three institutions: local governments, the US federal government and the military. They found that people were more willing to support long-term policy investments when those investments were to be made by institutions that they trust. In a study of Finnish voters, Christensen and Rapeli (2020) found that people do not always oppose policies with future potential benefits. Instead, people tend to care more about the costs involved and the likelihood of obtaining future potential benefits, and less about *when* those benefits will be realised.

Taken as a whole, there is little direct evidence that voters, or people more generally, are inherently myopic when it comes to policy preferences. It is especially notable that the few studies which explicitly examine voter myopia at the individual-level do not find much support for the myopic voter hypothesis. These studies tend to show, instead, that trust is a more decisive factor. In what follows, instead of conducting survey experiments focused on specific long-term policies, I conduct a comparative analysis of political myopia among people in four different groups: voters, non-voters, elected politicians and unelected public officials.

Measuring Political Myopia

Survey experiments have been used to analyse public support for specific policy investments, but these studies do not provide a general measure of political myopia. We know almost nothing about whether voters want politicians to focus on the present or the future more generally in their policymaking decisions. And we know even less about whether political elites are themselves myopic. In experimental studies, subjects have been asked to choose between specific short-term and long-term policy options, but those choices are likely to be topic-sensitive and context-dependent, and thus cannot be taken as evidence of a more generalised form of political myopia. Importantly, voters' specific policy preferences are largely a function of partisan cues, and, as such, they may be subject to change (e.g., Slothuus and Bisgaard 2020). But voters and political elites might, nevertheless, have more general, and stable, views about how near-term concerns should be balanced with future ones (Christensen and Rapeli 2020; see also Rapeli et al. 2021).

The analysis presented in this chapter uses two surveys: a citizen survey of voters and non-voters in Finland (CS), and a survey of Finnish decision makers (DS). Both surveys included a twelve-item battery designed to measure general levels of political myopia. These measures seek to capture the extent to which voters and elites think that decision-making should focus on the present versus the future. (For more details about the twelve-item battery see Rapeli et al. 2021.)

The current study uses the following four survey measures from the original twelve-item index. The choice options range from strongly agree to strongly disagree:

1. decision makers ought to solve future problems;
2. voters should be willing to reduce their standard of living for the sake of the future;
3. future living conditions ought to be accounted for today;
4. decision makers ought to invest in the future, even if taxpayers face costs now.

In the following analyses these four questions are combined into an additive scale of political myopia. In both surveys, the items have reasonably high Cronbach's alpha (CS = .757, DS = .642) and inter-item correlations.[1] Additionally, factor analysis shows that the items load on a single factor in both surveys, suggesting that the questions can be used as a unidimensional measure.[2]

In what follows, I use the scale described above in a two-step analysis. It begins with group-level comparisons between political elites and the citizens. Differentiating between voters and non-voters is important because non-voters typically have little or no influence on the actions of politicians. Differentiating between voters and decision makers is important because only the latter group are involved in making policy directly.

The second step of the analysis examines individual-level predictors of myopia among voters and non-voters. The dependent variable in this second analysis is the same as the one used in the first analysis, although it is coded positively so that higher values indicate less voter myopia. The following individual-level variables will be examined as possible drivers of myopia: empathy, political trust, sociodemographic factors and party support.

Empathy

Empathy involves sympathising with others and striving to understand their views and feelings (Walter 2012). Empathy influences how people evaluate others and whether they are willing to help them (Davis 1996). According to psychologists, there are at least two basic dimensions of empathy: (1) *affective empathy*, which refers to an individual's reactions to other people's emotions; and (2) *cognitive empathy*, which refers to an individual's ability to understand other people's perspectives (Walter 2012).

Empathy – or rather the lack of it – may be a reliable predictor of myopia. Those who can understand the perspectives of others, may be better able to take into consideration the potential interests and perspectives of future others. The ability to do so, might, in turn, be associated with more future-regarding political beliefs. To measure empathy, I use eight survey items from the Questionnaire for Cognitive and Affective Empathy (QCAE: Reniers et al. 2011). These items were then translated into Finnish. The battery includes measures of both cognitive and affective empathy.

Political Trust

Previous research has concluded that trust in political institutions is the strongest single predictor of support for long-term policies (e.g., Jacobs and Matthews 2012, 2017). The reason is that people who trust political institutions, also trust them to deliver whatever policy benefits have been promised. When those benefits lie in the distant future the role of political trust becomes crucial because long-term promises are often difficult to fulfil. No one knows what will happen in the future and people must trust policymakers to remain focused on trying to achieve long-term objectives, even as governments, circumstances and expectations change.

In the following analyses, I employ a composite measure of 'institutional trust' (Hooghe 2011). It consists of measures of trust in parliament, the judicial system, public officials, politicians, political parties, the government and the European Union. Each indicator is measured using a scale running from 0 to 10. These measures are then combined into an additive index. The index has high scalability (Cronbach's alpha of .935, inter-item correlations between .539 and .889), and the indicators load on a single factor.

Sociodemographic Factors

Sociodemographic factors may be another source of myopia. Age is an obvious candidate, although the expected direction of the relationship between age and myopia is not clear. We might expect young people to be future-regarding because they have more (expected) remaining lifetime. Consequently, they might care more about the farther future than older people because they assume they will experience it personally. Youth is also associated with risk-taking (e.g., Bommier 2006), and since investing in the future is always risky, young people may be more willing to take whatever actions may be required to make the future better. There are, however, reasons to think that older people might be more future-regarding than younger people. Studies have shown that priming older people to think about end-of-life considerations also encourages them to think more closely about the legacies they are leaving for future generations (Wade-Benzoni et al. 2012).

Having children or grandchildren might arouse a similar sense of responsibility for the future. In the following analyses, age is included as an independent variable and having children or grandchildren is combined into a single measure called 'offspring'.

To capture the impact of socioeconomic factors, I include measures of both gross annual income and formal education in my analyses. Those with higher incomes may be more willing to invest in the future because they do not need all of their financial resources to meet their present needs.

Education is used as a proxy for political sophistication. Given that the future is unknown and uncertain, and future-regarding actions are always politically, socially, economically and technically complex, those with higher levels of education may have more nuanced understandings of the choices involved in making long-term decisions and intertemporal trade offs.

Party Support

Political ideology is another relevant variable. In Finland, political parties are aligned along the traditional left–right spectrum and thus provide a reasonably good measure of political ideology. However, the direction of the expected relationship between ideology and myopia is not clear: each side of the political spectrum in Finland is associated with policies and beliefs that might be considered future-regarding. Leftist ideology, for example, is currently associated with environmentalism (e.g., Sargisson et al. 2020). As such, voters of the Green League and the two major parties of the left, the Social Democratic Party and the Left Alliance, may be more future-regarding than right-wing voters. On the other hand, those who vote for right-wing parties (i.e., the Finns Party, National Coalition and the Centre Party) are typically in favour of reducing the national debt, which can also be considered a future-regarding policy issue.

Analysis

Table 11.1 compares the opinions of non-voters, voters, elected politicians, and unelected public officials on four measures of myopia.

Table 11.1 Agreement with long-term policymaking
(% of respondents)

	Non-voters	Voters	Elected Politicians	Unelected Public Officials
Decision makers ought to solve future problems.	81.5	87.9	96.3	98.6
Voters should be willing to reduce their standard of living for the sake of the future.	53.2	62.5	87.2	90
Future living conditions ought to be accounted for today.	72.5	78.3	93.8	91.8
Decision makers ought to invest in the future, even if taxpayers face costs now.	51.5	61.7	85.7	90.9

Notes:
- Voters: respondents who said they voted in the latest parliamentary elections, *n* = 1,285.
- Non-voters: respondents who said they did not vote in the latest parliamentary elections, *n* = 399.
- Respondents who were not old enough to vote or did not want to say were excluded: altogether 110 individuals, or 5.8% of the entire sample.
- Elected politicians: *n* = 164.
- Unelected public officials: *n* = 500.
- Question wordings in Table are translations and also shortened versions of the original Finnish wordings: 'Päätöksentekijöiden on jo nyt pyrittävä ratkomaan vuosikymmenten päässä siintäviä ongelmia'; 'Nykyäänestäjien on oltava valmiita tinkimään elintasostaan, jos tulevien sukupolvien hyvinvointi sitä vaatii'; 'Päättäjien on panostettava tulevaisuuden ongelmien ratkomiseen, vaikka siitä aiheutuisi lisäkustannuksia nykyisille veronmaksajille'.

The key patterns in Table 11.1 are obvious. Non-voters are more myopic than voters, and both those groups are significantly more myopic than elected politicians and unelected public officials. Nevertheless, a majority *in all four categories and on each of the four questions* supports the more future-regarding options. Over 80 per cent of non-voters agree that decision makers should-concern themselves with solving problems. Over 70 per cent of non-voters also agree that future living conditions should be considered in today's policymaking processes. When asked whether today's voters should reduce their standards of living in order to improve living conditions in the future, support drops to a little over 50 per cent among non-voters and to a little over 60 per cent among voters. A comparable – but less substantive – drop occurs among the decision makers, but the levels of support in those groups remain remarkably high at around 90 per cent.

Figure 11.1 shows the means and distributions of attitudes across the four groups on the political myopia index. There is some support for the myopic voter argument in these data, but it is not overwhelming. Voters and non-voters *are* more myopic than decision makers – and non-voters are significantly more myopic than voters – but contrary to the expectations of the democratic myopia thesis, neither group is focused primarily on the present. What is more, there are no significant differences between elected and unelected officials. This finding challenges the assumptions of those who have argued that electoral pressures make politicians more myopic than unelected bureaucrats or technocrats.

In the next step of the analysis, the focus turns to individual-level predictors of political myopia in the citizen sample. (Decision makers are excluded from this analysis because the DS did not include the same demographic questions as the CS.)

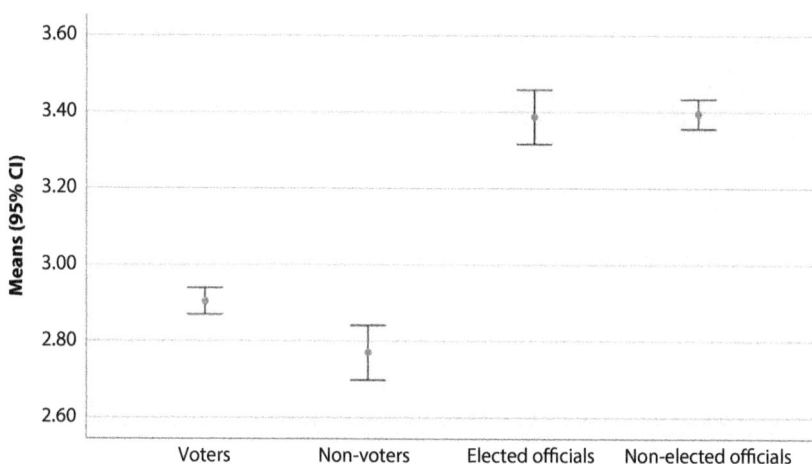

Figure 11.1 Myopic attitudes: group means and confidence intervals (95%). *Note:* The original scale ranging between 0 and 16 has been rescaled to values between 0 and 4.

The dependent variable in the following analyses is the political myopia index used above. As in the previous analysis, higher values indicate lower levels of myopia. All of the independent variables included in the models have values ranging from 0 to 1 in order to facilitate comparisons of their relative impacts. The results are displayed in two figures, which show the point estimates from linear regressions with confidence intervals at the 0.05 level. (The complete regression tables are included in the appendix at the end of the chapter.)

Figure 11.2 shows the effects of empathy, political trust, and sociodemographic variables on political myopia.

As shown in previous research, the single most significant factor influencing political myopia is political trust. In this analysis, those who have higher levels of trust in political institutions and decision makers are significantly less myopic than those with lower levels of trust. Empathy is also associated with being more future-regarding. This suggests that an ability and willingness to take the wellbeing of others into consideration is associated with also taking the future

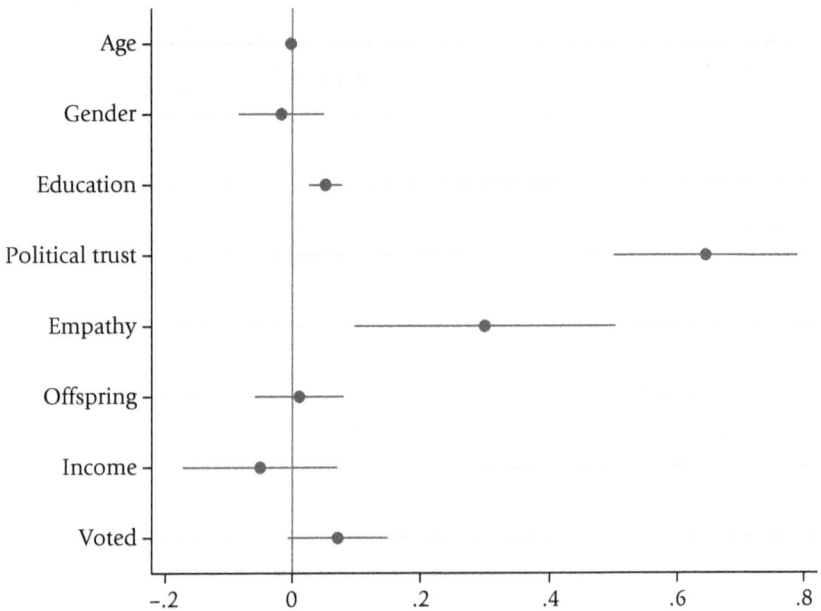

Figure 11.2 Predictors of political myopia

into account. The education variable is also significant, showing that those with more education are less myopic.

Interestingly, once other factors are taken into account, the differences in myopia between voters and non-voters that were observed in the previous analysis are no longer statistically significant. And many of the sociodemographic factors that seem like they should be strongly related to political myopia are not. Income, age and whether one has children or grandchildren, do not significantly affect political myopia. Gender, which was included as a standard control variable, is also insignificant in the analysis.

Figure 11.3 examines the relationship between party support and political myopia among voters in the CS. The regressions included control variables for age, gender and education (see appendix). Figure 11.3 shows that there is a clear political divide when it comes to considering the future. Voters of the Finns Party deviate from the rest with a strong preference for the present, whereas voters of the Green League and the Left Alliance differ from the rest due to their strong preference for the future. The estimates are not statistically significant for the other parties.

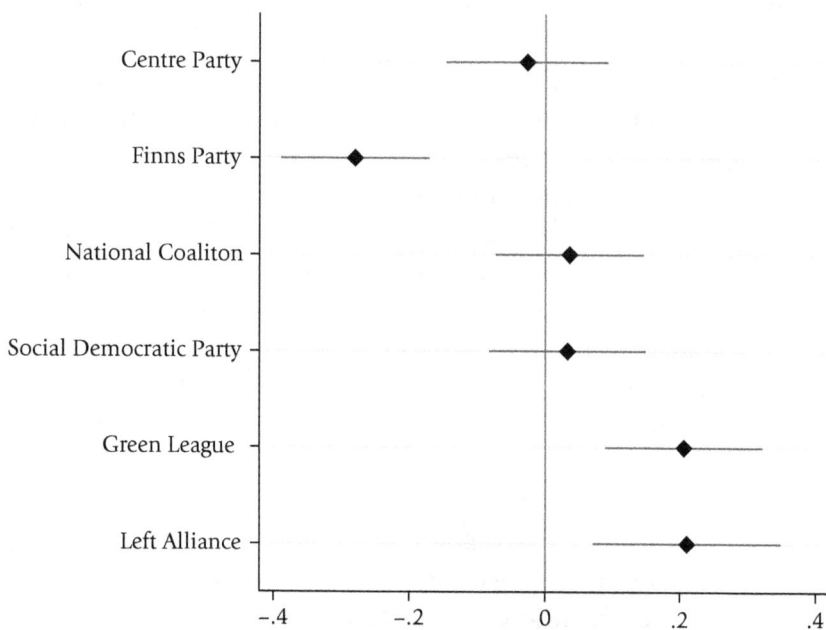

Figure 11.3 Party support and political myopia

Discussion

Many scholars and other commentators have argued that democracies are short-sighted because voters themselves are myopic. Empirical support for this claim has rested mainly on findings from survey experiments and psychological research, both of which show evidence of myopia in processes of preference formation. But survey experiments, which have examined attitudes towards specific (hypothetical) policies, have not provided strong support for the myopic voter argument more generally. Instead, these studies have shown that trust matters more than myopia itself. Rather than being myopic, voters tend to prefer near-term policy benefits when they do not trust their political elites or institutions to deliver on long-term promises.

The findings presented in this study show that voters and non-voters in Finland *are* more myopic than elected and unelected decision makers. In that sense, the findings support the myopic voter argument. Nevertheless, a majority of people in all four groups – voters, non-voters, elected politicians and unelected public officials – supported the more future-regarding options in the political myopia index. In this sense, the findings reported here challenge the myopic voter argument, which claims that short-sighted voters put pressure on decision makers to favour the present over the future. There is little evidence that voters in Finland as a whole favour the present over the future. Those who are less trusting, have lower levels of education, are less empathetic or are supporters of the Finns Party, are more focused on the present than others, but those groups do not represent a majority of the voting (or non-voting) public in Finland. Citizens and decision makers tended to be less future-oriented when they were asked about making lifestyle adjustments for the sake of the future, but even those considerations did not significantly affect their orientations towards the future.

The results reported here nevertheless illustrate that decision makers in Finland – both elected and unelected officials – have some work to do to convince voters and non-voters that it is important to consider the future as well as the present in policymaking more generally. A majority of people in Finland already support that approach, but a significant minority of voters and non-voters do not. One option for addressing this issue would be for decision makers and citizens to discuss long-term issues with each other in deliberative forums (e.g., Smith, Chapter 8; Setälä et al., Chapter 12, both this volume). Further research will be needed to determine whether decision makers can, in fact, encourage the voting public to support specific long-term policy initiatives through deliberative processes.

The findings on empathy reported here are also suggestive of future research opportunities. As explained above, political trust has been identified as one of the most significant factors affecting support for long-term policy initiatives. In this study, empathy is identified as another significant variable. Using a different version of the political myopia index, Rapeli et al. (2021) reported a positive relationship between empathy and future-orientation, but this result was not statistically significant. This suggests that the impact of empathy on myopia is sensitive to measurement choices, and thus requires further investigation. Nevertheless, the role of empathy in this context opens up interesting possibilities for future research. Political scientists have not yet explored all of the possible connections between psychological predispositions and political myopia. Empathy is a measure of sensitivity towards the needs and perspectives of others, but when, why and to what extent empathetic understandings extend to future others in political contexts is still unknown.

Other research projects might explore the connection between education and myopia more closely. High levels of formal education *could* be associated with an ability to understand the inevitable complexities associated with thinking about the future and acting in future-regarding ways. But education might instead be a proxy for social position. Those who are highly educated may feel more secure in their social and economic lives and thus freer to think and act in future-regarding ways without jeopardising their immediate needs.

Nor do we know much about how political myopia interacts with partisanship or political ideology. This study has shown that there are significant differences in future-orientation among voters of different parties in Finland. These findings do not, however, tell us whether supporters of left-wing parties are more future-regarding in other countries as well or *why* this could be the case. As explained above, parties on all parts of the ideological spectrum have political interests, policy commitments and worldviews that might favour the present in some cases and the future in others.

In summary, policymaking in Finland does not appear to be driven by the voter myopia problem. Citizens are more myopic than decision makers, but neither group is focused exclusively on the present. What is more, as Koskimaa (Chapter 11, this volume) explains, the Finnish policymaking elite has constructed an extensive structure to ensure that the concerns of the future are taken into consideration in policymaking processes at the national level. These future-regarding policy processes, which are highly developed in Finland, have been established primarily by and for unelected public officials, who have plenty of manoeuvring space in their policy decisions, regardless of what the voters want. The results reported in this chapter show that these unelected public officials in Finland are not focused primarily on the present. What is more, while they have the capacity to act in future-regarding ways against the interests of voters, they may not need to do so because voters themselves are not especially myopic in Finland. Future research should explore which came first in the Finnish case: a future-regarding political bureaucracy that has, in some ways, influenced public support for future-regarding action; or a relatively supportive public that has not actively opposed future-regarding decision-making processes. One might conjecture that the story involves both of these dynamics working in conjunction with each other.

Finland is an interesting case study in political myopia precisely because it challenges familiar expectations about myopic citizens, elected representatives and unelected officials. We do not know whether similar patterns will be evident in other countries. To explore this further, we will need to conduct comparative studies of political myopia in other democratic systems. But to do that we will need general, rather than policy-specific, measures of political myopia, like the ones used in this analysis.

Appendix

Table 11.A1 Predictors of political myopia

	Coef.	SE	t	P > |t|	95% CI	
Age	−.0022994	.0010689	−2.15	0.032	−.0043962	−.0002026
Gender	−.0172667	.034263	−0.50	0.614	−.0844813	.0499479
Education	.0521809	.0131843	3.96	0.000	.0263168	.0780449
Political trust	.6451642	.0739947	8.72	0.000	.5000072	.7903212
Empathy	.3002103	.1033303	2.91	0.004	.0975048	.5029157
Offspring	.010942	.0356228	0.31	0.759	−.05894	.080824
Income	−.050705	.0618059	−0.82	0.412	−.1719511	.070541
Voted	.0710902	.0397345	1.79	0.074	−.0068578	.1490382
Constant	2.289046	.0883718	25.90	0.000	2.115685	2.462407

$N = 1{,}359$; $F = 17.58^{***}$; $R^2 = .094$

Table 11.A2 Party support and political myopia

	Coef.	SE	t	P > |t|	[95% Conf. Interval]	
Centre	−.0267285	.0610857	−0.44	0.662	−.1465902	−.0931332
Finns Party	−.2802034	.0553923	−5.06	0.000	−.3888934	−.1715134
Natl Coalition	.0364236	.0560523	0.65	0.516	−.0735616	−.1464088
SDP	.0332761	.0590146	0.56	0.573	−.0825216	−.1490739
Green League	.2059974	.0592301	3.48	0.001	.0897768	−.3222181
Left Alliance	.2104641	.0707723	2.97	0.003	.0715955	−.3493326
Age	−.0020285	.0010302	−1.97	0.049	−.0040499	−7.12e−06
Gender	−.0283712	.0347971	−0.82	0.415	−.0966496	−.0399072
Education	.0597713	.0135296	4.42	0.000	.0332236	−.0863189
Constant	2.823722	.0762931	37.01	0.000	2.674021	−2.973424

$N = 1{,}078$; $F = 13.00^{***}$; $R^2 = .09$

Notes

1. CS: correlations range between .369 and .494. DS: correlations range between .235 and .440.
2. CS: eigenvalue 2.326, factor loadings range between .732 and .797. DS: eigenvalue 1.937, factor loadings range between .590 and .796.

TWELVE

Deliberative Minipublics and Climate Change Policy

Maija Setälä, Katariina Kulha and Hilma Sormunen

Introduction

As pointed out in previous chapters, the Finnish political system's capacity for future-regarding governance hinges on an advanced foresight system that includes experts and stakeholders in policy-making. Finnish citizens tend to have high levels of trust in experts and political institutions (Bäck and Kestilä-Kekkonen 2019), and this seems to be a crucial factor behind the success of Finland's elite-driven policymaking system. However, only cautious steps have been taken to make the Finnish policymaking system more participatory, and the country, more generally, seems to be lagging behind the 'deliberative wave' that has increased deliberative participation in other countries (OECD 2020). Against this backdrop, this chapter aims to calibrate the potential contributions of deliberative minipublics in policymaking processes on climate change in Finland.

Minipublics are small deliberative forums that consist of randomly selected participants who come together to engage in informed deliberations on specific policy issues. They are normally designed to represent the demographic or political diversity of the populations from which the participants are drawn (Setälä and Smith 2018). There are small-scale minipublics such as Citizens' Juries and Consensus Conferences, which typically include only a few dozen participants, and large-scale minipublics such as Citizens' Assemblies, which may include hundreds of participants.

Previous studies show that participation in minipublics enhances learning (Setälä et al. 2010), understanding of different viewpoints (Luskin et al. 2014), empathy (Grönlund et al. 2017) and long-term thinking (Kulha et al. 2021). In this respect, minipublics have proved to be an effective way to involve citizens in policymaking on complex and long-term issues. However, there are many outstanding questions regarding the roles of deliberative minipublics in policymaking and the ways in which minipublics might be 'coupled' with other representative institutions (Hendriks 2016).

Climate change is a prime example of a future-regarding problem. In order to address climate change, policymakers must understand the future consequences of various policy options, and they must be able to forge long-term commitments among political elites, citizens and other stakeholder groups. In recent years, there has been a proliferation of deliberative minipublics on climate issues in various countries and at different levels of governance. The aim of these minipublics is to enhance public understanding of climate issues, promote fairness in policies aimed at transitioning to carbon-neutral societies, and thereby support the legitimacy of climate actions more generally. The most notable examples are the UK Climate Assembly and the French Citizens' Convention on Climate, both of which were expected to facilitate just transitions to carbon-neutral societies (see, e.g., Farrell et al. 2019; Elstub et al. 2021; Smith, Chapter 8, this volume). Civil society activists and movements, most notably Extinction Rebellion, have actively promoted the use of deliberative minipublics in the development of climate mitigation policies (Devaney et al. 2020). In some cases, minipublics have been institutionalised. Ministers in Scotland's government, for example, are obligated to establish citizens' assemblies when considering matters related to climate change.

In this chapter, we examine the Finnish Citizens' Jury on Climate Actions, which took place in spring 2021. We analyse the background conditions of the jury, the jury process itself, and perceptions of the jury among participants and policymakers. Those who established the jury were motivated by concerns about the legitimacy of controversial climate policy measures proposed by the government – measures that will directly affect the everyday lives of people living in Finland if they are adopted. Our analysis shows that the jury was able to articulate disagreements among participants while also proposing constructive solutions to the long-term problem of climate change. The jury can thus be regarded as an example of a successful 'anticipatory minipublic'. As MacKenzie and Warren (2012: 121) explain, anticipatory minipublics 'function as checkups on trust, particularly in areas where the conditions of trust are in danger of erosion'. In this chapter, we argue that there is a case to be made for employing anticipatory minipublics in Finland on climate change, and other long-term issues, in the future.

Background: Routine Corporatism in Finland

Finland has a multiparty parliamentary system with proportional representation, and a long tradition of grand coalition governments that often include parties from both sides of the traditional left–right political spectrum. Inter-party negotiations among these diverse ideological groups play an important role in Finnish politics, especially at the stage when governmental programmes are drafted (Vesa et al. 2018). The Finnish political system has other features that encourage and support inclusive policymaking. It has been characterised as a system of 'routine', 'expansive' and 'soft' corporatism because interest groups and civil society organisations have access to working groups preparing policies as well as to parliamentary committees (Teräväinen-Litardo 2015; Vesa et al. 2018).

There are, however, questions about whether the Finnish system is adequately inclusive of all the different types of voices in civil society. Access to policymaking processes has been largely limited to established economic groups such as business organisations and trade unions (Vesa et al. 2018). These organisations rarely engage in public deliberation. Instead, they exert their influence by participating in extra-parliamentary working groups, and by forging direct contacts with civil servants, especially those in ministries (Vesa et al. 2018; Vesa et al. 2020). According to Teräväinen-Litardo (2015: 178), there is a 'lack of a critical public space that would operate independently in relation to the actively inclusive state'. Policy processes in Finland have also been criticised for not being transparent enough. It is often unclear why some arguments made by stakeholder groups influence policy while other arguments and groups do not (Airaksinen and Albrecht 2019).

Regardless of such criticisms, the Finnish political system enjoys high levels of support among the general public. In particular, the level of political trust in Finland is very high when compared with other countries. This may be explained by certain features of the Finnish political system, such as low levels of corruption, the multi-party system and coalition governments, as well as societal factors, such as Finland's egalitarian political culture and the country's rel-atively low levels of income inequality (Bäck and Kestilä-Kekkonen 2019). However, like other countries, Finland has experienced a decline in political trust in recent decades (Citrin and Stoker 2018). Support for the populist Finns Party, for example, is associated with lower levels of trust in political institutions, the media and other knowledge-based institutions such as universities (Saarinen et al. 2019).

Despite these declines, the Finnish people generally express high levels of trust in their institutions, and this may explain why there have not been strong pressures to renew or reform the political system to make it more participatory. Nevertheless, there are some novel participatory mechanisms in the Finnish system. Governmental agencies frequently use a specially designed website to engage individuals and civil society associations in public hear-ings on policy proposals and drafts of legislation.[1] The problem with this system is that only the most active civil society actors normally take advantage of these opportunities. In addition, the citizens' agenda initiative provides opportunities for people to influence the parliamentary decision-making agenda. According to the Finnish Constitution, 50,000 citizens can make a legislative initiative for the parliament, which is then obliged to deal with the initiative like any other law proposal. The citizens' initiative has been immensely popular among the public and has engaged those segments of the society that are usually less active in politics, for example, young people (Christensen et al. 2017).

Deliberative minipublics are rarely used in Finnish politics. So far, only four small minipublics have been used to provide input on government policy – and these were used in a purely consulta-tive capacity. This situation may be explained by scepticism among

Finnish political elites. According to a recent survey, political elites in Finland remain rather critical of the idea of using, let alone empowering, minipublics (Koskimaa and Rapeli 2020). Members of interest groups are even more sceptical. As Koskimaa and Rapeli (2020: 649) explain: 'As policy experts representing particular societal interests, they might be afraid of losing influence over the policy process if ordinary citizens are given a stronger voice.'

Goals and Tools of Finnish Climate Policy

In addition to stakeholders, experts play an important role in policymaking in Finland. A recent study shows that scientific knowledge has become increasingly central in climate change policy in Finland over the last two decades (Kukkonen and Ylä-Anttila 2020). Over this period, the role of scientific experts in policymaking has been institutionalised. For example, the 2015 Climate Change Act established a Climate Change Panel consisting of fifteen researchers from various scientific disciplines. The panel provides independent scientific expertise to governments on climate change policy.

The 2015 Climate Change Act specified the overall goals of Finland's national climate policies, as well as the key planning and steering mechanisms needed for the achievement of these targets. The act referenced other policy documents that specify concrete steps to be taken, including the Long-Term Plan for Climate Change Policy and the Medium-Term Climate Change Policy Plan. The latter plan outlines concrete measures for emissions reductions in 'effort sharing sectors', which include sectors that are not part of the EU Emissions Trading system – that is, housing, agriculture, transportation and waste management. This plan must be approved by the government once during every governmental term. The Medium-Term Plan extends approximately fifteen years into the future, laying out important policy trajectories well beyond the regular electoral cycle. The first Medium-Term Climate Change Policy Plan was completed in 2017, setting an emissions reduction target of 39 per cent by 2030.

Finnish climate policy was made even more ambitious after the 2019 parliamentary elections. After those elections, a five-party coalition was formed that included the Social Democrats, the Centre Party, the Green Party, the Left League and the Swedish-Speaking

People's Party. The governmental programme that was negotiated set an ambitious goal of achieving carbon neutrality by 2035. In order to meet this target, the Medium-Term Plan would have to include larger emissions reductions than previously planned (Government of Finland 2019). The new target also became the basis of a new Climate Change Act, which was passed by the parliament in spring 2022.

As in other countries, Finland's plan for emissions reductions raises issues about fairness and legitimacy (Devaney et al. 2020). The concern is that some groups or people may have to pay disproportionately higher costs than others in the transition to a carbon-neutral society. To address such concerns, the Finnish government established a Climate Policy Roundtable, which included key stakeholder groups, such as trade unions and business associations, representatives of various non-governmental organisations, such as youth organisations, as well as scientific experts. The purpose of the Round Table was to help to craft climate policies that will be broadly acceptable to the public at large.

The Ministry of the Environment, which was responsible for drafting the Climate Policy Plan was aware of potential legitimacy problems related to some of the measures included in the plan. In anticipation of such concerns, a series of public consultations were held which engaged particular segments of the population who would be directly affected. A public survey about the plan was also conducted. The survey was open for public comments in early 2021 and 18,000 responses were received. This survey did not engage a representative sample of the population, but the process made it clear that certain measures included in the plan – such as raising taxes on the fossil fuels used in transportation and for heating homes – would face public opposition and would be regarded as unfair by many people. These results echoed concerns raised in public discussions that climate policies would hit low-income households and those living in sparsely populated areas the hardest.

In spring 2021, the Ministry of the Environment and the Round Table commissioned a Citizens' Jury to provide input on the development of the new Medium-Term Climate Change Policy Plan. This was the first nationwide deliberative minipublic on climate policies in Finland. The Citizens' Jury was charged with the task of deliberating controversial climate policy measures in the areas of transportation, housing and food. Officials at the Ministry of the Environment prepared a list of fourteen measures that could potentially be included in the new Medium-Term Plan. These measures were selected because they would have direct and visible impacts on many individuals. Nine of these measures were related to transportation and traffic, three concerned housing and two concerned food.

The Citizens' Jury was designed to 'defuse' potential controversies before they became salient. In this sense, it can be regarded as an example of an 'anticipatory minipublic' (MacKenzie and Warren 2012). Compared with other climate assemblies, the Finnish jury had a rather narrow and precise agenda. It was charged with deliberating only a limited set of climate policies that were already being considered by the Ministry of the Environment. Nevertheless, the jury met for only three days in total, so a limited scope was necessary to ensure that meaningful outputs could be produced in a short period of time (cf. Elstub et al. 2021).

The Jury Process and Its Outcome

Members of the Finnish Citizens' Jury on Climate Actions were recruited by mail. In total, 8,000 randomly selected Finnish citizens aged from 18 to 80 were invited to participate. Stratified random sampling was then used to select a fifty-member jury from among those who expressed an interest in participating. The stratification criteria included age, gender, place of residence and level of education. One place on the jury was reserved for a member of the Sámi people because the initial sampling procedure could not be guaranteed to include anyone from this indigenous group. This member was therefore recruited in a separate process. Jury members were paid €150 each for their time and efforts (Kulha et al. 2022).

Of the fifty people selected to take part in the jury, thirty-seven confirmed their participation and thirty-three completed the process. The composition of the jury accurately reflected the Finnish population in terms of gender, age and place of residence, although men and younger people were slightly over-represented, and some regions lacked representation. People with higher levels of education were over-represented, and none of the participants had an education below secondary level. People with low levels of education have been under-represented in other online deliberations in Finland as well (Kulha et al. 2021; Värttö et al. 2021).

Participants in the jury were asked to consider the following question: 'How can climate measures affecting consumers be implemented in a fair yet effective way?' After deliberating the issues, the jury was asked to formulate a common statement on each of the fourteen proposed measures identified by the Ministry of the Environment. Due to Covid-19 restrictions, the jury convened online using Zoom instead of meeting in person. They met in April 2021 for one evening and one weekend. Before the first meeting, participants were given information packages about the fourteen climate measures selected by the Ministry of the Environment. The information included estimates about the costs and likely effectiveness of each of these measures, as well as information about Finnish climate policies more generally, the Medium-Term Plan and the country's emissions reduction targets.

During the first meeting, participants listened to presentations about Finnish climate policies, the jury process itself, and the principles of deliberation. They also reflected upon the fairness of the proposed climate measures. The jurors were then divided into five small groups and asked to formulate questions that experts would be asked to answer later in the process. The jury deliberations and the small groups discussions were guided by trained facilitators.

The second day began with presentations from experts who were asked to answer the questions the participants had formulated the day before. After this, the participants discussed issues of justice and fairness in climate change policy and notes from each of these discussions were then present to the jury in a plenary session. The small groups then deliberated the fourteen climate measures selected by the Ministry of the Environment. Each group inspected and deliberated two or three of the measures at a time, and the measures were circulated between groups until each group had deliberated each one. At the end of the second day, all the notes and comments produced by the groups were sent to the experts so that they could identify and correct any factual errors.

The third and final day was devoted to writing the jury's collective statements. These were drafted by the participants in their small groups and were informed by their previous deliberations and the feedback the participants had received from experts. Each group wrote collective statements for two or three of the fourteen measures. Their drafts were then presented to the plenary where all members of the jury had opportunities to suggest changes. When changes were suggested, they were deliberated and then voted on using a simple majority rule.

In addition to their collective statements about each of the fourteen measures, the jury prepared a general statement about the fairness of climate policies. In this case, each small group drafted suggestions for general principles of fairness to be included in the jury's statement, and the final text of the statement was compiled in plenary. Due to time constraints, various parts of the statement were developed in deliberations, but they were mainly adopted without voting – although the statement as a whole was approved in a final vote. Participants were invited to include dissenting opinion in the jury's report, and two jury members did so. The most controversial issues discussed in the dissents pertained to taxation.

Overall, the jury's statement expressed a willingness among members to reduce carbon emissions (Kulha et al. 2022: 10), although it did express concerns about the fairness of several of the measures identified by the Ministry of the Environment. While positive incentives such as subsidies and tax deductions were preferred to tax increases, the jury acknowledged that higher emissions should result in higher taxation. Their statement also emphasised the need to address regional differences, as well as the differential impacts that climate action will have on various groups, such as the elderly, the Sámi and people with low incomes. Access to information – on financial support for energy conversions, for example – was regarded as vital for the successful and fair implementation of the measures. Finally, the statement contained several suggestions on how to improve or broaden the scope of the draft measures. For example, the jury suggested that government subsidies for the purchase of new electric cars should be extended to include used electric cars and hybrid vehicles (Kulha et al. 2022: 12).

Before finishing the process, the jury participants were asked to complete an opinion survey. Table 12.1 summaries their responses. Even though climate policy is often technically, politically and temporally complex, 75 per cent of the participants believed that they had learned enough about the topic to formulate a considered opinion; 85 per cent said that taking part in the process had helped them to understand how climate policies would affect different demographic groups; and all the participants agreed that everyone's opinions were respected and listened to during the discussions. The members broadly agreed that the documents produced by the jury reflected their own views and the views of other participants, but they were less united on whether their statements would have any significant impact on policy decisions: 57 per cent of the jury members thought that their statement would have an impact on decision-making; 18 per cent were unsure; and 24 per cent (a substantial minority) disagreed with this statement.

After the process was complete, the jury's collective statement was presented to the Climate Policy Roundtable. It was also delivered to officials at the Ministry of the Environment, along with a report about the jury process itself. These documents were considered among other preparatory materials during the drafting of the new Medium-Term Climate Change Policy Plan.

A draft of this new plan was published in December 2021 and the finalized plan was accepted by the government in June 2022. It refers to the jury's statement eight times altogether, along with mentions of other participatory events. The plan discusses the jury's views on the impacts of fossil fuel tax increases, subsidies for climate-friendly food options, the divergent impacts that climate policies will have on different regions and individuals in Finland, as well as the jury's advice about consumer guidance. In their formal response to the jury, the Ministry of the Environment highlighted that the jury's advice to provide information and positive incentives to consumers was taken into account in the drafting of the Medium-Term Plan.

The Evaluation of the Citizens' Jury: Policymakers' Views

In this section, we examine how the Citizens' Jury was perceived by public officials and stakeholders. What do they think about

Table 12.1 Participants' opinions on the jury and its statement ($N = 33$)

	Completely Agree (%)	Partly Agree (%)	Cannot Say (%)	Partly Disagree (%)	Completely Disagree (%)
The subject of the jury was difficult.	21	52	3	21	3
Everyone's opinions were respected and listened to during the discussions.	82	18	0	0	0
During the jury I learned enough to form a considered opinion on the matter.	30	45	9	15	0
Taking part in the jury helped me to understand the impacts climate policies have on different demographic groups.	36	48	0	15	0
The jury succeeded in deliberating justice from diverse viewpoints.	36	55	0	3	6
The jury's statement reflects my own views well.	27	61	0	9	3
The jury's statement reflects the views of the participants well.	36	55	3	6	0
I think that the jury's statement will have an impact on decision-making.	15	42	18	15	9

the potential for minipublics to be used in the drafting of climate policy plans? In order to answer this question, we conducted semi-structured interviews with two officials at the Ministry of the Environment and five members of the Climate Policy Roundtable. These were the two bodies responsible for commissioning the jury and responding to its statement.

We asked our interviewees about their attitudes towards minipublics in general, the future potential uses of these processes, and the potential benefits and challenges of using them in the drafting of climate policy plans. We also asked our interviewees for their opinions on whether the Citizens' Jury will – or should – have any impact on the government's climate plan. There were questions about the representativeness of the jury, its legitimacy as a democratic process, and the role that the jury might play in relation to other forms of citizen and stakeholder engagement. The length of the interviews varied from between ten minutes to more than thirty.

The transcripts from each interview were analysed separately. Similarities and differences were identified and relevant statements from each interview were categorised into themes. In our analyses we tried to identify both manifest and latent meanings in the interviewees' statements. The questions we asked were influenced by academic discussions about minipublics, and the themes and sub-themes we identified have also been informed by these discussions. Table 12.2 summarises four main themes and several sub-themes, each of which is discussed below.

Expectations and Attitudes towards the Jury

The people we interviewed expressed generally positive views about the potential uses of minipublics in policymaking processes. They were happy, and even pleasantly surprised, with the results of the Citizens' Jury. Many commended the clarity of the jury's statement, as well as the jury's ability to focus on the topic at hand. Many of the interviewees also pointed out that the process could be improved in various ways, which is not surprising because this was the first nationwide minipublic on climate issues in Finland. Nevertheless, the interviewees generally agreed that engaging people and listening

Table 12.2 Analysis of interviews

1. Expectations and attitudes towards the Citizens' Jury and its results			
1.1 The jury provided a clear result	1.2 Minipublics are important in principle		
2. Benefits and impacts of minipublics			
2.1 Citizens can provide original ideas and viewpoints	2.2 Minipublics increase the legitimacy of political decision making	2.3 Deliberation adds value to citizen participation	2.4 Uncertainty about the impact of the Citizens' Jury
3. Minipublics in relation to other forms of public engagement			
3.1 Deliberation and representativeness distinguish minipublics from other forms of public engagement	3.2 Minipublics are a complementary method alongside other methods of public engagement	3.3 More experience with organising minipublics is required	
4. The challenges of minipublics			
4.1 Minipublics require a lot of resources	4.2 It is difficult to make minipublics truly representative	4.3 There is a lack of understanding about minipublics	4.4 Minipublics cannot be used to tackle every issue

to their concerns is important in principle, and minipublics are a potentially effective way to do so – especially on issues such as climate change that will affect all people and will require high levels of public support and acceptance to be dealt with in effective and legitimate ways. As one interviewee stated, 'I'm sure we all know that it's crucial that citizens support these climate actions, so that we don't get these Yellow Vests movements and all that's been seen around the world.'

The people we interviewed saw many potential benefits associated with minipublics, but many were nonetheless unsure what role minipublics should play in future policymaking processes. The interviewees agreed that minipublics might be used to generate public acceptance and support legitimacy, but they were not all convinced that minipublics should play a role in shaping the substance of climate policies.

Benefits and the Impact of Minipublics

According to our interviewees, minipublics are useful because they are representative institutions that give policymakers opportunities to hear from different types of people with wide-ranging views. Many pointed out that it is often possible to know what stakeholder groups will say in advance of public hearings, precisely because stakeholders typically have well-formulated and public views on policy proposals. Minipublics, by contrast, bring many different types of people together and their deliberations can produce completely new ideas – or new solutions to old problems or political impasses – that governments and stakeholders had not considered. As one interviewee remarked: 'Maybe [deliberation in minipublics] brings the reality closer. It's more thoughtful than what the members of parliament who work as ministers hear from their own stakeholders. In a way, politics disappears from it.' The interviewees also saw minipublics as a means of testing the legitimacy and public acceptance of policy proposals, and thereby demonstrating, to the public at large, that diverse concerns were being heard and taken into account in policymaking processes.

The interviewees also liked the fact that minipublics provide *informed* public input. The members of the Citizens' Jury had opportunities to learn about climate change and the government's climate policies. They listened to experts and asked them questions, and they deliberated the issues with each other. According to the interviewees the learning, information-gathering and deliberative aspects of the process added value to the policy inputs the jury provided. The participants learned a lot about the issues, but they were also able to focus their attention on questions or concerns where their input was most needed.

As with the participants themselves, however, the interviewees were divided on whether the Citizens' Jury would have any direct impact on the government's climate change policies. One interviewee said that the jury would not have much impact on the government's policies. Another said that it would only send 'weak signals' to the government. Other interviewees thought that the jury's statement would be taken into account in the development of the new Medium-Term Plan, and that the process was not organised merely for show.

Many of our interviewees said that it would be difficult to clearly identify the policy impacts of the Citizens' Jury. As one remarked: 'It's difficult to display the clear connection between certain matters, showing that this Citizens' Jury affected this certain matter specifically, but what can be said is that the jury has influenced the impact assessment part, when matters concerning social acceptability, equality and so on has been considered.' Thus, while most interviewees were uncertain about whether the jury would have any direct – and discernible – policy impacts, they generally agreed that the jury could potentially have such impacts and had, in fact, played a role in helping the government anticipate potential legitimacy problems.

Minipublics in Relation to Other Forms of Public Engagement

Our interviewees identified two main benefits of minipublics: representation and deliberation. They saw minipublics as being more legitimate and useful because they are typically more representative and deliberative than other engagement processes. While acknowledging that minipublics are resource-intensive, our interviewees saw them as an improvement over other more traditional forms of public engagement, such as open questionnaires and public hearings. Such processes typically engage only those who are already active in politics, and those who have strong (and often fixed) opinions on the issues being addressed. The random invitation processes that are used to populate minipublics help to ensure that a plurality of voices and views are heard in these processes, and those who are usually politically passive may be encouraged to participate.

Despite the advantages of minipublics, our interviewees also emphasised the value of other more traditional forms of engagement. Minipublics are time-consuming and resource-intensive for both organisers and participants. This means that they cannot be used in every situation and many people will be unable to participate, even if they would like to do so. As such, our interviewees thought that other, less time-consuming engagement options, such as opinion surveys and public hearings, should also be available. They saw minipublics as a complementary option to be used alongside these other methods. According to one interviewee, it is important to ensure that no single engagement process is 'too dominating'. Instead, we should take advantage of the strengths of different engagement methods which can then help to compensate for the weaknesses of others. Minipublics do not identify and quantify existing preferences or beliefs like opinion surveys. Instead, they produce informed deliberative outputs that reflect the shared concerns and opinions of representative groups of people. Public hearings, however, give people opportunities to have their voices (and existing opinions) heard by policymakers. Our interviewees also described the Citizens' Jury as a 'reality check' on whether the views expressed by non-governmental organisations and stakeholders were consistent with – and acceptable to – the public at large. In short, while many of our interviewees emphasised the importance of holding public hearings for citizens and stakeholders, they saw minipublics as an especially effective way to bring forward the views and concerns of ordinary people.

Our interviewees expressed generally positive views about minipublics, but none was explicitly in favour of formally incorporating them into policymaking processes. Some thought that more experimentation would have to be done before giving minipublics a more formal and influential role in policymaking processes. According to one interviewee, the Citizens' Jury on Climate Actions might encourage policymakers to use minipublics in the future, but it would be 'premature to say whether they would become statutory . . . I think that there's [a] need to first try them out more broadly and analyse the experiences.' Others argued that minipublics should be used only on an ad hoc, case-by-case basis to ensure the efficient use of public resources when there is a genuine interest or need to have deliberative public input in policymaking processes.

Challenges of Minipublics

One of the challenges of using – and institutionalising – minipublics has to do with the fact that the method is largely unknown among Finnish public officials, politicians, media and citizens. Our interviewees thought that people may be negative or sceptical towards forms of public engagement – like minipublics – that are unfamiliar and not well understood. As one interviewee stated: 'We needed to explain the added value and function [of the Citizens' Jury] to other ministries on a pretty specific level.' But the Citizens' Jury was novel for many of our interviewees as well, and this might help to explain some of the uncertainty they expressed about the possible or preferred ways of using minipublics in policymaking processes.

The representativeness of the Citizens' Jury was identified as one of its strengths, but there were also some critical concerns expressed about this aspect of the process. Some of our interviewees were happy with the composition and size of the jury. Others pointed out that thirty-three people is a relatively small group that cannot be expected to represent all relevant views on a complex issues like climate change policy. As one person stated: 'I don't think it's really possible to summarise the will of over five million people with any method ... I think that with [minipublics] it's however possible to produce viewpoints that other methods necessarily cannot.'

Many scholars and practitioners emphasise the opportunities for learning and deliberation that minipublics create. As mentioned above, deliberation can sometimes produce new insights or solutions to political impasses that have not been previously considered. Some of our interviewees, however, thought it may be difficult for a deliberative minipublic to produce new insights on complex issues like climate change policy in a relatively short period of time, even if participants engage in effective deliberations with each other. One interviewee pointed out that although many participants in the jury became better informed on climate policy, they may not have learned enough to grasp the full complexity of the problem and the policy options. Another interviewee was concerned that while the members of the jury had learned a lot and deliberated with each other, other members of the public who did not have those experiences might not be willing to accept – or able to understand – the recommendations made by the jury (see e.g., Lafont 2015).

Discussion: Prospects of Deliberative Minipublics in Finnish Climate Policies

The 'soft' corporatist tradition in Finland – which engages interest groups and stakeholders in policymaking processes – continues to be important. However, the role of scientific expertise has become more important in particular areas of policymaking, especially in climate policies. Some scholars worry that insufficient attention has been given to social justice concerns in the development of those policies (Teräväinen-Litardo 2015: 187–8). The Citizens' Jury on Climate Actions can be seen as a response to those concerns. It was tasked with assessing the fairness of fourteen measures to address climate change in Finland, each of which would affect individuals directly and have significant impacts on the distribution of public goods, subsidies and costs. It is not surprising, then, that substantial concerns about fairness and justice were expressed in the jury's final statement.

The Citizens' Jury was designed to scrutinise the government's climate action plans, and to provide feedback on how those plans might be improved and made more acceptable to the public at large. It was used to 'test' the legitimacy of policy proposals, but it was not – in this case – used an incubator of new policy ideas. In many respects it was a modest attempt to bridge the gap between citizens and elites in policymaking processes on climate change. The number of participants was small, the process lasted for only three days and it was conducted online (due to Covid-19 restrictions). The jury was also limited in its mandate: the participants were asked to comment on a pre-defined set of policy proposals, but they were not empowered to shape those proposals or recommend new ones.

Despite these limitations, the jury voiced numerous concerns about how the government's policy plans might be received by the public. Experts, for example, have emphasised consumption taxes as an efficient means of steering consumers towards sustainable options. The Citizens' Jury, however, expressed a strong preference for tax incentives and subsidies over tax increases, and those preferences were taken into account in the drafting of the government's new Medium-Term Plan. In this respect, the jury may have played a role in making the plan more acceptable to the public at large.

The jury also provided rationales and justifications for the collective recommendations that they made, and this is not something that can be obtained from other engagement processes like surveys or public hearings. At the same time, the public visibility of the jury was rather low, which means that most people in Finland have not considered the rationales, justifications or recommendations the jury produced. The jury has not triggered new public debates on climate change. Nor has it changed public perceptions about the nature of policymaking on this issue. However, it is not self-evident that minipublics *need* to play such public roles in policymaking processes. They can also enhance the legitimacy of those processes – and especially policy outcomes – by influencing how decision makers think about the issues and how they craft their policies.

There are reasons to think that those who were interviewed for this chapter would be among the strongest supporters of the Citizens' Jury on Climate Actions. After all, the jury was commissioned by the very people we interviewed, civil servants at the Ministry of the Environment and members of the Climate Policy Roundtable. Nevertheless, many of our interviewees were rather reserved about whether minipublics should be institutionalised and empowered. This finding is consistent with other studies of Finnish elites, who tend to be rather cautious and conservative about new public engagement processes (e.g., Koskimaa and Rapeli 2020). In Finland, existing channels for stakeholder participation seem to 'crowd out' new forms of participation such as deliberative minipublics.

But traditional elite-driven models of policymaking may not be sufficient to maintain the legitimacy of long-term decision-making in Finland. As explained above, Finland has enjoyed – and relied on – high levels of public trust in governments, institutions and experts. There is, however, some danger that the economic losses and lifestyle changes that will be required to achieve carbon-neutrality will erode trust in government officials, institutions and experts. This, in turn, could lead to a legitimacy crisis and the rise of populist backlash against the established, elite-driven system. It may be too optimistic to expect a dramatic and rapid increase in the number of deliberative processes in Finland, but deliberative minipublics, as we have argued, are one means of potentially mitigating the erosion of public trust while forging and supporting public commitments to ambitious climate policies. Unfortunately, the tension between technocracy and populism, which has been evident in many other established democracies, has not been effectively addressed in Finland either.

Note

1. See at: www.lausuntopalvelu.fi.

THIRTEEN

Conclusion: Future-Regarding Governance – Four Tensions and a Research Agenda

Michael K. MacKenzie, Simo Kyllönen and Maija Setälä

Introduction

The study and practice of future-regarding governance is in its infancy. Most of us are aware that our individual and collective decisions will affect the future in various ways, but our political institutions were not designed to deal with future issues or the long-term consequences of our decisions. Our political systems and practices are playing catch-up with our developing understanding of ourselves as temporal actors (i.e., beings that act both *within* our own times and *across* time when our actions have long-term consequences).

This book takes a wide view of the challenges and possibilities of future-regarding governance in democratic systems. It deals with conceptual challenges and possibilities, research methodologies and institutional design. The book also takes a deep dive into the practical politics of Finland's governmental foresight system, which is the most advanced and institutionalised system of its kind. Much of the existing literature on future-regarding governance looks at supplementary institutions that could be added to our existing democratic systems to make them more future-regarding. The scholars who have contributed to this book have tried to think more expansively about the future-regarding possibilities in our existing institutions, and how those might be leveraged on their own, or integrated with supplementary institutions, to make our democratic systems more future-regarding.

It is our hope that this book – and this concluding chapter – will inspire others to work in the challenging field of future-regarding governance. There is a lot of conceptual, methodological, practical and political work that needs to be done. In this concluding chapter, we outline some of our thoughts on the study and practice of future-regarding governance. In the next section, we identify four tensions that need to be (continually) navigated if we are going to have some chance of achieving our shared long-term objectives. In the last section of the chapter, we outline a research agenda that would help to advance the study of future-regarding governance. We invite other scholars to take on these research projects. There is more than enough work to go around.

Tensions

The study of future-regarding governance – like the study of politics more generally – is characterised by tensions. Tensions exist between various desirable goods that cannot be simultaneously maximised because the production of one often comes at the expense of another. For the most part, these are not dialectical tensions: they cannot be resolved through negation and the subsequent synthesis of something entirely new. The tensions we are addressing here are not the sort that should be resolved, eliminated or negated. Instead, they are tensions that can, and must, be continually navigated such that the goods that are in tension can be balanced against each other and both obtained, at least to some extent. These tensions must be *continually* navigated because the balances between them will shift over time with changing expectations, beliefs and political exigencies.

Think, for example, of the tension between freedom and equality. Both are desirable goods but they often (although not always) trade off against each other. The more equality we want in the economic realm, for example, the less freedom we will have in that realm (although we might gain more freedoms of other types when higher levels of economic equality are obtained). The political task is to figure out how to balance these goods against each other such that we can obtain acceptable or appropriate amounts of each. But what may be considered acceptable or appropriate is likely to differ between political societies and over time within each society or community.

In what follows, we discuss four common tensions in future-regarding governance: (1) long-term investments versus majority rule; (2) reversibility versus commitment; (3) independence versus politicisation; and (4) trust versus critique. Each of these goods are desirable in one way or another. As a result, we can expect – and actually want – these tensions to continue to exist in our democratic systems. The political task is to figure out how these tensions can be navigated, rather than eliminated, such that acceptable or appropriate – but probably always shifting – accommodations between them can be achieved and maintained over time.

Long-Term Investments versus Majority Rule

Perhaps the most fundamental tension has to do with the conflicts that inevitably arise between the present and the future. Democratic systems are supposed to be responsive to the needs and concerns of those who are affected by collective decisions (see, e.g., Warren, Chapter 1, this volume). If a majority are opposed to investing in the future, it will be difficult to do so even if they also acknowledge that it would be the right or proper thing to do – or that it would be better for their future selves and future others.

This tension is at the heart of many critiques of democracy. Scholars such as Bell (2016), Randers (2012), and many others have argued that authoritarian governments may be needed to make our societies more future-regarding. Authoritarian governments would be able to impose unpopular but necessary long-term policies on unwilling publics for their own good. But even if this argument is correct (which it probably is not), this is not an option in a democratic system. Moreover, different types of democratic systems are not, in practice, equally short-sighted or incapable of making long-term investments (e.g., Caluwaerts and Vermassen, Chapter 9, this volume; Jacobs 2011).

This line of inquiry raises the following question: can we have future-regarding *democratic* governments? That is, can we have governments that are both future-regarding and remain responsive to the demands and interests of (contemporary) affected publics? In this book we argue that the tension between future-regarding collective action and majority rule – or democratic responsiveness more generally – is not as omnipresent as many scholars and commentators have assumed.

This tension rests on at least two assumptions that need unpacking. The first assumption is that the interests of the future (as a whole) will be opposed to the interests of the present (as a whole) on many (or most) political issues or decisions. The second is that the majority of people will therefore have few incentives to act in future-regarding ways and many incentives to oppose policy investments aimed at benefiting the future (especially if those investments would be costly in the near term).

The idea that making long-term investments will primarily benefit the future at the expense of the present is an oversimplification. Even climate change mitigation policies – which are often taken as the quintessential example of this by scholars (see, e.g., Bell 2016; Randers 2012) – do not necessarily have these characteristics. When we invest in making our societies more environmentally sustainable, we *are* investing in the future, but we are also making changes that may have immediate benefits, such as making our cities more liveable by making them more walkable and less polluted.

It is likewise important to recognise that the present is diverse, and the future will be too. Policy decisions on temporally complex issues (such as climate change or pandemic response and preparedness) are likely to affect different groups within current publics in divergent ways. And the longer-term consequences of our decisions will affect different groups within future publics in divergent ways as well. This means that we cannot assume that people will have little motivation to act in future-regarding ways, or that everyone will have the same motivation not to. Some groups within the present might have interests that align with the potential interests of future others. Those people might therefore have strong incentives to act in ways that would benefit those future others (and themselves). It is simplistic to assume that the interests of the present and the future will be commonly and uniformly opposed to each other.

It is, of course, possible that majorities may in some instances be against long-term policy investments even if those investments would be better for society, or humanity more generally, over time. But there are reasons why this possibility should not be read as an indictment against the possibilities of making long-term decisions in democratic systems. First, authoritarian leaders may also, in some instances, be opposed to making long-term policy investments, which means that inaction on such policies is not a problem that exists only in democracies.

Secondly, and relatedly, inclusive decision-making processes can help to encourage rather than inhibit future-regarding collective action. Authoritarian leaders might invest in the future, or they might decide not to. There is little anyone outside the narrow confines of the powerful can do to influence a leader's decisions in a truly authoritarian regime. But even when authoritarian leaders decide to invest in the future, they will be investing only in their particular visions of what desirable futures might be like. By contrast, inclusive democratic processes make it possible for whole communities to forge *shared* visions of desirable futures. It may be politically difficult to develop and sustain truly future-regarding majorities, but inclusive democratic decision-making processes are the only means we have for figuring out how collective decisions are likely to affect – and whether they will be acceptable to – different types of people in the present *and in the future* (Setälä et al., Chapter 12, this volume; MacKenzie 2021b: ch. 5).

Thirdly, in a democracy the decisions of a majority must be considered decisive for some period of time, but there must always be opportunities for majorities forged at one time to be overturned by future majorities. As Moore (Chapter 3, this volume) argues, the reversibility of democratic decisions can make it more difficult to act in future-regarding ways, but this aspect of democracy is also an essential ingredient *for* successful future-regarding action. The fact that democratic decisions *must* be regularly reconsidered and *can* be reversed by new majorities, means that there will always be opportunities in democratic systems for groups who are in favour of making long-term investments to persuade others that this is what should be done.

Fourthly, in practice, it is often minorities – rather than majorities – that are the source of myopic decision-making in democratic systems. Most democracies are, in fact, more responsive to the demands of wealthy and well-connected individuals and groups or entities, such as corporations, than they are to the publics they are meant to serve (e.g., Gilens 2012). If wealthy and well-connected actors have objectives that they wish to pursue at the expense of the longer-term interests of society, they will often be able to do so in democratic systems (e.g., MacKenzie 2021b: ch. 1). Influential minorities will have incentives to pursue their own near-term and long-term objectives, even if these policies are good for those minorities but bad for society (or the world) as a whole. By contrast, inclusive decision-making processes, and especially those that are deliberative, can help to ensure that any collective decisions that are made are not inconsistent with the potential interests of society as a whole, both now and in the future. As Caluwaerts and Vermassen (Chapter 9, this volume) show in their analysis, democracies tend to be more, not less future-regarding when more people are involved and when diverse majorities (in the form of coalition governments) are required for policymaking.

Reversibility versus Commitment

In addition to any tensions that might exist between the long-term interests of society and the near-term preferences of contemporary publics, there is also a potential tension in democratic systems between reversibility and commitment. As explained above, one of the definitional features of a democracy is that everything – every decision, every term in office – is, and must be considered, provisional. There are no 'final' decisions in democratic politics, there are only temporary decisions to proceed which must be revisited in the future and may be overturned at any time. Provisionality is an essential component of what it means to say that an entity (an individual or collectivity) is autonomous, self-directing, or 'has a will'. At the same time, in order to achieve future-regarding goals individuals and collectivities must make commitments that are not, in fact, overturned before those goals can be reached.

Eerik Lagerspetz (Chapter 2, this volume) argues that future-regarding action may be inhibited when collective commitments to act are inconsistent with collective decisions (or indecisions) about

258 / Michael K. MacKenzie, Simo Kyllönen and Maija Setälä

how to act. The same sets of actors might be committed to shared long-term objectives while being unable to forge majorities in support of any of the options for achieving those objectives.

Alfred Moore (Chapter 3, this volume) emphasises the tension between commitment (or steadfastness) and reversibility (or flexibility). He argues that long-term decision-making will be inhibited if we veer too close to either one of these extremes. We will not achieve our long-term (individual or collective) goals if we remain dogmatically committed to objectives or means that are rendered irrelevant or undesirable by changing circumstances. But nor will we reach our long-term goals if we are continually changing course in haphazard ways, flitting from one thing to another without reason, analysis or intentionality.

How can these tensions be navigated in democratic systems? Lagerspetz argues that when collectivities identify shared goals but fail to identify acceptable means for acting, the latter choice, regarding means, may be taken off the democratic agenda. For example, if a collectivity decides that something should be done to mitigate climate change, but it cannot agree on *what* should be done, that decision, regarding means, might be given to bureaucrats or other experts. Lagerspetz argues that this would not violate the democratic agency of the collectivity; it would, instead, *uphold* that agency because it would make democratic action possible in the face of an impasse regarding the means of action. It would, in other words, make it possible for the collectivity to act *on its own intentions*, which is precisely what is needed for the realisation of agency. This response is not inconsistent with the design of many existing and proposed future-regarding institutions, such as the expert-driven components of the Finnish foresight system (Koskimaa, Chapter 10, this volume), or the expert commissions proposed by Landwehr (Chapter 6, this volume).

An alternative response to the impasse identified by Lagerspetz is to go back at the problem with more deliberation, negotiation, persuasion and other politicking. If a collectivity has a will to act but cannot decide how to act, then it may have to re-engage politically to try to figure out an acceptable (if not unanimously agreed-upon) means of acting. This would be a *more* democratic means of responding to the impasse that Lagerspetz identifies, because it would not require identifying and transferring decision-making power to unelected officials. But 'getting back to politics' is also likely to be the more obvious and thus more common response to these sort of impasses. When we cannot agree on appropriate means to achieve shared (or agreed-upon) ends, we typically keep arguing, deliberating or bargaining until we identify some broadly acceptable options for acting. This does not mean that more politicking will, in fact, produce a solution to any particular impasse. In some instances, as Lagerspetz implies, we will not have time for potentially endless political processes; in some cases, we will *just have to act* even if we cannot agree on how to act – and transferring certain decisions to expert bodies may be a (potentially legitimate) means of doing so. Nevertheless, 'getting back to politics' is the first response to the sort of impasses that Lagerspetz identifies, and democratic politics can thus be understood as both a potential barrier to long-term decision-making (when politics does not produce a solution to impasses), and a potential support for long-term decision-making (when inclusive democratic processes can forge strong commitments to act as well as agreements on how to act) (e.g., Setälä et al., Chapter 12, this volume).

Moore's contribution to this debate hinges on the role of competition in helping democratic societies to navigate the tension between reversibility and commitment. Moore (Chapter 3, this volume) frames this issue as an epistemic challenge: we need to remain committed to our long-term objectives *and* to effective means for achieving those objectives, but it is a posture of fallibility, which is underwritten by the presumption of provisionality in democratic politics, which compels us to continually return to those objectives and means to reassess them and change them when necessary. Partisan competition, especially when it is combined with inclusive practices of deliberation, helps to ensure that the democratic principle of provisionality is made a reality. Without groups competing for influence and power, democratic systems – like authoritarian ones – might get locked into ends or means that are rendered inappropriate or irrelevant by changing circumstances. At the same time, it should be possible (although difficult) to forge and maintain commitments to long-term objectives in competitive, inclusive and provisional democratic processes *when* doing so makes sense or can be justified to all (or most) of those involved. In Moore's account, democracy has mechanisms to navigate the tensions between reversibility and commitment built right into its DNA. His contribution is to emphasise the role that party competition – and politicisation – plays in creating both the epistemic conditions and the pragmatic incentives needed for those tensions to be navigated successfully over time.

Independence versus Politicisation

There is also a tension in future-regarding governance – and governance more generally – between independence and politicisation. Independent institutions are those that are supposed to operate outside the normal processes of partisan politics. Examples include constitutional courts, central banks and non-partisan electoral boundaries commissions. Political – or politicised – institutions are those that are predicated on conflict and competition. Issues become politicised when people disagree about what should be done and take sides. The most familiar politicised institutions are political parties and elected legislatures.

If the challenges of future-regarding governance have to do with provisionality, short electoral cycles, alternating governments and thus political uncertainty more generally, institutions that are designed to operate independently from those dynamics may be one means of making our democratic systems more future-regarding. Independence helps to ensure that long-term policy objectives can be achieved because independent institutions are not subject to electoral pressures and, in many cases, simple legislative majorities cannot change their mandates. There are several examples of independent institutions that have been given special mandates to act in future-regarding ways. These include independent Offices for Future Generations (OFGs), pension funds or other public funds that aim to benefit the present and the future. One notable example is the Norwegian Petroleum Fund, which is an independently managed sovereign wealth fund that was specially designed to save wealth generated by the country's oil and gas production for future generations. Currently, it is the largest sovereign wealth fund in the world (Takle 2021).

Independent institutions may be needed to bring some measure of (limited) certainty to the uncertain world of politics, but politicisation is needed to ensure that collective decisions: (1) adequately reflect the interests (or potential interests) of all those affected; (2) effectively navigate and anticipate potential conflicts between groups; and (3) identify and balance trade-offs between goods or objectives that cannot be jointly achieved. We need independent institutions that can process information and act outside the fray of politics if we are going to achieve our shared long-term objectives, but we need politicised institutions to legitimise those collective decisions and ambitions and regularly re-establish that legitimacy over time.

The tension between independence and politicisation is on display in this book. Moore (Chapter 3), MacKenzie (Chapter 7), and Caluwaerts and Vermassen (Chapter 9) emphasise politicised institutions and practices, such as party competition, democratic leadership, public engagement and coalitional government. Others, such as Lagerspetz (Chapter 2), Landwehr (Chapter 6), Smith (Chapter 8) and Koskimaa (Chapter 10), emphasise independent institutions such as expert panels, OFGs and non-partisan bureaucracies. The literature on future-regarding institutions more generally tends to emphasise independence over politicisation (e.g., Boston 2016a; Gonzáles-Ricoy and Gosseries 2016). But as with the other tensions, what is needed are political processes that continually strive to balance these goods while making appropriate adjustments over time. As such, those who are interested in future-regarding institutional design should think more carefully about how these two goods – independence and politicisation – can be achieved simultaneously within specific institutions or democratic processes, or separately in different but interacting parts of a democratic system.

The Finnish foresight system has both independent and politicised components. The Futures Dialogue is a politicised process in the sense that it involves, and is initiated by, an elected, multiparty government. The Committee for the Future (CF), which responds to the government's Report on the Future, is also politicised because it comprises elected members of parliament from multiple parties – although it is supposed to assess the government's Report on the

Future in a collaborative non-politicised manner. Other parts of the Finnish foresight system – the ministerial reviews and the foresight networks – ensure that independent experts such as bureaucrats, scientists, academics and policy analysts have a formal and institutionalised role in policymaking processes involving long-term decisions (Koskimaa, Chapter 10, this volume).

The minipublics discussed in this volume by Smith (Chapter 8) and Setälä et al. (Chapter 12) combine independence and politicisation into a single institution. Minipublics are designed to operate independently from partisan politics and electoral cycles. The members of a minipublic are randomly selected and they enter the process as individuals rather than as representatives of political parties or positions. At the same time, the purpose of a minipublic is to bring people with different perspectives and lived experiences together to deliberate contentious (i.e., politicised) issues.

There are proposals for other future-regarding institutions that would combine independence and politicisation. Smith (2021), for example, argues that OFGs, such as those in Hungary and Wales, could be combined with minipublics. The OFGs, which are typically headed by individuals, would operate on an independent, non-partisan basis, while the minipublics would be used to provide the OFGs with insight into the political (i.e., conflictual) dimensions of future issues or problems.

MacKenzie (2016b, 2021b) has argued that a randomly selected second chamber could function as a future-regarding institution, especially if the members of this chamber were given a special mandate to represent the future. This institution would operate independently from the fray of partisan politics. As with a minipublic, the members of a randomly selected chamber would not enter the process as partisan representatives and they would not be subject to the political imperatives of re-election. But the chamber would create a space for a diverse group of representatives to deliberate contentious and temporally complex issues while making future-regarding decisions. These examples suggest that it may be possible to create institutions – or processes – that are both politicised (in some respects) and capable of acting independently from the short-term dynamics associated with election cycles and electoral uncertainty.

Trust versus Critique

There is also a tension in democratic systems between public trust and critique. There are several reasons why we need to have trust in governments and experts if we are going to achieve our shared long-term objectives. First, we need to have good reasons to believe that governments will keep the promises they make. If our governments promise to invest in long-term initiatives, we must trust that those investments will be made, and that they have some reasonable prospect of being maintained long enough to do some good. If our political systems are corrupt – if, for example, they siphon public money into the pockets of government officials and their friends – we will have good reasons to oppose long-term investments even if we think that making those investments would, in principle, be the right thing to do. This is an especially acute concern when it comes to long-term initiatives that involve saving fungible assets – such as public pensions or sovereign wealth funds – that may be ransacked by current or future government officials for their own near-term (or personal) objectives.

Secondly, we need to have trust in experts to address long-term issues and problems. We need to trust that experts are motivated to act in the public interest (as they understand it) and that they are capable of doing so. Many of the long-term issues and problems that we face – such as pandemics and climate change – are both technically and politically complex (e.g., Hansson, Chapter 4, this volume). Experts, such as virologists, epidemiologists, ecologists and climate scientists, are needed to anticipate and navigate those and other long-term issues. But most people, including elected officials, do not have the time or the expertise that would be required to make independent judgements about the quality of the advice provided by experts. In this situation, some degree of warranted trust is needed. This does not mean that political power should be delegated to experts to make largely autonomous decisions about appropriate means for achieving long-term collective objectives. Experts should not, for example, be empowered to make decisions about how to balance competing interests, values or preferences. As Moore and MacKenzie (2020) argue, we need inclusive democratic, and probably deliberative, processes to sanction and legitimise

264/ Michael K. MacKenzie, Simo Kyllönen and Maija Setälä

collective decisions, even when – or *especially* when – those decisions are ultimately predicated on expert analyses that are technically sophisticated and largely inscrutable (at least in their details)
to non-experts. In these circumstances, we will have to trust that
the experts are acting in the public interest, that they are, in fact,
knowledgeable, and that they are not being compromised by (obvious) conflicts of interest if we are going to successfully deal with
technically complex problems such as pandemics, climate change,
and most of the other long-term problems and issues that we face.

But scepticism and critique are equally important – albeit less
widely acknowledged – requirements for successful future-regarding
collective action. Trust, of course, can always be abused. We *need* to
trust that government officials, for example, will not plunder our
long-term investments, but we also need to employ mechanisms –
such as scrutiny, oversight, accountability and critique – to help to
ensure that they do not do so now or in the future.

Trust can also discourage people from seriously considering new
or emerging information, even though doing so is critically important if we are going to adjust our actions appropriately to meet
our long-term objectives as circumstances change. Trust might also
make people less willing to listen to critiques, especially those that
are unpopular but might nevertheless be plausible or important.
This can make effective deliberation more difficult while also reducing the diversity of opinions or options considered when decisions
are being made – which may, in turn, reduce the epistemic quality
of those decisions, even when they *are* made by genuine experts.

Conversely, critique, which is born from a lack of trust, is a pre-
requisite for change. We need trust to maintain the course that we
are on, but we need critique to change our direction when we think
(or suspect) we might be going the wrong way. Democracies, when
they are working well, have a built-in capacity to change direction
when it becomes necessary or desirable to do so – even as they
might also do so when it is not necessary or desirable (Runciman
2013). This capacity is supported by institutional structures, such as
competitive elections and independent media systems, that make
empowered social critique possible.

But critique can also help support legitimacy and trust rather
than just challenge it. The very fact that a policy or public action

has survived genuine (and ongoing) critical assessments may be a good reason to think that the policy should be maintained rather than changed. This is akin to the logic of the peer-review process where specialists critique the contributions of other specialists, and any contributions that survive those assessments can then be considered legitimate even by non-specialists. Mark E. Warren (1996) makes a similar argument with respect to democratic authority, in which genuine and always present possibilities for critique can give people good reasons to accept claims to authority in democratic systems. This legitimising function of critique is crucially important when it comes to future-regarding action because, in order to help ensure that long-term investments are maintained, even as governments and personnel change over time, societies need reasons to (continue to) think that those investments *should* be maintained. Effective practices of democratic critique can help to provide those reasons and assurances.

As with the other tensions discussed in this chapter, societies need to maintain an always-probably-shifting balance between trust and critique if they are going to successfully achieve their long-term objectives. Trust and critique (together) can help to secure the commitments that are required for successful future-regarding collective action, but critique also plays an essential role in helping to keep democratic systems nimble enough to change course when necessary or desirable. Independent institutions can help to support trust when they reliably produce desirable outcomes (as when central banks successfully keep inflation low), and when people have reasons to believe that the actors within those institutions are not compromised, corrupted or conflicted.

Many of the institutions discussed in this book, such as OFGs, expert panels and foresight networks, aim to support public trust by ensuring that long-term issues are considered and assessed by independent actors. However, other political institutions and practices, such as oversized coalitions, also support trust by subjecting policy plans and programmes to scrutiny from diverse and critical partisan actors.

The Finnish foresight system – which is a focus of this book – is predicated more on trust than critique. Finland has enjoyed decades of good governance and low levels of corruption. There are also many good reasons for people to trust the judgements of experts and political elites in the Finnish system because those elites are generally quite future-regarding even when they are not intimately involved in the foresight system itself (Rapeli, Chapter 11, this volume). Nevertheless, as argued above, expert-driven policy processes often fail to adequately consider diverse public interests and concerns.

Trust may be further undermined – even when diverse publics' interests are adequately considered – if the decisions of experts are not regularly challenged and tested through open and critical inquiry. There are, indeed, some indications that the high levels of trust that have characterised the Finnish system for decades may be eroding (Setälä et al., Chapter 12, this volume). One factor behind this development may be an increasing gap between political elites – experts, bureaucrats and elected officials – and everyone else. When technically complex issues, such as climate change, become politically divisive, partisan commitments and material interests may come to affect the judgements that people make about the trustworthiness of policy experts and other elites. In such situations, new, more inclusive (and non-expert) foresight mechanisms, such as minipublics, may provide avenues for maintaining trust (e.g., MacKenzie and Warren 2012; Warren and Gastil 2015) as well as possibilities for critique and redirection.

Future-regarding democratic systems must strive to maintain an always-probably-shifting balance between these two democratic goods: trust and critique. They will also have to navigate the other tensions that we have discussed in this section, as well as any others that may be identified by other scholars or practitioners working in this field.

A Research Agenda

In addition to identifying the tensions associated with future-regarding governance, there are several other components of a future research agenda that would, in our view, help to advance this field. First, more attention needs to be paid to the conceptualisation and measurement of political myopia and future-regarding governance. Secondly, we need typologies of different types of temporally complex issues, each of which may be associated with different political challenges and possibilities. Thirdly, while scholars have tended to focus on failures of future-regarding governance, such as the many failures of climate change mitigation, we also need detailed studies of good long-term governance, such as the global efforts that have been made to reduce the use of ozone-depleting chlorofluorocarbons (CFCs). Fourthly, although Finland has one of the most advanced governmental foresight systems in the world, the Finnish model cannot be easily replicated elsewhere. More research needs to be done on which aspects of the Finnish system are relevant, or not, in other political or cultural contexts. We also need more research on the deficiencies or vulnerabilities of the Finnish foresight system. Lastly, we need to pay closer attention to the exigencies of political reform. Scholars tend to focus on what should *ideally* happen, but we also need activists and experienced political operatives to make change happen.

Conceptualisation and Measurement

The conceptual complexities associated with studying the future make measuring political myopia and future-regarding governance inherently difficult. When we study the future, we are focused on something that does not (yet) exist but will be created by our own actions or inactions. But it is often difficult to identify which actions – whether individual or collective – should be considered future-regarding, and which should be considered myopic.

Consider, for example, Finland's decision to bury nuclear waste in a deep hole in the bedrock. This storage facility has been designed to hold up to one hundred years of waste production, and it must be made secure for tens of thousands of years (Ialenti 2020). Given these timeframes, this project must be considered future-regarding. But it could, nevertheless, be considered myopic because it provides the country with a reason to serve its own short-term power needs with nuclear energy for the next one hundred years. Perhaps it would be more future-regarding to stop producing nuclear waste altogether. On the other hand, nuclear power might be considered future-regarding because it does not produce carbon emissions, even though it does saddle future generations with toxic waste.

This example illustrates the conceptual difficulties we are facing here. How can we develop valid and reliable measures of political myopia or future-regarding governance if we cannot say with confidence which issues or decisions are, in fact, future-regarding? What is needed are some general criteria for identifying which *aspects* of decisions are future-regarding and which are not.

In their comparative analysis of future-regarding governance, Caluwaerts and Vermassen (Chapter 9, this volume), employ two measures of intergenerational justice. Each has several dimensions that measure different aspects of the concept, including social supports for both younger and older generations, as well as measures of environmental, economic and fiscal sustainability. In their analysis, environmental policy is not being used as a unidimensional proxy for intergenerational justice. But as Caluwaerts and Vermassen acknowledge, there are other policy areas that could be included in measures of intergenerational justice. These include policies to protect biodiversity, investments in education or other scientific or cultural institutions, efforts to make cities more liveable and affordable, policies to mitigate generational reproductions of inequality, and protections for stable (or just) political institutions. But even if a measure of intergenerational justice were to include all (or most) of the relevant policy areas – which as MacKenzie (2021a) has argued might be *all* policy areas – it will be difficult to unambiguously identify which decisions within those areas are *more* or *less* future-regarding – given the fact that most individual and collective decisions, as illustrated above with the example of nuclear power, are likely to be future-regarding in some respects while myopic in others. To meet this challenge, future measures of intergenerational justice – or future-regarding governance – might employ a points system *within* each issue area, whereby the future-regarding aspects of any decisions would be given *merit* points, while the myopic dimensions of those decisions would be given *demerit* points. Although labour-intensive, such an approach would produce a more detailed and nuanced measure of future-regarding governance than those that are currently available.

Rapeli (Chapter 11, this volume) has developed a battery of survey questions designed to measure whether individuals are future-regarding or myopic. He shows that elites and non-elites in Finland are not as myopic as many observers have expected people, in general, to be. Nevertheless, non-elites in Finland are more myopic than either elected officials or bureaucrats. These findings challenge the conventional wisdom that people – both elites and non-elites – care more about the present than the future, but these findings have not yet been replicated in other political or social contexts, such as in the United States or China where people and elites face very different incentives and operate within distinct political cultures.

Although Rapeli has developed a useful measure of political myopia that may be deployed by others, there are some methodological challenges and practical considerations that need to be addressed. Most importantly, measuring general attitudes towards the future is not at all sufficient for understanding when – or whether – people will be willing to act to benefit the future. Those who are likely to experience economic losses because of climate change mitigation, for example, may be less willing to accept those policies even if they think it is important, in principle, to consider the potential interests of future others. These people would not be considered myopic in Rapeli's analysis even if they were to *act* myopically when given the option to support or oppose climate policies.

One option may be to use experimental methods to explore not only *who* is myopic but *when* or under which conditions they are more or less likely to act in future-regarding ways. MacKenzie and Caluwaerts (2021) show that those who deliberated in a laboratory experiment were more likely to say they would be willing to pay near-term costs (such as increases to gas taxes) for future potential benefits (such as those associated with climate change mitigation). In their study, however, no real money was at stake for the participants. In the future, experimental researchers might employ willingness-to-pay measures that have some real costs at stake for the participants. This approach would give us a better sense of not only who is willing to *consider* the future, but who is willing to *act* in future-regarding ways.

It should be acknowledged, however, that a willingness to pay near-term (financial) costs is only one dimension of future-regarding decision-making. As this book makes clear, future-regarding actions can produce any combination of near-term and long-term costs (which are often unevenly distributed between groups both within and between generations) and benefits (which are also, often, unevenly distributed). This fact makes measuring political myopia challenging because it means that *some* of those who are willing to act for the future might be acting in their own short-term interests while doing so, while others may be willingly sacrificing their short-term interests for the benefit of others. Who is being *more* future-regarding in this case, and does it matter? It is unclear. What is clear is that these two groups cannot be easily distinguished from each other using willingness-to-pay measures.

It may be tempting to throw up our hands and say that we cannot develop adequate, reliable, and conceptually valid measures of political myopia and future-regarding governance. We think that this would be the wrong approach. Social scientists have developed reliable and valid measures of other hard-to-measure social, political and psychological constructs, and we have faith that such measures of political myopia and future-regarding governance are not beyond our reach, even though the challenges are admittedly formidable.

Typologies of Temporally Complex Issues

Researchers should also consider developing typologies of temporal complexity. These would specify the temporal reach or timeframes of different issues. They would outline how the costs and benefits associated with solving problems in different issue areas are distributed both *within* and *between* generations. They would specify the nature or 'shape' of each issue, such as whether it is a cumulative problem like climate change, which becomes more acute over time in small (or imperceptible) increments; or whether it is an intermittent problem such as a pandemic or natural disaster, each of which are largely dormant problems before they become rapidly acute. Researchers should also consider the political imperatives associated with temporal complexity. Do the issues cross, for example, jurisdictional boundaries or can they be largely, or even partly, addressed within existing political units?

It is also important to acknowledge that not all temporally complex issues are problems. Societies make many positive investments in the future, such as the creation of parks, museums, pension plans and education systems. These efforts might help to solve contemporary problems (such as a lack of access to education), but the impetuous for such investments is often a desire to do good – to make the present and the future better.

Hansson (Chapter 4, this volume) has developed a typology of two temporally complex issues: pandemics and climate change. He identifies several similarities and differences between them but concludes that climate change is the more difficult issue to deal with because of its causal, epistemic, temporal and political dimensions. Future researchers might extend Hansson's analysis to include a range of other temporally complex issues such as budget deficits and public debts, urban planning, education spending, welfare state development and maintenance, income inequality, natural disaster preparedness, nuclear weapons, nuclear waste, structural racism and artificial intelligence, to name just a few examples. A comprehensive typology of temporal complexity will help to facilitate research on future-regarding governance. It will provide insight into which issue areas or topics are most difficult to deal with in democratic systems, and which political institutions might be needed to address those issues most effectively. A typology of temporal complexity would also help to facilitate the development of new measurement tools that can consistently and reliably distinguish myopic decisions from future-regarding ones.

Case Studies of Future-Regarding Governance

A related research programme might explore successful examples of future-regarding governance in democratic systems. Scholars in this field have tended to focus on the problem cases, and there are many good reasons for doing so. Temporally complex problems such as climate change pose a real threat to the long-term survival of humanity and other species. And there are *many* other problem cases. We produce nuclear waste without adequate plans for how that waste can be stored safely for tens of thousands of years.

We allow plastics and other contaminants to enter our environmental systems without much thought for the long-term consequences for our future selves, future others, the natural environment or other animals. We fail to prepare for pandemics and natural disasters. We underinvest in public goods such as education. We are, generally, quite bad at future-regarding governance.

Nevertheless, there are also successes that should be studied. Many municipalities in industrialised countries, for example, have adopted long-term initiatives to correct the mistakes made by urban developers in the mid-twentieth century. Many cities in North America, in particular, are safer, cleaner, more walkable, transit-friendly, more liveable and, in general, more pleasant than they were forty or fifty years ago.

Democratic governments have made long-term investments in social welfare programmes, public health care systems and public pension plans. Norway has used a considerable portion of its oil and gas wealth to create a huge sovereign wealth fund (Takle 2021). This fund ensures that the wealth generated by natural resources is shared across generations and not usurped by the relatively small number of generations involved in the extraction and development of those resources. If it is well-managed in the future (as it has been thus far) it could, in principle, exist in perpetuity for the benefit of all future generations of Norwegians. As explained above, Finland has made a conscious effort to build a containment system for nuclear waste that could, in principle, last for tens of thousands of years (Ialenti 2020).

The point of the matter is this: there *are* examples of successful future-regarding governance in democratic systems. Our failures are more numerous and indisputably important – and we can, and have, learned a lot from them. But we can learn a lot from our successes as well. In-depth case studies of these successes would help us better understand how future-regarding democratic governance might be done. Such studies can give us insight into the role that specific individuals, institutions or practices may have played in challenging or overcoming political myopia. What role did future-regarding leaders play in these cases? Can myopic political actors, such as voters or elites, be incentivised to make – and sustain – long-term investments? How have successful long-term

investments, such as Norway's sovereign wealth fund, been protected from the plundering of future governments? Analyses of
these and other examples of successful future-regarding governance
can tell us a lot about what works and why, which is something that
we still know very little about.

Learning from the Finnish Example

This book adopts a wide view of future-regarding governance, but
the most detailed case studies in the book focus on the example
of Finland. While much has been learned from the Finnish example, there are numerous questions that are not addressed in this
book. One outstanding question is whether – or which parts of –
the Finnish foresight system might be successfully and effectively
adopted elsewhere.

It is probably a good idea, for example, to ensure that the parts of
any foresight system are networked together like they are in Finland
(see Koskimaa, Chapter 10, this volume). Networking is important because future-regarding decisions that are made in one issue
area (such as education) will necessarily depend on decisions that
are – or *will* be – made in other issue areas (such as those having
to do with taxation and government revenues). Networking helps
to ensure that future-regarding objectives and decisions in various
issue areas are not decided in isolation from each other – which, in
turn, helps to prevent the various parts of a foresight system from
working at cross-purposes to each other.

Finland has made a conscious effort to integrate future-regarding
considerations into regular policymaking institutions. The Finnish
foresight system is institutionalised, and this makes governance in
that country more future-regarding than it is in most other places.
However, most of the actors within the Finnish foresight system
are not empowered to *make* future-regarding policies. Instead,
they have a form of soft power: they must persuade other decision
makers to act in future-regarding ways. Thus, the Finnish foresight
system does not create strong practical or pragmatic incentives for
elected officials to more seriously consider and act upon the potential interests of future others, especially when those interests are
perceived to be in conflict with the interests of the present.

The soft power of the Finnish foresight system may be sufficient in the context of an inclusive, multi-party system that seems to support long-term governance more generally. Such soft power may be less influential in more competitive and polarised democratic systems which provide fewer incentives for negotiation and collaboration between parties and interests. Moreover, the Finnish people have historically expressed high levels of trust in government officials and experts. An expert-driven foresight system on the Finnish model might be considered less legitimate – and thus rendered less effective – in less trusting political societies. Scholars should therefore think about how democratic institutions in low-trust societies, such as the United States or France, might be made more future-regarding. In low-trust societies it may be necessary to build trust *within* future-regarding institutions through inclusion, deliberation and critique. MacKenzie and Warren (2012), for example, have argued that deliberative minipublics – like those discussed in this volume by Smith (Chapter 8) and Setälä et al. (Chapter 12) – can help societies to anticipate and navigate trust 'trouble spots'. Inclusive and deliberative minipublics give those who are not involved in those processes reasons to believe that who are involved are capable, well-informed and acting in the public interest. Given these attributes, minipublics may be an effective option for future-regarding governance in both low- and high-trust societies.

The Politics of Democratic Reform

Researchers and activists also need to think more carefully – and strategically – about the politics of democratic reform. If we want to make our democratic systems more future-regarding, we will have to think about the political actions that need to be taken to make those reforms a reality. Institutions that would empower some people to act as special representatives of the future would, in most cases, also *disempower* – or at least counterbalance the influence of – those who have power in our current systems. It is inherently difficult to make reforms that shift the balance of power from one set actors to another because those with power to make public decisions also (normally) have the power to prevent or delay any institutional reforms that would weaken their powers.

Any comprehensive programme for democratic reform must, as a first step, identify potential agents of change (i.e., political actors who are capable, willing or incentivised to do what may be necessary to make change happen). MacKenzie (Chapter 7, this volume) argues that future-regarding democratic leaders can play a role in making change happen, but he does not say who those leaders might be, where they may be found, or what might incentivise them to act in future-regarding ways.

Who will be the agents of change when it comes to future-regarding democratic reform? And why might they be incentivised to make reforms happen? Who will benefit most from those reforms, and how can those people (if they exist) be encouraged to take up the cause? We do not have good answers to these questions. Scholars have proposed reforms that would help to make our democratic systems more future-regarding, and we may be able to identify agents of change. But we will need savvy politicians and activists to take on these roles, and define them for themselves, if future-regarding democratic reforms are going to happen. The politics of each reform programme will be different – some will be more successful than others, and it is likely that no reform programme will be realised in quite the way that scholars might have imagined or recommended. Nevertheless, academic studies of future-regarding governance – quantitative, qualitative and speculative ones – can help to set the parameters for a democratic reform agenda by specifying what it is we should be aiming at.

REFERENCES

Aalto-Lassila, A. 2008. 'Eduskunnan tulevaisuusvaliokunnan synty. Kansalaisaloitteesta vakinaiseksi valiokunnaksi', Master's thesis, University of Helsinki.

Abizadeh, Arash. 2012. 'On the Demos and its Kin: Nationalism, Democracy, and the Boundary Problem', *American Political Science Review* 106(4): 867–82.

Achen, Christopher H. and Larry M. Bartels. 2016. *Democracy for Realists: Why Elections do not Produce Responsive Government*. Princeton, NJ: Princeton University Press.

Afsahi, Afsoun. 2020. 'Toward a Principle of Most Deeply Affected', *Philosophy and Social Criticism* 48(1): 40–61.

Agnew, John. 2020. 'Dying from Ideology: the Spatial Paradox of Trump's "Populism" in the Time of Covid-19', *Semestrale di studi e ricerche di geografia* 32(2): 9–21.

Ahvenharju, Sanna, Laura Pouru-Mikkola, Matti Minkkinen and Toni Ahlqvist (2020). 'Tulevaisuustiedon lähteillä: analyysi ennakointi-raporteista ja tulevaisuuden ilmiöistä'. Helsinki: Eduskunnan tule-vaisuusvaliokunnan julkaisuja. 6/2020, available at: https://www.edusk unta.fi/FI/naineduskuntatoimii/julkaisut/Documents/tuvj_6+2020. pdf.

Airaksinen, Jussi and Albrecht, Eerika. 2019. 'Arguments and their Effects: A Case Study on Drafting the Legislation on the Environmental Impacts of Peat Extraction in Finland', *Journal of Cleaner Production* 226: 1004–12.

Allington, Daniel, Bobby Duffy, Simon Wessely, Nayana Dhavan and James Rubin. 2020. 'Health-protective Behaviour, Social Media Usage and Conspiracy Belief during the COVID-19 Public Health Emergency', *Psychological Medicine*, 1–7.

Anckar, Dag. 1996. 'The Intensity Problem between Beneficent Rule and Responsive Rule', in *Society, the Body, and Well-Being: Essays in Honour of Elienne Riska*, eds Kirsti Suolinna, Elizabeth Ettorre and Eero Lahelma. Åbo: Åbo Akademi, 1–33.

Anderson, Elizabeth. 2006. 'The Epistemology of Democracy', *Episteme* 3(1/2): 8–22.

Anderson, Thomas R., Ed Hawkins and Philip D. Jones. 2016. 'CO_2, the Greenhouse Effect and Global Warming: From the Pioneering Work of Arrhenius and Callendar to Today's Earth System Model', *Endeavour* 40(3): 178–87.

Andrews, Josephine T. 2002. *When Majorities Fail: The Russian Parliament, 1990–1993*. Cambridge: Cambridge University Press.

Andrić, Vuko. 2020. 'Is the All-Subjected Principle Extensionally Adequate?' *Res Publica* 23(3): 387–407.

Arendt, Hannah. [1954] 1987. *Between Past and Future: Eight Exercises in Political Thought*. Harmondsworth: Penguin.

Arendt, Hannah. 1958. *The Human Condition*. Chicago: University of Chicago Press.

Arendt, Hannah. 1961. *Between Past and Future: Eight Exercises in Political Thought*. London: Penguin.

Armingeon, Klaus, Virginia Wenger, Fiona Wiedemeier, Christian Isler, Laura Knöpfel, David Weisstanner and Sarah Engler. 2020. *Comparative Political Data Set 1960–2018*. Zurich: Institute of Political Science, University of Zurich, available at: https://www.cpds-data.org, last accessed 1 September 2021.

Arneson, Richard J. 2004. 'Democracy is Not Intrinsically Just', in *Justice and Democracy*, eds Keith Dowding, Robert E. Goodin and Carole Pateman. Cambridge: Cambridge University Press, 40–58.

Arrhenius, Gustaf. 2005. 'The Boundary Problem in Democratic Theory', in *Democracy Unbound*, ed. Folke Tersman. Stockholm: Stockholm Universitet, 14–29.

Arrhenius, Svante. 1896. 'On the Influence of Carbonic Acid in the Air upon the Temperature of the Ground', *Philosophical Magazine and Journal of Science* 41(251): 237–76.

Arter, David. 2000. 'The Model for Parliaments in the Future? The Case of the Finnish Committee for the Future', *Politiikka* 42(3): 149–63.

Arter, David. 2015. 'A "Pivotal Centre Party" Calls the Shots: The 2015 Finnish General Election', *West European Politics* 38(6): 1345–53.

Atehortua, Nelson A. and Stella Patino. 2021. 'COVID-19, a Tale of Two Pandemics: Novel Coronavirus and Fake News Messaging', *Health Promotion International* 36(2): 524–34.

Bächtiger, André and John Parkinson. 2019. *Mapping and Measuring Deliberation*. Oxford: Oxford University Press.

Bächtiger, Andre, John Dryzek, Jane Mansbridge and Mark E. Warren. 2018. *The Oxford Handbook of Deliberative Democracy*. Oxford: Oxford University Press.

Bäck, Maria and Elina Kestilä-Kekkonen. 2019. *Poliittinen ja sosiaalinen luottamus: Polut, trendit ja kuilut*. Valtiovarainministeriön julkaisuja 2019:31.

Barber, Benjamin R. 1984. *Strong Democracy: Participatory Politics for a New Age*. Berkley: California University Press.

Bartels, Larry M. 2009. *Unequal Democracy: The Political Economy of the New Gilded Age*. Princeton, NJ: Princeton University Press.

Batson, C. Daniel, Bruce D. Duncan, Paula Ackerman, Terese Buckley, and Kimberly Birch. 1981. 'Is Empathic Emotion a Source of Altruistic Motivation?' *Journal of Personality and Social Psychology* 40(2): 290–302.

Batson, C. Daniel, Shannon Early and Giovanni Salvarani. 1997. 'Perspective-taking: Imagining how Another Feels versus Imaging How You Would Feel', *Personality and Social Psychology Bulletin* 23: 751–8.

Batson, C. Daniel, Marina P. Polycarpou, Eddie Harmon-Jones, Heidi J. Imhoff, Erin C. Mitchener, Lori L. Bednar, Tricia R. Klein and Lori Highberger. 1997. 'Empathy and Attitudes: Can Feeling for a Member of a Stigmatized Group Improve Feelings Toward the Group?' *Journal of Personality and Social Psychology* 72(1): 105–18.

Batson, C. Daniel, David A. Lishner, Amy Carpenter, Luis Dulin, Sanna Harjusola-Webb, E. L. Stocks, Shawna Gale, Omar Hassan and Brenda Sampat. 2003. '". . . As You Would Have Them Do Unto You": Does Imagining Yourself in the Other's Place Stimulate Moral Action?' *Personality and Social Psychology Bulletin* 29(9): 1190–1201.

Baume, Sandrine. 2018. 'Rehabilitating Political Parties: An Examination of the Views of Hans Kelsen', *Intellectual History Review* 28(3): 425–49.

Bechtel, Michael M. and Jens Hainmueller. 2011. 'How Lasting is Voter Gratitude? An Analysis of the Short- and Long-Term Electoral Returns to Beneficial Policy', *American Journal of Political Science* 55(4): 852–68.

Beerbohm, Eric. 2015. 'Is Democratic Leadership Possible?' *American Political Science Review* 109(4): 639–52.

Begley, Sharon. 2007. 'The Truth about Denial', *Newsweek*, 13 August.

Bell, Daniel A. 2016. *The China Model: Political Meritocracy and the Limits of Democracy*. Princeton, NJ: Princeton University Press.

Bellamy, Richard. 2012. 'Democracy, Compromise and the Representation Paradox: Coalition Government and Political Integrity', *Government and Opposition* 47(3): 441–65.

Bello, Piera and Vincenzo Galasso. 2021. 'The Politics of Ageing and Retirement: Evidence from Swiss Referenda', *Population Studies* 75(1): 3–18.

Benhabib, Seyla. 1994. 'Deliberative Rationality and Models of Democratic Legitimacy', *Constellations* 1(1): 26–52.

Berenguer, Jamie. 2007: 'The Effect of Empathy in Proenvironmental Attitudes and Behaviors', *Environment and Behavior* 39(2): 269–83.

Bergman, Timo. 2011. '"Tapahtumien kulkua on mahdotonta ennustaa". Mahdollisuudet, haasteet ja uhat ministeriöiden tulevaisuusnäkemyksissä koskien väestön ikärakenteen kehitystä Suomessa', Master's thesis, University of Jyväskylä.

Bernauer, J., M. Bühlmann, A. Vatter and M. Germann. 2016. 'Taking the Multidimensionality of Democracy Seriously: Institutional Patterns and the Quality of Democracy', *European Political Science Review* 8(3): 473–94.

Bertelsmann Stiftung. 2019. *Social Justice in the EU and OECD. Index Report 2019*. Gütersloh: Bertelsmann Stiftung.

Bhatia, Sharey, Jey H. Lau and Timothy Baldwin. 2021. 'Automatic Classification of Neutralization Techniques in the Narrative of Climate Change Scepticism', Proceedings of the 2021 Conference of the North American Chapter of the Association for Computational Linguistics: Human Language Technologies, 2167–75.

Bidadanure, Juliana. 2016. 'Youth Quota's, Diversity, and Long-Termism', in *Institutions for Future Generations*, eds I. González-Ricoy and A. Gosseries Oxford: Oxford University Press, 83–97.

Bloom, Paul. 2016. *Against Empathy: The Case for Rational Compassion*. New York: HarperCollins.

Böhm, Katharina, Claudia Landwehr and Nils Steiner. 2014. 'What Explains "Generosity" in the Public Financing of High-tech Drugs?' *Journal of European Social Policy* 24(1): 39–55.

Bohman, James. 1998. 'Survey Article: The Coming of Age of Deliberative Democracy', *Journal of Political Philosophy* 6(4): 400–25.

Bohman, James. 2003. 'Deliberative Toleration', *Political Theory* 31(6): 757–79.

Bohman, James. 2010. *Democracy Across Borders: From Dêmos to Dêmoi*. Cambridge MA: MIT Press.

Bohman, James. 2012. 'Representation in the Deliberative System', in *Deliberative Systems: Deliberative Democracy at the Large Scale*, eds Jane J.

Mansbridge and John Parkinson. Cambridge: Cambridge University Press, 72–94.

Bommier, Antoine. 2006. 'Uncertain Lifetime and Intertemporal Choice: Risk Aversion as a Rationale for Time Discounting', *International Economic Review* 47(4): 1223–46.

Boston, Jonathan. 2016a. *Governing for the Future: Designing Democratic Institutions for a Better Tomorrow.* Bingley: Emerald Group Publishing.

Boston, Jonathan. 2016b. 'Anticipatory Governance: How Well is New Zealand Safeguarding the Future?' *Policy Quarterly* 12(3): 11–24.

Boston, Jonathan. 2021. 'Assessing the Options for Combatting Democratic Myopia and Safeguarding Long-term Interests', *Futures* 125: 102668.

Boston, Jonathan, John Wanna, Vic Lipski and Justin Pritchard. 2014. *Future-Proofing the State: Managing Risks, Responding to Crises and Building Resilience.* Canberra: ANU Press.

Boykoff, Maxwell T. and Jules M. Boykoff. 2004. 'Balance as Bias: Global Warming and the US Prestige Press', *Global Environmental Change* 14(2): 125–36.

Brady, Henry E., Sidney Verba and Kay L. Schlozman. 1995. 'Beyond SES: A Resource Model of Political Participation', *American Political Science Review* 89(2): 271–94.

Bratman, Michael E. 2009. 'Intention, Practical Rationality, and Self-Governance', *Ethics* 119(3): 411–43.

Bratman, Michael E. 2012. 'Time, Rationality, and Self-Governance', *Philosophical Issues* 22: 73–88.

Brennan, Jason. 2017. *Against Democracy.* Princeton, NJ: Princeton University Press.

Brewer, Paul R., Kimberly Gross and Timothy Vercellotti. 2018. 'Trust in International Actors', in *The Oxford Handbook of Social and Political Trust,* ed. Eric M. Uslaner. Oxford: Oxford University Press, 657–86.

Brulle, Robert J. 2018. 'The Climate Lobby: A Sectoral Analysis of Lobbying Spending on Climate Change in the USA, 2000 to 2016', *Climatic Change* 149(3/4): 289–303.

Bruneau, Emile G. and Rebecca Saxe. 2012. 'The Power of Being Heard: The Benefits of "Perspective-Giving" in the Context of Intergroup Conflict', *Journal of Experimental Social Psychology* 48(4): 855–66.

Budge, Ian. 2005. 'Direct and Representative Democracy: Are They Necessarily Opposites?' UNDESA, International Conference on Engaging Communities. Brisbane, Australia, 14–17, available at: http://unpan1. un.org/intradoc/groups/public/documents/UN/UNPANO21106.pdf, last accessed 24 April 2007.

Bussu, Sonia, Adrian Bua, Rikki Dean and Graham Smith. 2022.

'Embedding Participatory Governance', *Critical Policy Studies*, 1–13, published online, DOI: 10.1080/19460171.2022.2053179.

Calvillo, Dustin P., Bryan J. Ross, Ryan J. B. Garcia, Thomas J. Smelter and Abraham M. Rutchick. 2020. 'Political Ideology Predicts Perceptions of the Threat of Covid-19 (and Susceptibility to Fake News about It)', *Social Psychological and Personality Science* 11(8): 1119–28.

Caney, Simon. 2016. 'Political Institutions for the Future: A Fivefold Package', in *Institutions for Future Generations*, eds I. González-Ricoy and A. Gosseries. Oxford: Oxford University Press, 135–55.

Caney, Simon. 2018. 'Justice and Future Generations', *Annual Review of Political Science* 21: 475–93.

Cann, Heather W. and Leigh Raymond. 2018. 'Does Climate Denialism Still Matter? The Prevalence of Alternative Frames in Opposition to Climate Policy', *Environmental Politics* 27(3): 433–54.

Caramani, Daniele. 2020. 'Introduction: The Technocratic Challenge to Democracy', in *The Technocratic Challenge to Democracy*, eds Eri Bertsou and Daniele Caramani. London: Routledge.

Carmichael, Jason T., Robert J. Brulle and Joanna K. Huxster. 2017. 'The Great Divide: Understanding the Role of Media and Other Drivers of the Partisan Divide in Public Concern Over Climate Change in the USA, 2001–2014', *Climatic Change* 141: 599–612.

Castiglione, D. and Mark E. Warren. 2019. 'Rethinking Democratic Representation: Eight Theoretical Issues and a Post-script', in *The Constructivist Turn in Political Representation*, eds L. Disch, N. Urbinati and M. van de Sande. Edinburgh: Edinburgh University Press, 21–47.

Cheng, Vincent C. C., Susanna K. P. Lau, Patrick C. Y. Woo and Kwok Yung Yuen. 2007. 'Severe Acute Respiratory Syndrome Coronavirus as an Agent of Emerging and Reemerging Infection', *Clinical Microbiology Reviews* 20(4): 660–94.

Cho, Renee. 2020. 'COVID-19's Long-term Effects on Climate Change: For Better or Worse', Earth Institute, Columbia University, available at: https://blogs.ei.columbia.edu/2020/06/25/covid-19-impacts-climate-change, last accessed 25 October 2020.

Christensen, Henrik S. and Lauri Rapeli. 2020. 'Immediate Rewards or Delayed Gratification? A Conjoint Survey Experiment of the Public's Policy Preferences', *Policy Sciences* 54: 63–94.

Christensen, Henrik S., Maija Jäske, Maija Setälä and Elias Laitinen. 2017. 'The Finnish Citizens' Initiative: Towards Inclusive Agenda-Setting?' *Scandinavian Political Studies* 40(4): 411–33.

Cikara, Mina, Emile G. Bruneau and Rebecca R. Saxe. 2011. 'Us and Them:

Intergroup Failures of Empathy', *Current Directions in Psychological Science* 20(3): 149–153.

Citrin, Jack and Laura Stoker 2018. 'Political Trust in a Cynical Age', *Annual Review of Political Science* 21: 49–70.

Coate, Stephen and Stephen Morris. (1999). 'Policy Persistence', *American Economic Review* 89(5): 1327–36.

Cohen, Joshua. 1998. 'Democracy and Liberty', in *Deliberative Democracy*, ed. Jon Elster. Cambridge: Cambridge University Press, 185–231.

Convention Citoyenne pour le Climat. 2019, available at: https://www.conventioncitoyennepourleclimat.fr/en, last accessed 25 October 2021.

Cook, John, Naomi Oreskes, Peter D. Doran, William R. L. Anderegg, Bart Verheggen, Ed W. Maibach, J. Stuart Carlton, Stephan Lewandowsky, Andrew G. Skuce and Sarah A. Green. 2016. 'Consensus on Consensus: a Synthesis of Consensus Estimates on Human-caused Global Warming', *Environmental Research Letters* 11(4): 048002.

Coppedge, Michael, John Gerring, Carl H. Knutsen, Staffan I. Lindberg, Jan Teorell, David Altman and Daniel Ziblatt. 2020a. V-Dem Country-Year Dataset v10. Varieties of Democracy (V-Dem) Project.

Coppedge, Michael, John Gerring, Carl H. Knutsen, Staffan I. Lindberg, Jan Teorell, David Altman and Daniel Ziblatt. 2020b. V-Dem Codebook v10. Varieties of Democracy (V-Dem) Project, available at: https://www.v-dem.net/en/data/data, last accessed 1 September 2021.

Dahl, Robert A. 1956. *A Preface to Democratic Theory*. Chicago: University of Chicago Press.

Dahl, Robert A. 1961. *Who Governs? Democracy and Power in an American City*. New Haven, CT: Yale University Press.

Dahl, Robert A. 1971. *Polyarchy. Participation and Opposition*. New Haven, CT: Yale University Press.

Dahl, Robert A. 1989. *Democracy and its Critics*. New Haven, CT: Yale University Press.

Dale, D. and T. Subramaniam. 2020. 'Fact Check: A List of 28 Ways Trump and His Team have been Dishonest about the Coronavirus', *CNN*, 11 March 2020, available at: https://edition.cnn.com/2020/03/11/politics/fact-check-trump-administration-coronavirus-28-dishonest/index.html, last accessed 26 October 2020.

Daniels, Norman. 2012. 'Reasonable Disagreement about Identified vs. Statistical Victims', *Hastings Center Report* 42(1): 35–45.

Daniels, Norman and James E. Sabin. 1997. 'Limits to Health Care: Fair Procedures, Democratic Deliberation, and the Legitimacy Problem for Insurers', *Philosophy and Public Affairs* 26(4): 303–50.

Daniels, Norman and James E. Sabin. 2008. 'Accountability for Reasonableness: An Update', *British Medical Journal* 337.

Davis, Jenny L. and Toni P. Love. 2017. 'Self-in-Self, Mind-in-Mind, Heart-in-Heart: The Future of Role-taking, Perspective-taking, and Empathy', *Advances in Group Processes* 34: 151–74.

Davis, Mark H. 1980. 'A Multidimensional Approach to Individual Differences in Empathy', *JSAS Catalog of Selected Documents in Psychology* 10(85).

Davis, Mark H. 1996. *Empathy: A Social Psychological Approach.* Boulder, CO: Westview.

Delli Carpini, Michael and Scott Keeter. 1996. *What Americans Know about Politics and Why it Matters.* New Haven, CT: Yale University Press.

d'Entrèves, Maurizio P. 2006. '"To Think Representatively": Arendt on Judgment and the Imagination', *Philosophical Papers* 35(3): 367–85.

Deschouwer, Kris. 2006. 'And the Peace Goes On? Consociational Democracy and Belgian Politics in the Twenty-First Century', *West European Politics* 29(5): 895–911.

Devaney, Laura, Diarmuid Torney, Pat Brereton and Martha Coleman. 2020. 'Ireland's Citizens' Assembly on Climate Change: Lessons for Deliberative Public Engagement and Communication', *Environmental Communication* 14(2): 141–6.

Dobson, Andrew. 1996. 'Representative Democracy and the Environment', in *Democracy and the Environment*, eds William M. Lafferty and James Meadowcroft. Cheltenham: Edward Elgar, 124–39.

Dobson, Andrew. 2007. 'Environmental Citizenship: Towards Sustainable Development', *Sustainable Development* 15(5): 276–85.

Dowlen, Oliver. 2008. *The Political Potential of Sortition.* Exeter: Imprint Academic.

Dryzek, John S. and Alex Y. Lo. 2015. 'Reason and Rhetoric in Climate Communication', *Environmental Politics* 24(1): 1–16.

Dryzek, John S. and Simon Niemeyer. 2008. 'Discursive Representation', *American Political Science Review* 102(4): 481–93.

Dryzek, John S., Andre Bächtiger, Simone Chambers, Joshua Cohen, James N. Druckman, Andrea Felicetti, James S. Fishkin et al. 2019. 'The Crisis of Democracy and the Science of Deliberation: Citizens can Avoid Polarization and Make Sound Decisions', *Science* 363(6432): 1144–6.

Du, Xinming, Xiaomeng Jin, Noah Zucker, Ryan Kennedy and Johannes Urpilainen. 2020. 'Transboundary Air Pollution from Coal-fired Power Generation', *Journal of Environmental Management* 270(1): 110862.

Dufva, Mikko and Toni Ahlqvist. 2015. 'Miten edistää hallituksen ja eduskunnan välistä tulevaisuusdialogia?' *Valtioneuvoston selvitys ja tutkimustoiminnan julkaisusarja* 17/2015 (November).

Dulic, Aleksandra, Jeanette Angel and Stephen Sheppard. 2016. 'Designing Futures: Inquiry in Climate Change Communication', *Futures* 81: 54–67.

Dunn, John. 1993. 'Preface', in *Democracy: The Unfinished Journey*, ed. John Dunn. Oxford: Oxford University Press.

Eckersley, Robyn. 2004. *The Green State: Rethinking Democracy and Sovereignty*. Cambridge, MA: MIT Press.

Ekeli, Kristian S. 2005. 'Giving a Voice to Posterity: Deliberative Democracy and Representation of Future People', *Journal of Agricultural and Environmental Ethics* 18(5): 429–50.

Ekeli, Kristian S. 2009. 'Constitutional Experiments: Representing Future Generations through Submajority Rules', *Journal of Political Philosophy* 17(4): 440–61.

Ekins, Richard. 2012. *The Nature of Legislative Intent*. Oxford: Oxford University Press.

Elsässer, Lea, Svenja Hense and Armin Schäfer. 2018. *Government of the People, by the Elite, for the Rich: Unequal Responsiveness in an Unlikely Case*, MPIfG Discussion Paper 18/5. Max Planck Institute for the Study of Societies: Cologne.

Elstub, Stephen, Jayne Carrick, David M. Farrell and Patricia Mockler. 2021. 'The Scope of Climate Assemblies: Lessons from the Climate Assembly UK', *Sustainability* 13(20): 11272.

Estlund, David. 2008. *Democratic Authority: A Philosophical Framework*. Princeton, NJ: Princeton University Press.

Farrell, David M., Jane Suiter and Clodagh Harris. 2019. '"Systematizing" Constitutional Deliberation: the 2016–18 Citizens' Assembly in Ireland', *Irish Political Studies* 34(1): 113–23.

Farrell, Justin. 2016a. 'Corporate Funding and Ideological Polarization about Climate Change', *Proceedings of the National Academy of Sciences* 113(1): 92–7.

Farrell, Justin. 2016b. 'Network Structure and Influence of the Climate Change Counter-movement', *Nature Climate Change* 6(): 370–4.

Fernández-Llamazares, Álvaro, Raquel A. Garcia, Isabel Diaz-Reviriego, Maria Cabeza, Aili Pyhälä and Victoria Reyes-Garcia. 2017. 'An Empirically Tested Overlap between Indigenous and Scientific Knowledge of a Changing Climate in Bolivian Amazonia', *Regional Environmental Change* 17(8): 1673–85.

Fishkin, James S. 2018. *Democracy When the Public are Thinking: Revitalizing our Politics through Public Deliberation*. Oxford: Oxford University Press.

Font, Joan, Graham Smith, Carol Galais and Pau Alarcon. 2018. 'Cherry-picking Participation: Explaining the Fate of Proposals from Participatory Processes', *European Journal of Political Research* 57(3): 615–36.

Forster, Piers M., Harriet I. Forster, Matt J. Evans, Matthew J. Giddens, Cris D. Jones, Cristoph A. Keller, Robin D. Lamboll et al. 2020. 'Current and Future Global Climate Impacts Resulting from COVID-19', *Nature Climate Change* 10: 913–19.

Frankel, J. 2020. 'Covid-19 and the Climate Crisis are Part of the Same Battle', *The Guardian*, 2 October 2020, available at: https://www.theguardian.com/business/2020/oct/02/covid-19-and-the-climate-crisis-are-part-of-the-same-battle, last accessed 23 October 2020.

Frederick, Shane, George Loewenstein and Ted O'Donoghue. 2002. 'Time Discounting and Time Preference: A Critical Review', *Journal of Economic Literature* 40(2): 351–401.

Frinken, Julian and Claudia Landwehr. 2022. Information and deliberation in the Covid-19 crisis and in the climate crisis: how expertocratic practices undermine self-government and compliance. *Acta Politica*, 1–19, DOI: doi.org/10.1057/s41269-022-00267-2.

Fritschi, Tobias and Tom Oesch. 2008. *Volkswirtschaftlicher Nutzen von frühkindlicher Bildung in Deutschland. Eine ökonomische Bewertung langfristiger Bildungseffekte des Besuchs von Kindertageseinrichtungen.* Gütersloh: Bertelsmann Stiftung.

Fuji Johnson, Genevieve. 2007. 'Discursive Democracy in the Transgenerational Context and a Precautionary Turn in Public Reasoning', *Contemporary Political Theory* 6(1): 67–85.

Fülöp, Sándor. 2017. Interview. Future Generations Commissioner for Wales, 2021, available at: https://futuregenerations.wales.

Fung, Archon. 2013. 'The Principle of Affected Interests: An Interpretation and Defense', in *Representation: Elections and Beyond*, eds Jack H. Nagel and Rogers M. Smith. Philadelphia: University of Pennsylvania Press, 236–68.

Gál, Róbert I., Pieter Vanhuysse and Lili Vargha. 2018. 'Pro-elderly Welfare States within Child-oriented Societies', *Journal of European Public Policy* 25(6): 944–58.

Gallagher, Michael. 1991. 'Proportionality, Disproportionality and Electoral Systems', *Electoral Studies* 10(1): 33–51.

Gates, Bill. 2020. 'COVID-19 is Awful: Climate Change Could be Worse', 4 August 2020, available at: https://www.gatesnotes.com/Energy/Climate-and-COVID-19, last accessed 11 October 2020.

Gerber, Marlène, André Bächtiger, Susumu Shikano, Simon Reber and Samuel Rohr. 2018. 'Deliberative Abilities and Influence in a

Transnational Deliberative Poll (EuroPolis)', *British Journal of Political Science* 48(4): 1093–118.

Gerring, John and Strom C. Thacker. 2008. *A Centripetal Theory of Democratic Governance*. Cambridge: Cambridge University Press.

Giddens, Anthony. 1984. *The Constitution of Society*. Berkeley: University of California Press.

Gidley, Jennifer M. 2017. *The Future: A Very Short Introduction*. Oxford: Oxford University Press.

Gilens, Martin. 2005. 'Inequality and Democratic Responsiveness', *Public Opinion Quarterly* 69(5): 778–96.

Gilens, Martin. 2012. *Affluence and Influence: Economic Inequality and Political Power in America*. New York and Princeton, NJ: Russell Sage Foundation and Princeton University Press.

Glicksman, Robert L. 2010. 'Anatomy of Industry Resistance to Climate Change: a Familiar Litany', in *Economic Thought and US Climate Change Policy*, ed. David M. Driesen. Cambridge, MA: MIT Press, 83–105.

González-Ricoy, Iñigo. 2016. 'Constitutionalising Intergenerational Provisions', in *Institutions for Future Generations*, eds I. González-Ricoy and A. Gosseries. Oxford: Oxford University Press, 170–83.

González-Ricoy, I. and A. Gosseries (eds). 2016. *Institutions for Future Generations*. Oxford: Oxford University Press.

Goodhart, Michael E. 2018. *Injustice: Political Theory for the Real World*. New York: Oxford University Press.

Goodin, Robert E. 1992. *Green Political Theory*. Cambridge: Polity.

Goodin, Robert E. 1995. *Utilitarianism as a Public Philosophy*. Cambridge: Cambridge University Press.

Goodin, Robert E. 1996. 'Enfranchising the Earth, and its Alternatives', *Political Studies* 44(5): 835–49.

Goodin, Robert E. 2000. 'Democratic Deliberation Within', *Philosophy and Public Affairs* 29(1): 81–108.

Goodin, Robert E. 2003. *Reflective Democracy*. Oxford: Oxford University Press.

Goodin, Robert E. 2007. 'Enfranchising All Affected Interests, and Its Alternatives', *Philosophy and Public Affairs* 35(1): 40–68.

Goodin, Robert E. 2008. 'The Place of Parties', in *Innovating Democracy: Democratic Theory and Practice after the Deliberative Turn*, ed. R. E. Goodin. Oxford: Oxford University Press, 204–23.

Gorji, Shaghayegh and Ali Gorji. 2021. 'COVID-19 Pandemic: the Possible Influence of the Long-term Ignorance about Climate Change', *Environmental Science and Pollution Research* 28(13): 15575–9.

Government of Finland. 2019. 'Programme of Prime Minister Sanna Marin's Government 2019', Helsinki: Publications of the Finnish Government 2019:33, available at: https://julkaisut.valtioneuvosto.fi/bi tstream/handle/10024/161935/VN_2019_33.pdf.

Graham, Lori M. 2008. 'Reparations, Self-determination, and the Seventh Generation', *Harvard Human Rights Journal* 21(1): 47–104.

Grewal, David S. 2009. *Network Power: The Social Dynamics of Globalization.* New Haven, CT: Yale University Press.

Grönlund, Kimmo, Andre Bächtiger and Maija Setälä. 2014. *Deliberative Mini-Publics: Involving Citizens in the Democratic Process.* Colchester: ECPR Press.

Grönlund, Kimmo, Kaisa Herne and Maija Setälä. 2017. 'Empathy in a Citizen Deliberation Experiment', *Scandinavian Political Studies* 40(4): 457–80.

Grönlund, Kimmo, Kaisa Herne, Maija Jäske, Heikki Liimatainen, Lauri Rapeli, Jonas Schauman, Rasmus Siren, Mikko Värttö and Albert Weckman. 2020. 'Involving Citizens in the Planning of a Future City Center in Turku: Deliberative Citizens' Panel as a Democratic Innovation', City of Turku Urban Research Programme, Research Reports 4/2020, available at: https://www.turku.fi/sites/default/files/atoms/files/tutkim usraportteja_4-2020.pdf.

Groombridge, Brian. 2006. 'Parliament and the Future: Learning from Finland', *Political Quarterly* 77(2): 273–80.

Gundersen, Adolph G. 1995. *The Environmental Promise of Democratic Deliberation.* Madison: University of Wisconsin Press.

Gust, Ian D., Alan W. Hampson and Daniel Lavanchy. 2001. 'Planning for the Next Pandemic of Influenza', *Reviews in Medical Virology* 11(1): 59–70.

Gutmann, Amy and Dennis Thompson. 2004. *Why Deliberative Democracy?* Princeton, NJ: Princeton University Press.

Habermas, Jürgen. 1996. *Between Facts and Norms: Contributions to a Discourse Theory of Law and Democracy*, trans. W. Rehg. Cambridge, MA: MIT Press.

Hajer, Maarten A. and Peter Pelzer. 2018. '2050 – An Energetic Odyssey: Understanding "Techniques of Futuring" in the Transition Towards Renewable Energy', *Energy Research and Social Science* 44: 222–31.

Hanson, Lorelei. L. 2018. *Public Deliberation on Climate Change: Lessons from Alberta Climate Change Dialogues.* Edmonton: Alberta University Press.

Hansson, Sven O. 2015. 'Experiments before Science: What Science Learned from Technological Experiments', in *The Role of Technology in Science: Philosophical Perspectives*. ed. Sven O. Hansson. Dordrecht: Springer, 81–110.

Hansson, Sven O. 2017. 'Science Denial as a Form of Pseudoscience', *Studies in History and Philosophy of Science* 63: 39–47.

Hansson, Sven O. 2018a. 'Risk, Science and Policy: a Treacherous Triangle', *Ethical Perspectives* 25(3): 391–418.

Hansson, Sven O. 2018b. 'How Connected are the Major Forms of Irrationality? An Analysis of Pseudoscience, Science Denial, Fact Resistance and Alternative Facts', *Mètode Science Study Journal* 8: 125–31.

Hansson, Sven O. 2019. 'Farmers' Experiments and Scientific Methodology', *European Journal for Philosophy of Science* 9(3): 1–23.

Hansson, Sven O. 2020. 'Social Constructivism and Climate Science Denial', *European Journal for Philosophy of Science* 10(3): 1–27.

Hara, Keishiro, Ritsuji Yoshioka, Masashi Kuroda, Shuji Kurimoto and Tatsuyoshi Saijo. 2019. 'Reconciling Intergenerational Conflicts with Imaginary Future Generations: Evidence from a Participatory Deliberation Practice in a Municipality in Japan', *Sustainability Science* 14: 1605–19.

Harris, Clodagh. 2021. 'Looking to the Future? Including Children, Young People and Future Generations in Deliberations on Climate Action: Ireland's Citizens' Assembly 2016–2018', *Innovation: European Journal of Social Science Research* 34(5): 677–93.

Healy, Andrew and Neil Malhotra. 2009. 'Myopic Voters and Natural Disaster Policy', *American Political Science Review* 103(3): 387–406.

Heckscher, Albert. 1892. *Bidrag til grundlæggelse af en afstemningslære. Om methoderne ved udfindelse af stemmerflerhed i parlamenter (afsteming over ændringforslag m.v.) ved valg og domstole.* Københaven: Universitetsboghandler G. E. C. Gad.

Hendriks, Carolyn M. 2016. 'Coupling Citizens and Elites in Deliberative Systems: The Role of Institutional Design', *European Journal of Political Research* 55(1): 43–60.

Hepburn, Cameron, Brian O'Callaghan, Nicholas Stern, Joseph Stiglitz and Dimitri Zenghelis. 2020. 'Will COVID-19 Fiscal Recovery Packages Accelerate or Retard Progress on Climate Change?' *Oxford Review of Economic Policy* 36(Suppl.): S359–81.

Herman-Mercer, Nicole M., Elli Matkin, Melinda J. Laituri, Ryan C. Toohey, Maggie Massey, Kelly Elder, Paul F. Schuster and Edda A. Mutter. 2016. 'Changing Times, Changing Stories: Generational Differences in Climate Change Perspectives from Four Remote Indigenous Communities in Subarctic Alaska', *Ecology and Society* 21(3): 28.

Herne, Kaisa, Jari K. Hietanen, Olli Lappalainen and Esa Palosaari. 2022. 'How to Promote Altruistic Sharing? The Influence of Empathy and Veil of Ignorance on Dictator Game Behavior', *PloS One* 17(3): e0262196.

Heyward, Clare. 2008. 'Can the All-Affected Principle Include Future Persons? Green Deliberative Democracy and the Non-Identity Problem', *Environmental Politics* 17(4): 625–43.

Hiromitsu, Toshiaki. 2019. 'Consideration of Keys to Solving Problems in Long-Term Fiscal Policy through Laboratory Research', *International Journal of Economic Policy Studies* 13(1): 147–72.

Hirschman, Albert O. 1986. 'On Democracy in Latin America', *New York Review of Books*, 10 April.

Hobson, Kertsy and Simon Niemeyer. 2011. 'Public Responses to Climate Change: The Role of Deliberation in Building Capacity for Adaptive Action', *Global Environmental Change* 21(3): 957–71.

Hollingsworth, T. Déirdre, Neil M. Ferguson and Roy M. Anderson. 2007. 'Frequent Travelers and Rate of Spread of Epidemics', *Emerging Infectious Diseases* 13(9): 1288–94.

Holmes, Edward C., Andrew Rambaut and Kristian G. Andersen. 2018. 'Pandemics: Spend on Surveillance, not Prediction', *Nature* 558: 180–2.

Hooghe, Marc. 2011. 'Why There is Basically Only One Form of Political Trust', *British Journal of Politics and International Relations* 13(2): 269–75.

Hoque, Naimul. 2014. 'Analysing Sustainable Consumption Patterns: A Literature Review', *Development* 56(3): 370–7.

Huber, Evelyne, Charles Ragin, John D. Stevens, David Brady and Jason Beckfield. 2004. *Comparative Welfare States Data Set.* Northwestern University, University of North Carolina, Duke University and Indiana University.

Hume, David. [1739] 1948. 'A Treatise of Human Nature. Books II and III', in *Hume's Moral and Political Philosophy*, ed. Henry D. Aiken. Darien: Hafner, 1–169.

Huremović, Damir. 2019. 'Brief History of Pandemics (Pandemics Throughout History)', in *Psychiatry of Pandemics*, ed. Damir Huremović. Berlin: Springer, 7–35.

Ialenti, Vincent. 2020. *Deep Time Reckoning: How Future Thinking Can Help Earth Now.* Cambridge, MA: MIT Press.

Intergovernmental Panel on Climate Change (IPCC). 2015. *Climate Change 2014: Synthesis Report. Contribution of Working Groups I, II and III to the Fifth Assessment Report of the Intergovernmental Panel on Climate Change.* Geneva: IPCC.

Jacobs, Alan M. 2008. 'The Politics of When: Redistribution, Investment and Policy Making for the Long Term', *British Journal of Political Science* 38: 193–220.

Jacobs, Alan M. 2011. *Governing for the Long Term: Democracy and the Politics of Investment*. Cambridge: Cambridge University Press.

Jacobs, Alan M. 2016. 'Policy Making for the Long Term in Advanced Democracies', *Annual Review of Political Science* 19(1): 433–54.

Jacobs, Alan M. and J. Scott Matthews. 2012. 'Why do Citizens Discount the Future? Public Opinion and the Timing of Policy Consequences', *British Journal of Political Science* 42(4): 903–35.

Jacobs, Alan M. and J. Scott Matthews. 2017. 'Policy Attitudes in Institutional Context: Rules, Uncertainty, and the Mass Politics of Public Investment', *American Journal of Political Science* 61(1): 194–207.

Johnson, Genevieve F. 2008. *Deliberative Democracy for the Future: The Case of Nuclear Waste Management in Canada*. Toronto: University of Toronto Press.

Kahneman, Daniel. 2011. *Thinking, Fast and Slow*. New York: Farrar, Straus & Giroux.

Kahneman, Daniel and Amos Tversky. 2000. *Choices, Values, and Frames*. Cambridge: Cambridge University Press.

Kahneman, Daniel, Jack L. Knetsch and Richard H. Thaler. 1991. 'Anomalies: The Endowment Effect, Loss Aversion, and Status Quo Bias', *Journal of Economic Perspectives* 5(1): 193–206.

Kalichman, Seth C. 2009. *Denying AIDS: Conspiracy Theories, Pseudoscience, and Human Tragedy*. Berlin: Springer.

Kallbekken, Steffen and Sælen, Håkon. 2021. 'Public Support for Air Travel Restrictions to Address COVID-19 or Climate Change', *Transportation Research Part D: Transport and Environment* 93(3): 102767.

Kamijo, Yoshio, Asuka Komiya, Nobuhiro Mifune and Tatsujoshi Saijo. 2017. 'Negotiating with the Future: Incorporating Imaginary Future Generations into Negotiations', *Sustainability Science* 12: 409–20.

Karnein, Anja. 2016. 'Can We Represent Future Generations?' in *Institutions for Future Generations*, eds I. González-Ricoy and A. Gosseries. Oxford: Oxford University Press, 83–97.

Kelly, Heath. 2011. 'The Classical Definition of a Pandemic is not Elusive', *Bulletin of the World Health Organization* 89(7): 539–40.

Kelsen, Hans. 1929. *Vom Wesen und Wert der Demokratie. Zweite, umgearbeitete Auflage*. Tübingen: J. C. B. Mohr.

Kelsen, Hans. [1929] 2013. *The Essence and Value of Democracy*, eds Nadia Urbinati and Carlo Invernizzi Accetti, trans. Brian Graf. Lanham, MD: Rowman & Littlefield. (Orig.: *Vom Wesen und Wert der Demokratie*. 1929 rev. and expanded edn, orig. 1920. Translation based on 1929 edn.)

Kelsen, Hans. 1951. 'Science and Politics', *American Political Science Review* 45(3): 641–61.

Kendall, Willmoore and George W. Carey. 1968. 'The Intensity Problem and Democratic Theory', *American Political Science Review* 62(1): 5–24.

Kerr, J., C. Panagopoulos and S. van der Linden. 2021. 'Political Polarization on COVID-19 Pandemic Response in the United States', *Personality and Individual Differences* 179: 110892.

King, Andrew D. and Luke J. Harrington. 2018. 'The Inequality of Climate Change from 1.5 to 2 C of Global Warming', *Geophysical Research Letters* 45(10): 5030–3.

Kinski, Lucy and Kerry Whiteside. 2022. 'Of Parliament and Presentism: Electoral Representation and Future Generations in Germany', *Environmental Politics* 1–22, published online. DOI: 10.1080/09644016. 2022.2031441.

Knight, Jack and Melissa Schwartzberg, 2020. 'Institutional Bargaining for Democratic Theorists (or How We Learned to Stop Worrying and Love Haggling)', *Annual Review of Political Science* 23: 259–76.

Kohn, George C. 2008. *Encyclopedia of Plague and Pestilence: From Ancient Times to the Present*, 3rd edn. New York: Infobase.

Koirala, Pankaj, Raja R. Timilsina and Koji Kotani. 2021. 'Deliberative Forms of Democracy and Intergenerational Sustainability Dilemma', *Sustainability* 13(13): 7377.

Kornhauser, Lewis A. and Lawrence G. Sager. 1986. 'Unpacking the Court', *Yale Law Journal* 96(1): 82–117.

Kornhauser, Lewis A. and Lawrence G. Sager. 1993. 'The One and the Many: Adjudication in Collegial Courts', *California Law Review* 81(1): 1–59.

Koskimaa, Vesa and Lauri Rapeli. 2020. 'Fit to Govern? Comparing Citizen and Policymaker Perceptions of Deliberative Democratic Innovations', *Policy & Politics* 48(4): 637–52.

Koskimaa, Vesa and Tapio Raunio. 2020. 'Encouraging a Longer Time Horizon: The Committee for the Future in the Finnish Eduskunta', *Journal of Legislative Studies* 26(2): 159–79.

Koskimaa, Vesa and Tapio Raunio. 2022. 'Expanding Anticipatory Governance to Legislatures: The Emergence and Global Diffusion of Parliamentary Future Committees, manuscript under review.

Koskimaa, Vesa, Lauri Rapeli and Juha Hiedanpää. 2021. 'Governing through Strategies: How Does Finland Sustain a Future-oriented Environmental Policy for the Long Term?' *Futures* 125: 102667.

Krznaric, Roman. 2020. *The Good Ancestor: How to Think Long Term in a Short Term World*. New York: Penguin.

Kukkonen, Anna and Tuomas Ylä-Anttila. 2020. 'The Science–Policy Interface as a Discourse Network: Finland's Climate Change Policy 2002–2015', *Politics and Governance* 8(2): 200–14.

Kulha, Katariina, Mikko Leino, Maija Setälä, Maija Jäske and Stäffan Himmelroos. 2021. 'For the Sake of the Future: Can Democratic Deliberation Help Thinking and Caring about Future Generations?' *Sustainability* 13(10): 5487. DOI: 10.3390/su13105487.

Kulha, Katariina, Hilma Sormunen, Mikko Leino, Maija Setälä, Mari Taskinen and Maija Jäske. 2022. 'Final Report of the Citizens' Jury on Climate Actions', *Publications of the Ministry of the Environment* 2022:2, available at: http://urn.fi/URN:ISBN:978-952-361-218-1.

Laakso, Markk and Rein Taagepera. 1979. '"Effective" Number of Parties: A Measure with Application to West Europe', *Comparative Political Studies* 12(1): 3–27.

Lafont, Cristina. 2015. 'Deliberation, Participation and Democratic Legitimacy: Should Deliberative Minipublics Shape Public Policy?' *Journal of Political Philosophy* 23:1 (January): 40–63.

Lafont, Cristina. 2019. *Democracy Without Shortcuts: A Participatory Conception of Deliberative Democracy*. Oxford: Oxford University Press.

Lagerspetz, Eerik. 2014. 'Albert Heckscher on Collective Decision-Making', *Public Choice* 159(3/4): 327–39.

Lagerspetz, Eerik. 2016. *Social Choice and Democratic Values*. Heidelberg: Springer.

Lagerspetz, Eerik. 2017. 'Kelsen on Democracy and Majority Decision', *Archiv für Rechts- und Sozialphilosophie* 103(2): 155–79.

Landwehr, Claudia. 2015. 'Democratic Meta-Deliberation: Towards Reflective Institutional Design', *Political Studies* 63(S1): 38–54.

Landwehr, Claudia and Katharina Böhm. 2014. 'Strategic Institutional Design: Two Case Studies of Non-Majoritarian Agencies in Health Care Priority Setting', *Government and Opposition* 51(4): 632–60.

Lauth, Hans-Joachim. 2011. 'Quality Criteria for Democracy. Why Responsiveness is not the Key', *Zeitschrift für Vertgleichende Politikwissenschaft. Sonderheft* 1: 59–80.

Lee, Vernon J., Ximena Aguilera, David Heymann and Annelies Wilder-Smith. 2020. 'Preparedness for Emerging Epidemic Threats: a Lancet Infectious Diseases Commission', *The Lancet Infectious Diseases* 20(1): 17–19.

Lenton, Timothy M., Johan Rockström, Owen Gaffney, Stefan Rahmstorf, Katherine Richardson, Will Steffen and Hans J. Schellnhuber. 2019. 'Climate Tipping Points: Too Risky to Bet Against', *Nature* 575: 592–5.

Levenbook, Barbara Baum. 2020. 'A Puzzle about Legal Systems and Democratic Theory', *Jurisprudence* 11(2): 157–68.

Levine, Michael E. and Jennifer L. Forrence. 1990. 'Regulatory Capture, Public Interest, and the Public Agenda: Toward a Synthesis', *Journal of Law, Economics, & Organization* 6: 167–98.

Lewandowsky, Stephan. 2021. 'Liberty and the Pursuit of Science Denial', *Current Opinion in Behavioral Sciences* 42: 65–9.

Liberman, Nira and Yaacov Trope. 2008. 'The Psychology of Transcending the Here and Now', *Science* 322(5905): 1201–5.

Liebenberg, Louis. 1990. *The Art of Tracking: The Origin of Science*. Cape Town: David Philip.

Lijphart, Arend. 1984. *Democracies: Patterns of Majoritarian and Consensus Government in Twenty-one Countries*. New Haven, CT: Yale University Press.

Lijphart, Arend. 2012. *Patterns of Democracy: Government Forms and Performance in Thirty-Six Countries*. New Haven, CT: Yale University Press.

Lindblom, Charles E. 2002. *The Market System: What It Is, How It Works, and What to Make of It*. New Haven, CT: Yale University Press.

List, Christian. 2006. 'The Discursive Dilemma and Public Reason', *Ethics* 116(2): 362–402.

List, Christian and Philip Pettit. 2002. 'Aggregating Sets of Judgments: An Impossibility Result', *Economics and Philosophy* 18(1): 89–110.

List, Christian and Philip Pettit. 2011. *Group Agency: The Possibility, Design, and Status of Corporate Agents*. Oxford: Oxford University Press.

Loembé, Marguerite M. and John N. Nkengasong. 2021. 'COVID-19 Vaccine Access in Africa: Global Distribution, Vaccine Platforms, and Challenges Ahead', *Immunity* 54(7): 1353–62.

Loewenstein, George, Deborah Small and Jeff F. Strnad. 2005. 'Statistical, Identifiable and Iconic Victims and Perpetrators', *SSRN Electronic Journal*. DOI: doi.org/10.2139/ssrn.678281.

Longini Jr., Ira M., Paul E. M. Fine and Stephen B. Thacker. (1986). 'Predicting the Global Spread of New Infectious Agents', *American Journal of Epidemiology* 123(3): 383–91.

Lontzek, Thomas S., Yongyang Cai, Kenneth L. Judd and Timothy M. Lenton. 2015. 'Stochastic Integrated Assessment of Climate Tipping Points Indicates the Need for Strict Climate Policy', *Nature Climate Change* 5(5): 441–4.

Luntz, Frank. 2002. 'The Environment: a Cleaner, Safer, Healthier America', available at: https://www.sourcewatch.org/images/4/45/LuntzResearch. Memo.pdf, last accessed 25 October 2020.

Luskin, R. C., I. O'Flynn, J. S. Fishkin and D. Russell. 2014. 'Deliberating across Deep Divides', *Political Studies* 62(1): 116–35.

MacCallum, Gerald D. 1968. 'Legislative Intent', in Essays in *Legal Philosophy*, ed. Robert S. Summers, Berkeley: University of California Press, 237–73.

MacKenzie, Michael K. 2013. *Future Publics: Long-Term Thinking and Farsighted Action in Democratic Systems*. Vancouver: University of British Columbia.

MacKenzie, Michael K. 2016a. 'Institutional Design and Sources of Short-Termism', in *Institutions for Future Generations*, eds I. González-Ricoy and A. Gosseries. Oxford: Oxford University Press, 24–48.

MacKenzie, Michael K. 2016b. 'A General-Purpose, Randomly Selected Chamber', in *Institutions for Future Generations*, eds I. González-Ricoy and A. Gosseries. Oxford: Oxford University Press, 282–98.

MacKenzie, Michael K. 2018. 'Deliberation and Long-Term Decisions: Representing Future Generations', in *The Oxford Handbook of Deliberative Democracy*, eds Andre Bächtiger, John S. Dryzek, Jane Mansbridge and Mark E. Warren. Oxford: Oxford University Press, 251–81.

MacKenzie, Michael K. 2021a. 'There is No Such Thing as a Short-Term Issue', *Futures* 125: 102652.

MacKenzie, Michael K. 2021b. *Future Publics: Democracy, Deliberation, and Future Regarding Collective Action*. Oxford: Oxford University Press.

MacKenzie, Michael K. and Didier Caluwaerts. 2021. 'Paying for the Future: Deliberation and Support for Climate Action Policies', *Journal of Environmental Policy & Planning* 23(3): 317–31.

MacKenzie, Michael K. and Kieran O'Doherty. 2011. 'Deliberating Future Issues: Minipublics and Salmon Genomics', *Journal of Public Deliberation* 7(1): 1–27.

MacKenzie, Michael K. and Mark E. Warren. 2012. 'Two Trust-Based Uses of Minipublics in Democratic Systems', in *Deliberative Systems: Deliberative Democracy at the Large Scale*, eds Jane Mansbridge and John Parkinson. Cambridge: Cambridge University Press, 52–71.

Madhav, Nita, Ben Oppenheim, Mark Gallivan, Prime Mulembakani, Edward Rubin and Nathan Wolfe. 2018. 'Pandemics: Risks, Impacts, and Mitigation', in *Disease Control Priorities: Improving Health and Reducing Poverty*, eds Dean T. Jamison et al., 3rd edn. Washington, DC: World Bank Group, 315–45.

Maharana, Narayana, Suman K. Chaudhury, Manash Kumar S. and Chinmaya Mahapatra. 2020. 'Total Lockdown Due to COVID-19 Pandemic, Its Psychological and Behavioural Impact: a Survey in India', *Journal of Critical Reviews* 7(19): 8148–61.

Manin, Bernard. 1987. 'On Legitimacy and Political Deliberation', *Political Theory* 15(3): 338–68.

Manin, Bernard. 1997. *The Principles of Representative Government*. Cambridge: Cambridge University Press.

Mansbridge, Jane. 2003. 'Rethinking Representation', *American Political Science Review* 97(4): 515–28.

Mansbridge, Jane. 2012. 'On the Importance of Getting Things Done', *Political Science & Politics* 45(1): 1–8.

May, John D. 1978. 'Defining Democracy: A Bid for Coherence and Consensus', *Political Studies* 26(1): 1–14.

McKelvey, T. 2020. 'Coronavirus: Why are Americans so Angry about Masks?' *BBC News*, 20 July 2020, available at: https://www.bbc.com/news/world-us-canada-53477121, last accessed 25 October 2020.

McQuilkin, Jamie. 2019. 'Intergenerational Solidarity Index 2019', in *The Good Ancestor: How to Think Long Term in a Short-Term World*, by Roman Krznaric, available at: https://github.com/pipari/ISI, last accessed 25 April 2021.

Mendelberg, Tali and John Oleske. 2000. 'Race and Public Deliberation', *Political Communication* 17(2): 169–91.

Meyer, Kenneth L. 2019. 'Confronting the Pandemic Superthreat of Climate Change and Urbanization', *Orbis* 63(4): 565–81.

Miller, David. 2009. 'Democracy's Domain.' *Philosophy and Public Affairs* 37, 201–28.

Mittiga, Ross. 2021. 'Political Legitimacy, Authoritarianism, and Climate Change.' *American Political Science Review* 1–14, published online. DOI: 10.1017/S0003055421001301.

Montanaro, Laura. 2017. *Who Elected Oxfam?: A Democratic Defence of Self-Appointed Representatives*. Cambridge: Cambridge University Press.

Moore, Alfred. 2017. *Critical Elitism: Deliberation, Democracy, and the Politics of Expertise*. Cambridge: Cambridge University Press.

Moore, Alfred and MacKenzie, Michael K. 2020. 'Policymaking During Crises: How Diversity and Disagreement Can Help Manage the Politics of Expert Advice', *BMJ* 2020;371:m4039.

Moore, Alfred, Carlo Invernizzi-Accetti, Elizabeth Markovits, Zeynep Pamuk and Sophia Rosenfeld. 2020. 'Beyond Populism and Technocracy: The Challenges and Limits of Democratic Epistemology', *Contemporary Political Theory* 19(4): 730–52.

Morrell, Michael. E. 2010. *Empathy and Democracy: Feeling, Thinking and Deliberation*. University Park, PA: Pennsylvania State University Press.

Motta, Matt, Dominik Stecula and Christina Farhart. 2020. 'How Right-leaning Media Coverage of COVID-19 Facilitated the Spread of Misinformation in the Early Stages of the Pandemic in the US', *Canadian Journal of Political Science* 53(2): 335–42.

Müller, Jan-Werner. 2021. *Democracy Rules*. London: Penguin.

Muradova, Lala. 2020. 'Seeing the Other Side? Perspective-Taking and Reflective Political Judgements in Interpersonal Deliberation', *Political Studies* 69(3): 644–64.

Murto, Eero. 2014. *Virkamiesvaltaa? Ministerien ja virkamiesten väliset valtasuhteet Suomessa viime vuosikymmenten aikana.* Tampere: Tampere University Press.

Nair, Sreeja and Michael Howlett. 2017. 'Policy Myopia as a Source of Policy Failure: Adaptation and Policy Learning Under Deep Uncertainty', *Policy and Politics* 45(1): 103–18.

Nakagawa, Yoshinori, Koji Kotania, Mika Matsumoto and Tatsuyoshi Saijo. 2019. 'Intergenerational Retrospective Viewpoints and Individual Policy Preferences for Future: A Deliberative Experiment for Forest Management', *Futures* 105: 40–53.

Nakagawa, Yoshinori, Arai Real, Koji Kotani, Masanobu Nagano and Tatsuyoshi Saijo. 2019. 'Intergenerational Retrospective Viewpoint Promotes Financially Sustainable Attitude', *Futures* 114: 102454.

Nannestad, Peter and Martin Paldam. 2000. 'Into Pandora's Box of Economic Evaluations: A Study of the Danish Macro VP-function, 1986–1997', *Electoral Studies* 19(2/3): 123–40.

Nattrass, Nicoli. 2008. 'AIDS and the Scientific Governance of Medicine in Post-Apartheid South Africa', *African Affairs* 107(427): 157–76.

Newton, Kenneth and Jan W. Van Deth. 2016. *Foundations of Comparative Politics: Democracies of the Modern World.* Cambridge: Cambridge University Press.

Niemeyer, Simon and Julia Jennstål. 2016. 'The Deliberative Democratic Inclusion of Future Generations', in *Institutions for Future Generations*, eds I. González-Ricoy and A. Gosseries. Oxford: Oxford University Press, 247–65.

Nordhaus, William D. 1975. 'The Political Business Cycle', *Review of Economic Studies* 42(1): 169–90.

Norris, Pippa. 2012. *Making Democratic Governance Work: How Regimes Shape Prosperity, Welfare and Peace.* Cambridge: Cambridge University Press.

OECD (Organisation for Economic Cooperation and Development). 2020. *Innovative Citizen Participation and New Democratic Institutions: Catching the Deliberative Wave.* Paris: OECD Publishing.

Offe, Claus. 1996. *Modernity and the State. East, West.* Cambridge: Polity Press.

O'Grady, Cathleen. 2020. 'Jury Duty for Global Warming: Citizen Groups Help Solve the Puzzle of Climate Action', *Science* 370(6516): 518–21.

Olson, Mancur. 1965. *The Logic of Collective Action: Public Goods and the Theory of Groups.* Cambridge, MA: Harvard University Press.

Olson, Mancur. 1982. *The Rise and Decline of Nations: Economic Growth, Stagflation and Social Rigidities*. New Haven, CT: Yale University Press.

Ophuls, William and A. Stephen Boyan. 1992. *Ecology and the Politics of Scarcity Revisited: The Unraveling of the American Dream*. New York: Freeman.

Oreskes, Naomi and Erik M. Conway. 2010. *Merchants of Doubt: How a Handful of Scientists Obscured the Truth on Issues from Tobacco Smoke to Global Warming*. New York: Bloomsbury.

Oreskes, Naomi, Erik M. Conway and Matthew Shindell. 2008. 'From Chicken Little to Dr. Pangloss: William Nierenberg, Global Warming, and the Social Deconstruction of Scientific Knowledge', *Historical Studies in the Natural Sciences* 38(1): 109–52.

Oswald, Patricia A. 1996. 'The Effects of Cognitive and Affective Perspective-taking on Empathic Concern and Altruistic Helping', *Journal of Social Psychology* 136(5): 613–23.

Owen, David and Graham Smith. 2018. 'Sortition, Rotation, and Mandate: Conditions for Political Equality and Deliberative Reasoning', *Politics & Society* 46(3): 419–34. (Republished in *Legislature by Lot: Transformative Designs for Deliberative Governance*, eds John Gastil and Erik O. Wright. London: Verso Books, 2019.)

Pahl, Sabine and Judith Bauer. 2013. 'Overcoming the Distance: Perspective-Taking with Future Humans Improves Environmental Engagement', *Environment & Behavior* 45(2): 155–69.

Pahl, Sabine, Stephen Sheppard, Christine Boomsma and Christopher Groves. 2014. 'Perceptions of Time in Relation to Climate Change', *WIREs: Climate Change* 5(3): 375–88.

Parfit, Derek. 2017. 'Future People, the Non-Identity Problem, and Person-Affecting Principles.' *Philosophy and Public Affairs* 45:2 (September): 118–57.

Parkhill, Karen, Christina Demski, Catherine Butler, Alexa Spence and Nick Pidgeon. 2013. *Transforming the UK Energy System: Public Values, Attitudes and Acceptability, Synthesis Report*. London: UKERC.

Parkinson, John and Jane Mansbridge (eds). 2012. *Deliberative Systems: Deliberative Democracy at the Large Scale*. Cambridge: Cambridge University Press.

Pennock, James R. 1979. *Democratic Political Theory*. Princeton, NJ: Princeton University Press.

Persson, Torsten and Lars E. O. Svensson. 1989. 'Why a Stubborn Conservative would Run a Deficit: Policy with Time-Inconsistent Preferences', *Quarterly Journal of Economics* 104(2): 325–45.

Pettit, Philip. 2003a. 'Akrasia, Collective and Individual', in *Weakness of Will and Practical Irrationality*, eds Sarah Stroud and Christine Tappolet. Oxford: Clarendon, 68–96.

Pettit, Philip. 2003b. 'Deliberative Democracy, the Discursive Dilemma, and Republican Theory', in *Debating Deliberative Democracy*, eds James S. Fishkin and Peter Laslett. Oxford: Blackwell, 138–62.

Pettit, Philip. 2004a. 'Depoliticizing Democracy', *Ratio Juris* 17(1): 52–65.

Pettit, Philip. 2004b. 'A Dilemma for Deliberative Democrats', in *Deliberation and Decision*, eds Anne van Aaken, Christian List and Christian Luetge. Aldershot: Ashgate, 91–107.

Pettit, Philip. 2006. 'Democracy, National and International', *The Monist* 89(2): 301–4.

Phillips, Anne. 1995. *The Politics of Presence*. Oxford: Clarendon.

Pierson, Paul. 2004. *Politics in Time: History, Institutions, and Social Analysis*. Princeton, NJ: Princeton University Press.

Pitkin, Hanna F. 1967. *The Concept of Representation*. Berkely: University of California Press.

Pollitt, Christopher. 2008. *Time, Policy, Management: Governing with the Past*. Oxford: Oxford University Press.

Pouru, Laura, Matti Minkkinen, Burkhard Auffermann, Christopher Rowley, Maria Malho and Aleksi Neuvonen. 2020. 'Kansallinen ennakointi Suomessa', *Valtioneuvoston selvitys- ja tutkimustoiminnan julkaisusarja* 2020:17 (April).

Prime Minister's Office (PMO). 2007. 'Valtioneuvoston tulevaisuusselontekotyön kehittämismahdollisuuksia', *Valtioneuvoston kanslian julkaisusarja* 3:2007.

Prime Minister's Office (PMO). 2011. 'Valtioneuvoston ennakointiverkosto 2007–2011: Loppuraportti', *Valtioneuvoston kanslian julkaisusarja* 8:2011.

Prime Minister's Office (PMO). 2014. 'Yhteistä ja jatkuvaa ennakointia: Ehdotus kansalliseksi toimintatavaksi', *Valtioneuvoston kanslian julkaisusarja* 1:2014.

Prime Minister's Office (PMO). 2019a. 'Mahdollisuudet Suomelle', *Valtioneuvoston julkaisuja* 1:2019.

Prime Minister's Office (PMO). 2019b. 'Hallituksen strategisten johtamisvälineiden kehittämishankkeen suositukset', *Valtioneuvoston julkaisuja* 1:2019.

Proudhon, Pierre-Joseph. (1848/1867–70). 'Solution du problème social', in *Oeuvres completes* de P.-J. Proudhon, VI. Paris: A. Lacroix, Verboeckehove & Cie.

Przeworski, Adam. 1999. 'Minimalist Conception of Democracy: A Defense', in *Democracy's Value*, eds Shapiro Ian and Casiano Hacker-Cordon. Cambridge: Cambridge University Press, 23–55.

Przeworski, Adam. 2010a. *Democracy and the Limits of Self-Government*. Cambridge: Cambridge University Press.

Przeworski, Adam. 2010b. 'Consensus, Conflict, and Compromise in Western Thought on Representative Government', *Procedia Social and Behavioral Sciences* 2(5): 7042–55.

Ragazzoni, David. 2018. 'Political Compromise in Party Democracy: An Overlooked Puzzle in Kelsen's Democratic Theory', in *Compromise and Disagreement in Contemporary Political Theory*, eds Christian F. Rostboll and Theresa Scavenius. New York: Routledge, 95–112.

Ramboll 2013. *Tulevaisuusselonteon ennakointihankkeen arviointi*. Ramboll Management Consulting.

Randers, Jørgen. 2012. *2052: A Global Forecast for the Next Forty Years*. White River Junction, VT: Chelsea Green.

Rapeli, Lauri, Maria Bäck, Maija Jäske and Vesa Koskimaa. 2021. 'When Do You Want It? Determinants of Future-oriented Political Thinking', *Frontiers in Political Science* 3: 692913.

Rascovan, Nicolás, Karl-Göran Sjögren, Kristian Kristiansen, Rasmus Nielsen, Eske Willerslev, Christelle Desnues and Simon Rasmussen. 2019. 'Emergence and Spread of Basal Lineages of Yersinia pestis During the Neolithic Decline', *Cell* 176(1/2): 295–305.

Rask, Mikko, Richard Worthington and Minna Lammi. 2013. *Citizen Participation in Global Environmental Governance*. London: Routledge.

Rehm, Philipp, Jacob S. Hacker and Mark Schlesinger. 2012. 'Insecure Alliances: Risk, Inequality, and Support for the Welfare State', *American Political Science Review* 10(2): 386–406.

Reiman, Jeffrey. 2007. 'Being Fair to Future People: The Non-Identity Problem in the Original Position.' *Philosophy and Public Affairs* 35(1): 69–92.

Reiner Jr., Robert C., David L. Smith and Peter W. Gething. 2015. 'Climate Change, Urbanization and Disease: Summer in the City . . .', *Transactions of the Royal Society of Tropical Medicine and Hygiene* 109(3): 171–2.

Reniers, Renate, Rhiannon Corcoran, Richard Drake, Nick M. Shryane and Birgit A. Völlm. 2011. 'The QCAE: a Questionnaire of Cognitive and Affective Empathy', *Journal of Personality Assessment* 93(1): 84–95.

Revelle, Robert and Hans E. Suess. 1957. 'Carbon Dioxide Exchange between Atmosphere and Ocean and the Question of an Increase of Atmospheric CO_2 during the Past Decades', *Tellus* 9(1): 18–27.

Rice, D. 2020. 'Scientists are Seeing an "Acceleration of Pandemics": They are Looking at Climate Change', *US Today*, 10 September 2020, available at: https://eu.usatoday.com/story/news/nation/2020/09/10/climate-change-covid-19-does-global-warming-fuel-pandemics/5749582002, last accessed 11 October 2020.

Richardson, Henry S. 2002. *Democratic Autonomy: Public Reasoning about the Ends of Policy*. Oxford: Oxford University Press.

Riker, William H. 1982. *Liberalism against Populism*. San Francisco, CA: W. H. Freeman.

Rosanvallon, Pierre. 2011. *Democratic Legitimacy: Impartiality, Reflexivity, Proximity*. Princeton, NJ: Princeton University Press.

Rosenblum, Nancy, 2008. *On the Side of the Angels: An Appreciation of Parties and Partisanship*. Princeton, NJ: Princeton University Press.

Rosenbluth, Frances McCall and Ian Shapiro. 2018. *Responsible Parties: Saving Democracy From Itself*. New Haven, CT: Yale University Press.

Rosner, Sara and Jeff Schlegelmilch. 2020. 'Making the Connections: COVID-19 and Climate Change', available at: https://www.allianceber nstein.com/library/making-the-connections-COVID-19-and-climate-ch ange.htm, last accessed 26 October 2020.

Ross, Alf. 1952. *Why Democracy?* Cambridge, MA: Harvard University Press.

Rossi, Rodolfo, Valentina Socci, Dalila Talevi, Sonia Mensi, Cinzia Niolu, Francesca Pacitti, Antinisca Di Marco, Alessandro Rossi, Alberto Siracusano and Giorgio Di Lorenzo. 2020. 'COVID-19 Pandemic and Lockdown Measures Impact on Mental Health among the General Population in Italy', *Frontiers in Psychiatry* 11: 790.

Rothstein, Bo. 2005. *Social Traps and the Problem of Trust*. Cambridge: Cambridge University Press.

Rousseau, Jean-Jacques. [1758] 1973. 'A Discourse on Political Economy', in *The Social Contract and Discourses*. ed and trans. G. D. H. Cole. London: Dent, 115–53.

Rousseau, Jean-Jacques. [1758] 1973. 'Geneva manuscripts', in *The Social Contract and Discourses*, ed. and trans. G. D. H. Cole. London: Dent.

Rubenfeld, Jed. 2001. *Freedom and Time: A Theory of Constitutional Self-Government*. New Haven, CT: Yale University Press.

Rummens, Stefan. 2012. 'Staging Deliberation: The Role of Representative Institutions in the Deliberative Democratic Process', *Journal of Political Philosophy* 20(1): 23–44.

Runciman, David. 2013. *The Confidence Trap: A History of Democracy in Crisis from World War I to the Present*. Princeton. NJ: Princeton University Press.

Rutstein, David D. 1974. 'The Epidemiology and Control of Man-made Diseases', in *Annals of Life Insurance Medicine*, ed. E. Tanner. Berlin: Springer, 25–34.

Saarinen, Arttu, Aki Koivula and Teo Keipi. 2019. 'Political Trust, Political Party Preference and Trust in Knowledge-based Institutions', *International Journal of Sociology and Social Policy* 40(1): 154–68.

Saffon, Maria P. and Nadia Urbinati. 2013. 'Procedural Democracy, the Bulwark of Equal Liberty', *Political Theory* 41(3): 441–81.

Saijo, Tatsuyoshi. 2020. 'Future Design: Bequeathing Sustainable Natural Environments and Sustainable Societies to Future Generations', *Sustainability* 12(6): 6467.

Sands, Peter, Carmen Mundaca-Shah and Victor, J. Dzau. 2016. 'The Neglected Dimension of Global Security: A Framework for Countering Infectious-disease Crises', *New England Journal of Medicine* 374(13): 1281–7.

Sargisson, Rebecca J., Judith I. M. De Groot and Linda Steg. 2020. 'The Relationship between Sociodemographics and Environmental Values across Seven European Countries', *Frontiers in Psychology* 11: 2253.

Saunders, Ben. 2014. 'Democracy and Future Generations', *Philosophy and Public Issues* 4(2): 11–28.

Saward, Michael. 1994. 'Democratic Theory and Indices of Democratization', in *Defining and Measuring Democracy*, ed. Beetham David. London; Sage, 6–24.

Saward, Michael. 1998. *The Terms of Democracy*. Cambridge: Polity.

Schelling, Thomas. C. 1968. 'The Life You Save May be Your Own', in *Problems in Public Expenditure Analysis*, ed. Samuel. B. Chase, Jr. Washington, DC: Brookings Institution, 127–62.

Schmidt, Matthias. 2015. '150-km/h-Limit auf Autobahnen hätte eine knappe Mehrheit', *Yougov Survey*, 15 October 2015, available at: https://yougov.de/news/2015/10/15/150-kmh-limit-auf-autobahnen-hatte-ei ne-knappe-meh.

Schmitt, Carl. [1923] 1988. *The Crisis of Parliamentary Democracy*, trans. Ellen Kennedy. Cambridge, MA: MIT Press.

Scholz, John T. 1998. 'Trust, Taxes, and Compliance', in *Trust and Governance*, eds V. Braithwaite and M. Levi. New York: Russell Sage Foundation, 135–66.

Schroth, Olaf, Jeannette Angel, Stephen R. J. Sheppard and Aleksandra Dulic. 2014. 'Visual Climate Change Communication: From Iconography to Locally Framed 3D Visualization', *Environmental Communication* 8(4): 413–32.

Schuldt, Jonathon P., Sungjong Roh and Norbert Schwarz. 2015. 'Questionnaire Design Effects in Climate Change Surveys: Implications for the Partisan Divide', *ANNALS of the American Academy of Political and Social Science* 658(1): 67–85.

Seo, Hyeon S. 2017. *Reaching Out to the People? Parliament and Citizen Participation in Finland*. Acta Universitatis Tamperensis, 2264. Tampere: Tampere University Press.

Setälä, Maija, and Graham Smith. 2018. 'Deliberative Mini-publics and Deliberative Democracy', in *The Oxford Handbook of Deliberative Democracy*, eds Andre Bächtiger, John S. Dryzek, Jane Mansbridge and Mark E. Warren. Oxford: Oxford University Press.

Setälä, Maija, Kimmo Grönlund and Kaisa Herne. 2010. 'Citizen Deliberation on Nuclear Power: A Comparison of Two Decision-Making Methods', *Political Studies* 58(4): 688–714.

Setälä, Maija, Henrik Serup Christensen, Mikko Leino, Kim Strandberg, Maria Bäck and Maija Jäske. 2020. 'Deliberative Mini-publics Facilitating Voter Knowledge and Judgement: Experience from a Finnish Local Referendum', *Representation* (October), published online, DOI: 10.1080/00344893.2020.1826565.

Sevillano, Verónica, Juan I. Aragonés and P. Wesley Schultz. 2007. 'Perspective-taking, Environmental Concern, and the Moderating Role of Dispositional Empathy', *Environment and Behavior* 39(5): 685–705.

Shahar, Dan C. 2015. 'Rejecting Eco-authoritarianism, Again', *Environmental Values* 24:3 (June): 345–66.

Shaman, Jeffrey. 2018. 'Pandemic Preparedness and Forecast', *Nature Microbiology* 3(3): 265–67.

Shapiro, Ian. 2003. *The State of Democratic Theory*. Princeton, NJ: Princeton University Press.

Shapiro, Ian. 2016. *Politics against Domination*. Cambridge, MA: Harvard University Press.

Shapiro, Ian. 2017. 'Collusion in Restraint of Democracy: Against Political Deliberation', *Daedalus* 146(3): 77–84.

Shapiro, Scott J. 2011. *Legalism*. Cambridge, MA: Belknap Press.

Shearman, David J. C. and Joseph W. Smith. 2007. *The Climate Change Challenge and the Failure of Democracy*. Westport, CT: Praeger.

Sheppard, Stephen R. J. 2012. *Visualizing Climate Change: A Guide to Visual Communication of Climate Change and Developing Local Solutions*. London: Routledge.

Shih, Margaret, Elsie Wang, Amy T. Bucher and Rebecca Stotzer. 2009. 'Perspective-taking: Reducing Prejudice Towards General Outgroups and Specific Individuals', *Group Processes & Intergroup Relations* 12(5): 565–77.

Shih, Margaret, Rebecca Stotzer and Angélica S. Gutiérrez. 2013. 'Perspective-taking and Empathy: Generalizing the Reduction of Group Bias towards Asian Americans to General Outgroups', *Asian American Journal of Psychology* 4(2): 79–83.

Shoham, Shlomo. 2010. *Future Intelligence*. Gütersloh: Verlag Bertelsman Stifung.

Shope, Robert. 1991. 'Global Climate Change and Infectious Diseases', *Environmental Health Perspectives* 96:171–74.

Shrum, Trisha. 2016. 'The Salience of Future Climate Impacts and the Willingness to Pay for Climate Change Mitigation', Working Paper, Pershing Square Venture Fund for Research on the Foundation of Human Behavior and the Harvard Environmental Economics, available at: https://scholar.harvard.edu/files/trishashrum/files/salience_futurecli matebenefits.pdf.

Shwed, Uri and Peter S. Bearman. 2010. 'The Temporal Structure of Scientific Consensus Formation', *American Sociological Review* 75(6): 817–40.

Slothuus, Rune and Martin Bisgaard. 2020. 'How Political Parties Shape Public Opinion in the Real World', *American Journal of Political Science* 65(4): 896–911.

Small, Deborah A., George Loewenstein and Paul Slovic. 2007. 'Sympathy and Callousness: The Impact of Deliberative Thought on Donations to Identifiable and Statistical Victims', *Organizational Behavior and Human Decision Processes* 102: 143–53.

Smith, Adam. 2010. *The Wealth of Nations: An Inquiry into the Nature and Causes of the Wealth of Nations.* Petersfield, Hampshire: Harriman House.

Smith, Graham. 2003. *Deliberative Democracy and the Environment.* London: Routledge.

Smith, Graham. 2009. *Democratic Innovations: Designing Institutions for Citizen Participation.* Cambridge: Cambridge University Press.

Smith, Graham. 2020. 'Enhancing the Legitimacy of Offices for Future Generations: The Case for Public Participation.' *Political Studies* 68(4): 996–1013.

Smith, Graham. 2021. *Can Democracy Safeguard the Future?* Cambridge: Polity.

Song, Sarah. 2012. 'The Boundary Problem in Democratic Theory: Why the Demos Should Be Bounded by the State.' *International Theory* 4:1 (March): 39–68.

Spinoza, Benedictus (Baruch). ([1670] 1951). *Tractatus theologico-politicus,* trans. Robert H. M. Elwes. New York: Dover.

Spreeuwenberg, Peter, Madelon Kroneman and John Paget. 2018. 'Reassessing the Global Mortality Burden of the 1918 Influenza Pandemic', *American Journal of Epidemiology* 187(12): 2561–7.

Stanton, Tim. 2016. 'Popular Sovereignty in an Age of Mass Democracy: Politics, Parliament and Parties in Weber, Kelsen, Schmitt and Beyond', in *Popular Sovereignty in Historical Perspective,* eds Quentin Skinner and Richard Bourke. Cambridge: Cambridge University Press, 320–58.

Stoker, Gerry. 2014. 'The Myth of Democratic Myopia', paper presented at the 2016 ECPR General Conference, Glasgow.

Sultana, Farhana. 2021. 'Climate Change, COVID-19, and the Co-production of Injustices: A Feminist Reading of Overlapping Crises', *Social & Cultural Geography* 22(4): 447–60.

Takle, Marianne. 2021. 'The Norwegian Petroleum Fund: Savings for Future Generations?' *Environmental Values* 30(2): 147–67.

Tapio, Petri and Sirkka Heinonen. 2018. 'Focused Futures from Finland', *World Futures Review* 10(2): 111–35.

Teale, Chris. 2020. 'COVID-19 May Sport the Thinnest Silver Lining: a Cleaner Climate', *Smart Cities Dive*, 19 March 2020, available at: https://www.smartcitiesdive.com/news/coronavirus-impact-cities-climate-chan ge-efforts/574450, last accessed 23 October 2020.

Teräväinen-Litardo, Tuula. 2015. 'Negotiating Green Growth as a Pathway towards Sustainable Transitions in Finland', in *Rethinking the Green State: Environmental Governance Towards Climate and Sustainability Transitions*, eds Karin Bäckstrand and Annica Kronsell. London: Routledge.

Teschner, Na'ama. 2013. *Official Bodies that Deal with the Needs of Future Generations and Sustainable Development*. Jerusalem: Knesset Information and Research Center.

'The Medium-Term Climate Policy Plan' (in English). *Ympäristöministeriö*, available at: https://ym.fi/en/medium-term-climate-change-policy-plan, last accessed 15 October 2021.

'The Results of the Citizen Survey on Climate Policies' (in Finnish). *Ympäristöministeriö*, available at: https://ym.fi/-/ilmastokysely-viestinta-elintarvikkeiden-ilmastovaikutuksista-ja-panostukset-kevyen-liikente en-vayliin-naita-ilmastotoimia-suomalaiset-pitavat-hyvaksyttavimpina, last accessed 15 October 2021.

Thompson, Dennis F. 2010. 'Representing Future Generations: Political Presentism and Democratic Trusteeship', *Critical Review of International Social and Political Philosophy* 13(1): 17–37.

Thompson, Dennis F. 2011. 'Representing Future Generations: Political Presentism and Democratic Trusteeship', in *Democracy, Equality, and Justice*, eds Matt Matravers and Lukas Meyer. Abingdon: Routledge, 17–38.

Todd, Andrew R. and Adam D. Galinsky. 2014. 'Perspective-Taking as a Strategy for Improving Intergroup Relations: Evidence, Mechanisms, and Qualifications', *Social and Personality Psychology Compass* 8(7): 374–87.

Tonn, Bruce E. 2018. 'Philosophical, Institutional, and Decision-making Frameworks for Meeting Obligations to Future Generations', *Futures* 95: 44–57.

Tooze, Adam. 2020. 'Did Xi Just Save the World?' *Foreign Policy*, 25 September 2020, available at: https://foreignpolicy.com/2020/09/25/xi-china-climate-change-saved-the-world%E2%80%A8.

Trappenburg, Margo. 2005. 'In Praise of Stability: Justice between Generations', paper prepared for the ECPR Joint Sessions, Granada, 15–18 April 2005.

Tremmel, Jörg. 2015. 'Parliaments and Future Generations: The Four-Power-Model', in *The Politics of Sustainability: Philosophical Perspectives*, eds Dieter Birnbacher and May Thorseth. London: Routledge, 212–33.

UNAIDS (Joint United Nations Programme on HIC/AIDS). 2020. 'Global HIV & AIDS Statistics – 2020 Fact Sheet', available at: https://www.unaids.org/en/resources/fact-sheet, last accessed 25 October 2020.

United Nations. 2004. *A More Secure World: Our Shared Responsibility Report of the High-level Panel on Threats, Challenges and Change*. New York: United Nations.

Urbinati, Nadia. 2014. *Democracy Disfigured*. Cambridge, MA: Harvard University Press.

Urbinati, Nadia. 2019. *Me the People: How Populism Transforms Democracy*. Cambridge, MA: Harvard University Press.

Urbinati, Nadia and Mark Warren. 2008. 'The Concept of Representation in Contemporary Democratic Theory', *Annual Review of Political Science* 11: 387–412.

Uwasu, Michinori, Yusuke Kishita, Keishiro Hara and Yutaka Nomaguchi. 2020. 'Citizen-Participatory Scenario Design Methodology with Future Design Approach: A Case Study of Visioning of a Low-Carbon Society in Suita City, Japan', *Sustainability* 12(11): 4746.

Vanhuysse, Pieter. 2013. 'Measuring Intergenerational Justice: Toward a Synthetic Index for OECD Countries', in *Intergenerational Justice in Aging Societies: A Cross-national Comparison of 29 OECD Countries*, ed. Bertelsmann Stiftung. Gütersloh: Bertelsmann Stiftung, 10–43.

Vanhuysse, Pieter. 2014. *Intergenerational Justice and Public Policy in Europe*. Brussels: Observatoire Social Européen.

Vanhuysse, Pieter and Jörg Tremmel. 2018. 'Measuring Intergenerational Justice for Public Policy', in *The Routledge Handbook of Ethics and Public Policy*, eds Annabella Lever and Andrei Poama. Abingdon: Routledge, 472–86.

Varoufakis, Yanis. 2016. 'Why We Must Save the EU', *The Guardian*, 5 April 2016, available at: https://www.theguardian.com/world/2016/apr/05/yanis-varoufakis-why-we-must-save-the-eu.

Värttö, Mikko, Maija Jäske, Kaisa Herne and Kimmo Grönlund. 2021. 'Kaksisuuntainen katu', *Politiikka* 63(1): 28–53.

Verba, Sidney and Norman H. Nie. 1972. *Participation in America: Political Democracy and Social Equality.* New York: Harper & Row.

Vesa, Juho, Antti Gronow and Tuomas Ylä-Anttila. 2020. 'The Quiet Opposition: How the Pro-Economy Lobby Influences Climate Policy', *Global Environmental Change* 63: 102117.

Vesa, Juho, Anu Kantola and Anne S. Binderkrantz. 2018. 'A Stronghold of Routine Corporatism? The Involvement of Interest Groups in Policy Making in Finland', *Scandinavian Political Studies* 41(4): 239–62.

Vieten, Ulrike M. 2020. 'The "New Normal" and "Pandemic Populism": The COVID-19 Crisis and Anti-Hygienic Mobilisation of the Far-Right', *Social Sciences* 9(9): 165.

Vinke, Kira, Sabine Gabrysch, Emanuela Paoletti, Johan Rockström and Hans J. Schellnhuber. 2020. 'Corona and the Climate: a Comparison of Two Emergencies', *Global Sustainability* 3(E25): 1–7.

Vinx, Lars. 2007. *Hans Kelsen's Pure Theory of Law. Legality and Legitimacy.* Oxford: Oxford University Press.

Volk, Ulrich. 2020. 'Investing in a Green Recovery: The Pandemic is Only a Prelude to a Looming Climate Crisis', *Finance & Development*, 28–31.

Vorauer, Jacquie D. 2013. 'Chapter Two: The Case For and Against Perspective-taking', in *Advances in Experimental Social Psychology 48*, eds J. M. Olson and M. P. Zanna. Amsterdam: Elsevier Academic, 59–115.

Vorauer, Jacquie D. and Stacey J. Sasaki. 2014. 'Distinct Effects of Imagine-other versus Imagine-self Perspective-taking on Prejudice Reduction', *Social Cognition* 32: 130–47.

Wade-Benzoni, Kimberly A., Harris Sondak and Adam D. Galinsky. 2010. 'Leaving a Legacy: Intergenerational Allocations of Benefits and Burdens', *Business Ethics Quarterly* 20(1): 7–34.

Walter, Henrik. 2012. 'Social Cognitive Neuroscience of Empathy: Concepts, Circuits, and Genes', *Emotion Review* 4(1): 9–17.

Ward, Bob. 2020. 'Organisers of Anti-Lockdown Declaration have Track Record of Promoting Denial of Health and Environmental Risks', available at: https://www.lse.ac.uk/granthaminstitute/news/organisers-of-an ti-lockdown-declaration-have-track-record-of-promoting-denial-of-heal th-and-environmental-risks, last accessed 3 February 2022.

Warren, Mark E. 1996. 'Deliberative Democracy and Authority', *American Political Science Review* 90(1): 46–60.

Warren, Mark E. 2009. 'Governance-Driven Democratization', *Critical Policy Studies* 3(1): 3–13.

Warren, Mark E. 2014. 'Governance-Driven Democratization', in *Practices of Freedom: Democracy, Conflict and Participation in Decentred Governance,* eds S. Griggs, A. Norval and H. Wagenaar. Cambridge: Cambridge University Press, 38–59.

Warren, Mark E. 2017a. 'What Kinds of Trust Does a Democracy Need? Trust From the Perspective of Democratic Theory', in *Handbook of Political Trust*, eds S. Zmerli and T. van den Meer. Cheltenham: Edward Elgar, 33–52.

Warren, Mark E. 2017b. 'Trust and Democracy', in *The Oxford Handbook of Social and Political Trust*, ed. E. Uslaner. Oxford: Oxford University Press, 75–94.

Warren, Mark E. n.d. 'The Principle of All Affected Interests in Theory and Practice', in *Democratic Inclusion in a Globalized World: The Principle of All Affected Interests*, eds A. Fung and S. Gray. In preparation.

Warren, Mark E. and John Gastil. 2015. 'Can Deliberative Minipublics Address the Cognitive Challenges of Democratic Citizenship', *Journal of Politics* 77(2): 582–74.

Watts, Nick, Markus Amann, Nigel Arnell, Sonja Ayeb-Karlsson, Jessica Beagley, Kristine Belesova, Maxwell Baykoff et al. 2021. 'The 2020 Report of the Lancet Countdown on Health and Climate Change: Responding to Converging Crises', *The Lancet* 397(10269): 129–70.

Weale, Albert. 2018. *The Will of the People: A Modern Myth*. Cambridge: Polity.

Weaver, R. Kent. 1986. 'The Politics of Blame Avoidance', *Journal of Public Policy* 6(4): 371–98.

Whelan, Frederick G. 2018. *Democracy in Theory and Practice*. London: Routledge.

White, Jonathan and Lea Ypi. 2016. *The Meaning of Partisanship*. Oxford: Oxford University Press.

Wilenius, Markku. 2005. 'Yhteiskunnallisen ennakoinnin rooli tulevaisuuden haasteiden tunnistamisessa', *Tutu-julkaisuja* 1/2005.

Wolf, Stephan and Cameron Dron. 2020. 'The Effect of an Experimental Veil of Ignorance on Intergenerational Resource Sharing: Empirical Evidence from a Sequential Multi-person Dictator Game', *Ecological Economics* 175: 106662.

Wolkenstein, Fabio. 2019a. 'Agents of Popular Sovereignty', *Political Theory* 47(3): 338–62.

Wolkenstein, Fabio. 2019b. 'Review of "Responsible Parties: Saving Democracy From Itself"', *Constellations* 26(4): 658–60.

Wood, James W., Rebecca J. Ferrell and Sharon N. Dewitte-Aviña. 2003. 'The Temporal Dynamics of the Fourteenth-century Black Death: New Evidence from English Ecclesiastical Records', *Human Biology* 75(4): 427–48.

Wood, Matt and Matthew V. Flinders. 2014. 'Rethinking Depoliticization: Beyond the Governmental', *Policy & Politics* 42(2): 151–70.

Woodward, Calvin. 2020. 'AP Fact Check: Trump's Faulty Claims on Flu and Coronavirus', *Associated Press*, 7 October 2020, available at: https://apnews.com/article/virus-outbreak-donald-trump-ap-fact-check-anthony-fauci-flu-fe474f0c15f76adf324791a2cfc1e2bb, last accessed 26 October 2020.

World Commission on Environment and Development. 1987. *Our Common Future*. Oxford: Oxford University Press.

Young, Iris M. 2000. *Democracy and Inclusion*. Oxford: Oxford University Press.

INDEX

EU representative:
Easy Access System Europe
Mustamäe tee 50, 10621 Tallinn, Estonia
Gpsr.requests@easproject.com